Gump's Treasure Trade

ABRAHAM LIVINGSTON GUMP

December 13, 1869 — August 29, 1947

Portrait by Alfred Jonniaux, 1943
(Photograph by Frank van Eckhardt)

CAROL GREEN WILSON

~ *Gump's*

Treasure Trade

A STORY OF SAN FRANCISCO

THOMAS Y. CROWELL COMPANY · NEW YORK

To A. L.

Preface

SOME THIRTY-FIVE years ago I prepared a college paper entitled "The Commercial Call of China to California" for a course in transportation at Stanford University. The subject proved so intriguing that I planned to pursue it further as a master's thesis, but matrimony intervened. Now and then throughout a busy life I have written biography, the first one being the story of a Scotch Presbyterian missionary who devoted forty years to rescuing Chinese girls from yellow slavery in San Francisco's Chinatown.

The spell of the mysterious Orient continued to lure. It was natural, then, as opportunity came to know A. Livingston Gump, the nearly blind art dealer who devoted his years to a materialization of my own academic dream, that his experience should appeal to me as an appropriate part of the history of the city where art provided a common language as East met West.

It was late in his life when we were introduced. For that reason I knew him in a reminiscent mood. It became my privilege to transcribe into a notebook the memoirs of a man who refused to let physical handicap interfere with his vigorous participation in the evolving culture of a city where his father had found a roistering town peopled with ex-miners and vigilantes.

A.L. was often tired when I visited with him in those summer afternoons of 1947; the mind that had functioned so shrewdly and often brilliantly behind his clouded eyes was sometimes hazy as to dates and names. But it was clear in its purpose to the hour of his sudden death on August 29. I left that afternoon gratified because he had untangled some of the data obscure in former interviews, and pleased by his interest in my plans for a flight to the Middle East.

It has taken just a year to weave my way through the maze of memories Mr. Gump bequeathed; but I have had guidance and help from many aides. An attempt to list accurately all who have responded to calls for help would be impossible. His entire family and the whole Gump staff have answered patiently question after question. The older son, Robert, visualized through long hours of conference the father of his boyhood memories in an intimate revelation of A.L.'s unique personality; and Richard Gump added his interpretation of the business and artistic philosophy of the firm. Friends and acquaintances shared their pet Gump anecdotes; librarians from New York to San Francisco consulted files to verify minute details; and the entire manuscript had careful reading by Robert Gump, Ed Newell, Edythe Larsen (A.L.'s secretary for twenty years), Martin Rosenblatt, Dr. Frederick Vickery, director of the Crocker Art Gallery, and his talented wife Charlotte Beach Vickery, Miss Caroline Wenzel of the California State Library, and Mrs. Edna Parratt of the California Historical Society.

Source material has come from many persons and publications. I was fortunate in visiting with A.L.'s older sister, Mrs. William Bronner in New York about a year before her death, and from her derived a picture of San Francisco as she remembered it after fifty years absence. Her granddaughter, Elsie Godley, had compiled much of Mrs. Bronner's material in "Gump Family Sketches" for an English course at New York University. She generously supplied me with a copy.

A former colleague in Stanford alumni publications, Frank J. Taylor, shared with me the material he had published in various magazines, chiefly *The Saturday Evening Post,* some years ago when he collaborated with Mr. Gump in the story of "Jade Hunt" and "Plunging in Art."

Directors and librarians in all of San Francisco's art institutions helped me piece together that phase of the city's history. Special thanks should go to Bruce Porter, Haig Patigan, and Herbert Fleishhacker for early data; to Dr. Walter Heil, Thomas Carr Howe, Jr., Ching Wah Lee, Miss Katherine Ball, Dr. Grace McCann Morley, and Miss Neely Sullivan for specific information; and to Mrs. Franklin Hittell, Mrs. Charles Bradford Hudson, and her daughter Claire Hudson Brett, who loaned valuable memoranda.

Brother Cornelius' exhaustive volume, *Keith, Old Master of California* (G. P. Putnams' Sons, 1942) and *William Keith* by Eugene Neuhaus (University of California Press, 1938) have been invaluable references.

Two of my former professors at Stanford, Edgar Eugene Robinson and Payson J. Treat, responded cordially to requests for refresher facts and a master's thesis prepared under Dr. Robinson by Julia Lynch in 1937 on "The First Twenty-Four Hours of the San Francisco Earthquake and Fire" supplemented A.L.'s personal narrative of that disastrous morning.

For help in the preparation of the material on jade, I am indebted to Ed Newell, Martin Rosenblatt, and Joe Wheeler, as well as to such books as *Jade Lore* by John Goette (Kelly and Walsh Ltd.; Shanghai, Hong Kong, and Singapore; 1936), *Chinese Art*, vol. I, by Stephen W. Bushell (Victoria and Albert Museum, London, 1921), *Jade,* by Alice V. Petar (U.S. Bureau of Mines, Information Circular, 1936), and various other magazine articles clipped and filed by Mr. Rosenblatt.

Research on this project has taken me to the Huntington Library in San Marino, the Bancroft in Berkeley, the California State in Sacramento, and in San Francisco to the Public, Society of Pioneers, Historical, de Young, Wells Fargo, and Mechanics libraries.

For all the cooperation from whatever source I express deep gratitude. To my husband, who has devoted uncounted hours to listening and to constructive criticism, I can only say that the master's degree might have been won with less intrusion on his time!

C.G.W.

Contents

List of Illustrations

ABE GUMP began to live in a shadowy world when he was eleven. He first became aware of a dark cloud when the teacher moved his seat to the back of the classroom. Suddenly the figures on the blackboard disappeared. Frightened and puzzled, he did not join the other children at the noon recess. Instead, he grabbed his tin lunch pail and ran home.

He knew that his father, like all San Francisco merchants of the eighties, would be home for a hearty noon meal. For Abe, Solomon Gump had the answer to every question. But this situation baffled the vigorous art dealer. He had begun to build dreams around this fourth son of his. The boy seemed to have inherited his own love of beauty, his feel for treasure, his adventurous spirit. The second son in the large family, Lafayette, was already blind. Solomon could not bear to have another member become like that son, bright but ineffectual.

"We'll see Dr. Barkan at once," declared the father. But the bearded Hungarian, one of San Francisco's pioneer specialists, shook his head.

"Try the dark for a while," he ordered. "Keep the boy in a shuttered room for six weeks. Then take him out only after sundown."

Those were weeks of anguish. Abe was quick in his studies, alert in games. He pined for the books he had always devoured, those wonderful stories lining the shelves of the Bush Street Free Library where he and a few chosen companions used to dash every noon with their lunch boxes. Pent up in the boy were the ambitions of venturesome forbears, men and women who had left Old World homes to share in the new experiment in democracy. He lay in the dark, his energetic body rebelling against inactivity, and found his only solace in re-living the vivid tales his father told him in their evenings together.

Out of those nightly stories lasting impressions were stamped on the inner being of the child. He felt himself a participant in the drama of early San Francisco, the logical heir of his father's intense loyalty.

Solomon Gump could not qualify as a Pioneer. He had not arrived in California prior to January 1, 1850. But his determination to be part of the western city had coincided with his first sight of America. New York harbor was filled with clipper ships when the Gump family docked there in 1850. Seventeen-year-old Solomon was ready right then to join other adventurous young men who were jamming these full-rigged vessels departing for the new gold-crazed state just admitted to the Union.

But thirteen years elapsed before his opportunity came to see California. On a spring morning in 1863 Solomon, then thirty years old, stood at the rail of a Pacific Mail steamer approaching the Golden Gate. His eyes, lifting from the monotonous gray-blue swells of the Pacific, caught sight of a large square frame building perched on the edge of the steep cliff. A flag flew briskly from its high pole, and fluttering white kerchiefs indicated welcome from people crowded on a balcony supported on high posts. To the north, rising above sharp rocks and inviting green hills, a high mountain was darkly silhouetted, white puffs of fog drifting above its peak. To the south as the ship steered between jagged protecting palisades he saw trees and roofs of houses of the Presidio and beyond them nothing but endless rolling dunes. Their white sands were creased with gullies filled with billowing waves of lupin, soft yellow and deep blue. Dead ahead in the bay, now widening out from the narrow Gate, a huge forbidding island of rock stood guard.

The water, whipped into tiny white caps, broke against the curving shoreline where a few uninviting houses straggled in the mud, outposts of the city he had come so far to see. As the ship turned southward into the bay a forest of masts acclaimed the security of the port. Above the entrance to the cove which harbored them, a hill higher than the others on the irregular skyline attracted Solomon's eyes to a waving flag on its observation tower. Small stucco houses, blue, green, and pink, clung to its bayside slopes like little nests, giving the appearance of a Mediterranean coastal town. Along the edge of the greenish water he began to see a jutting network of wharves and wooden houses with streets leading up from the waterfront into a closely huddled city. So this was San Francisco, the magnet that had drawn him so far from his family waiting in the East!

Across the cove on the left was a large grassy island where brilliant poppies shone in the morning sun. A fellow voyageur standing by his side was returning from a visit to the East. Noting Solomon's eager interest, he explained that this was known as Goat Island and proceeded to recount a bit of local history. The new name, he told him, replaced the more attractive Spanish *Yerba Buena* when an early inhabitant, hungry for a change of diet, purchased some goats from an English trading vessel. Forced to find new pastures by angry neighbors whose shirts were being eaten off their clothes lines, the goats had been ferried to the island and there they had multiplied.

The steady plop-plop of the churning paddle wheels which had accompanied every thought during the past weary weeks gradually slowed and ceased as the vessel slipped into the long wooden dock. Solomon scanned the upturned faces of the waiting throng. There they were—his sister Gertrude and her husband David Hausmann with their three young children. Two years of adventure had made sturdy pioneers out of the timid youngsters he had escorted up the gangplank on the Hudson River dock that other April morning when he had so longed to sail west with them. They crowded close to Gertrude now as their uncle stepped onto the dock. Five voices, interrupted by the formalities of landing and collecting baggage, vied clamorously for news of their eastern home and family.

Then they all bundled into a waiting wagon and drove up the plank toll road that led from the docks up Folsom Street. Hausmann told Solomon proudly that their home was in one of the best residence districts—at the corner of Folsom and Hawthorn Streets.

That evening as they sat around the lamp-lit supper table Solomon asked,

"How did you know when our steamer would dock?"

"We saw the signal flags on the Merchants' Exchange. That's one of the first things you learn to look for around here," David informed his brother-in-law. "I understand that in the early gold rush days there were semaphores on Telegraph Hill—they called it Signal Hill then. That's the rocky point that you probably noticed as you turned into the cove this morning."

Solomon interrupted, "You mean the one where the pink houses are perched?"

"Yes," answered Hausmann. "In those days that was the first place where ships coming in the Golden Gate could be sighted. About 1852 a marine observation station was set up on Point Lobos, the rocky headland you passed as you entered the Gate. That same year the first telegraph line in California connected the Point Lobos station with the tower on Signal Hill and after that the name was changed to Telegraph Hill. Then the merchants of the city decided that they ought to get the word more quickly down town, so the wires were connected directly with our new Merchants' Exchange Building."

In years to come Solomon would watch for the arrival signals of his own cargoes from the far places of the world; but that night no such vision took his mind off the immediate task. He was in California to investigate business possibilities. If he saw a chance of success in the mirror business which David had started, he would have to write convincingly to his wife Louisa, waiting with their two baby girls in faraway New York. She had objected strenuously to any suggestion that they join the Hausmanns in the "horrid city" portrayed in Gertrude's homesick letters. She could not face the thought of "constant winds whirling sand about so that ladies are obliged to wear thick veils to protect their eyes," the lack of refined social life, houses built on mud flats. Nevertheless, when Gertrude's letters became too insistent, Louisa had agreed to let him make this exploratory trip.

From the start Solomon was intrigued with this raw western city. Life here never lacked color and excitement. It was like a Greenwich Fair on an expansive scale, with its flaunting signboards, booming gongs, and flying flags. Imbued with the drama of the scene, he soon felt that he belonged among its cosmopolitan citizens. Waiting in line to crowd the post office on Steamer Days, he rubbed shoulders with men from many states and nations. He listened to familiar Yankee expressions and drawling southern accents, while Spanish and Chinese, French and German added overtones of distant origin.

Son of a cultured Heidelberg linen merchant, Solomon Gump was immediately at home among the Europeans who had come early to share in the new far-western wealth. He worked with Hausmann making gilded cornices for mansions that were being built for men who had struck it rich in the mines, and mirrors for the many saloons. While his relatives pined for the "civilized life of New York," Solomon reveled in the fresh adventure of sharing in the making of a city.

From an older brother-in-law, Henry Cohn, who in 1856 had been the first of the clan to respond to the lure of the gold state, he had introductions to the newly rich from the Comstock. Because his own first business experience had been as a ship chandler in Apalachicola, Florida, he was familiar with trade and traders, and sometimes in the waterfront saloons he found sailors wearing jackets he had sold them years before.

These saloons first made the Hausmann business profitable. The visiting miner with his heavy bags of gold, the sailor with his sea pay, the lonely bachelor tired of his back-hall bedroom all sought recreation in the El Dorado, the Bella Union or "Pop" Sullivan's Hoffman House. As the saloon keepers prospered, they spent their money for decoration. Solomon sensed the making of a fortune as he supplied glistening mirrors and polished bars, plus the inevitable sculptured lady whose marble form shone in repeated reflections.

Those were turbulent days in San Francisco. Fights were frequent in the noisy saloons, whether tempers flared over too many aces or the question of loyalty to the cause of the Union or the Confederacy. Whatever the outcome, it usually meant business for the mirror shop. Flying bullets sometimes brought orders for redecoration of fancy back-bars installed only a few days before.

Solomon purchased an interest in the Hausmann shop. Then, in 1864, to the great relief of his homesick sister, he bought out his brother-in-law. Gertrude happily prepared to take her family back to New York; while across the continent Louisa was steeling herself for the ordeal of a trip to California.

Solomon was greatly relieved when he learned that his younger brother, Gustave, was coming west to represent Greenebaum and Company, a men's furnishing firm into which Henry Cohn had sunk part of the fortune he had taken east from the Comstock. Gus could shepherd the little family safely to their new home.

As Solomon thought of his wife's impending trip west he looked longingly at the daguerreotype he always carried with him. He wondered how she would appear after a whole year of separation. Would she ever be as pretty again as that sixteen-year-old belle who, with her twin sister, Eliza, had swept into the New York ballroom in her swishing hoop-skirted taffeta? How exactly alike they had looked that night, distinguished only by the flowers they wore, one a pink, the other a white camelia. A single look had aroused Solomon's ardor.

"I shall marry one of them!" he had said to his companion.

Now there was some trepidation in his heart as he thought of uprooting this daughter of the wealthy but tight-fisted Simeon Livingston from New York for a second time. The memory of their honeymoon year in the Deep South was not encouraging. Would the tearful homesick days she spent in Apalachicola be repeated in San Francisco? He recalled those heaving sobs when Louisa, fearful of the impending War Between the States, had insisted that they return to New York so that she would not have to bear their first child on "foreign soil." He thought again of her fright as they ran the blockade, passed Fort Sumter as it fell, and endured an Atlantic storm.

This time it was imperative that she like her new home. He must find as comfortable and attractive a dwelling as possible. With two baby girls to bring up, Louisa would be more fussy than ever about the environment in which they would live.

The house that Solomon selected was in a new part of town. The city had spread west as far as Union Square, where several large churches added architectural dignity and moral respectability. He found a small frame house on Geary Street above Powell and stocked its pantry well from the great market a few blocks away at Post and Market streets. He wondered how Louisa would react to the carcasses of bucks and bears that were often hanging in those stalls along with calves and enormous hogs. And would she care to eat the duck and seagull eggs which were displayed there in such quantities?

Solomon regarded himself as a well-established San Franciscan by the time his family was due. He belonged to Pacific Lodge, an early Masonic chapter in the West, was a contributor to Congregation Temple Emanu-el which had just erected a fine new synagogue on Sutter Street, and was active in the mercantile life of the busy city.

During the weeks while Louisa was en route, he read the shipping pages in the *Alta California* with sober anxiety. Attacks on shipping on the Atlantic Coast had increased with the intensity of the war between North and South. Warships now guarded all eastbound shipping from California with their cargoes of gold, and he was relieved to know that the *Sacramento* on which his family had sailed from New York was armed with one 100-pound and four 20-pound Parrott rifles. It had recently been reported that points along the Pacific Coast were believed to be favorable hiding places for Confederate ships and he knew only too well from his own blockade-running experiences how dangerous the whole long journey could be. Perhaps he should not have sent for Louisa until the war was over.

Then he looked about him at the beautiful bay, the fine new buildings of the growing city, the tidy little home he had all ready. Surely Louisa would respond to his own enthusiasm!

At last the flag he longed to see fluttered from the high pole on the Merchants' Exchange, and Solomon joined the pushing crowd on the Folsom Street dock to watch the great paddle-wheeled steamer head for the pier. His eyes strained for the faces he loved. When Louisa came down the gangplank he mustered all his cheerfulness to lift the gloom from her wan face. The journey had indeed been a dreadful one and Gus had had his hands full, between the babies and their seasick mother.

For the first few weeks Solomon was afraid that he was not going to be any more successful in arousing Louisa's enthusiasm than David Hausmann had been with Gertrude. The brown frame house was a poor substitute for the big pink brick home in Gramercy Park where she had spent this last year with her family. Still, this was her own, and Solomon's generosity was a stimulating contrast to the penury of her own father, who hid his wads of bills in odd corners so that his wife could not spend them on luxuries. Solomon enjoyed a hearty laugh when Louisa told him about her father's rage one cold fall day when her mother let her younger brother light the Clinton Airtight Furnace in the hall before the appointed date for winter fires. Her father had cached his wad in the furnace pipes that time!

Louisa insisted upon a few modern improvements in the San Francisco house as their family increased. The children were fascinated as they watched men digging a deep hole in the sandy yard for a new outhouse. Babies were born in quick succession in the first few San Francisco years, all sons—Alfred, Lafayette, and Sigmund. Henrietta and Bella—"the little New Yorkers" as their parents called them—enjoyed their playmates next door, grandchildren of the Stephen Franklins, whose house crowded close beside theirs in typical San Francisco style. Bella and Willie Franklin made a game of "touching hands" through their open windows. Sometimes they all played together in the square where pretty flowers grew behind the white picket fence. On Sundays lovely music floated down the street from the Starr King church.

The family soon grew too big for the little brown house. Just before the next baby was born the Gumps moved out to Eddy and Leavenworth. Here, on December 13, 1869, their fourth son arrived. They called him Abraham for Solomon's handsome father, master blower of the shophar of the synagogue in old Heidelberg, now a highly respected New York merchant. To this they added Louisa's maiden name of Livingston—a translation of the difficult German name Lebenstein which had bothered Simeon's Connecticut neighbors when he ran a farm and general store near Hartford before he became a prosperous New York dry goods dealer.

The little boy, whose imposing name was naturally shortened to Abe, was born the same year that the completed transcontinental railroad finally brought San Francisco into direct communication with the distant East. Raymond-Whitcomb tours from Boston brought trainloads of curious travelers to see the famed Pacific Coast. Men of all types poured into the western terminus. Some sought work, some health. All were adventurers in varying degrees. Most of them stayed to build substantial firms into the business fabric of the community.

Solomon's business had been keeping pace with the fast-moving times. Hausmann had added picture framing to the making of mirrors and gilded cornices before he left. The year after Louisa arrived, in 1865, Solomon began yearly buying trips to Europe, selecting fine Italian marbles for mantels and garden pedestals. By 1866 the small shop on Clay and Leidesdorf became inadequate and he moved to Sansome Street.

The Gump store now had "S. & G." above its door. Following the custom of his forefathers, Solomon had invited his younger brother to join him, giving him a third interest in the business, free of any obligations. Gustave brought to the establishment a solid foundation in merchandising. He had acquired this understanding of business under the Greenebaums and with the Straus firm, with whom he had worked in Macon, Georgia—the same men who later bought Macy's in New York.

The Gump brothers eventually had a new line. Solomon always returned from his European trips carrying baggage bulging with pieces of fine porcelain, delicate figurines, carved animals. Their house, already too small for the necessities, was so overcrowded that practical Louisa protested over the influx of useless knickknacks. Solomon began to carry his treasures to the office.

"Is that for sale?" a newly rich caller asked one morning as he bargained with Solomon over the cornices and matching mirrors to be custom made for his elaborate home.

Soon other customers began buying the vases, porcelains, and figurines which decorated Solomon's desk. *Objets d'art* from "S. & G. Gump" became a mark of distinction.

Now the firm branched out on a large scale. Solomon purchased the business of the pioneer art dealers Jones, Wool, and Sutherland, importers of fine engravings and artists' supplies from Europe. This merger added greatly to the prestige of the Gump store, as well as to its resources. The older firm had started in 1855. At the first Mechanics Fair held in 1857 they had been awarded a diploma for two frames, the best specimens of their class produced or manufactured in California. Their display had included two large frames, one "elaborately wrought specimen gilded with much taste, and another smaller of superior style." There was also an oval gilt frame manufactured in the East but finished and gilded in San Francisco.

During the Civil War this firm had exhibited a collection of beautiful statuettes in plaster—by Rogers of New York—illustrating events of soldier life. These works were held by local art critics as "worth more than a passing notice, exhibiting as they do a force of character and expression of truth to nature that tells the story far better than the artist could have done in words."

By the time the Gumps came into possession, Jones, Wool, and Sutherland had expended some ten thousand dollars in a "suburban enterprise"—a substantial brick edifice where they manufactured the increasing number of frames demanded by the growing population. The building was way out on Market Street, between Seventh and Eighth!

The five oval lathes on the main floor of this factory turned out wooden frames to hold stilted portraits of San Francisco's early citizens and the huge ovoid mirrors which reflected the gaiety of the rich young city.

Upstairs in the gilding rooms where these frames were finished the Gump children spent enchanted hours watching workers sweep up leavings of pure gold, and helped screen them from the dust. The new generation of Gumps was literally born into the business, for it was on the scales used to weigh this retrieved gold that each new Gump baby—Abe, Goldina, William—was weighed by a young apprentice, Sam Smith, who later became foreman of that important department.

Soon Solomon began to provide pictures for the frames that Sam gilded. On one of his earliest trips to Europe he came under the spell of a beautiful artist's model in the Latin Quarter of Paris. She was so lovely that leading painters of the day competed to reproduce her graceful form. Solomon stocked up with these pictures; but once back in San Francisco Louisa would not have them in the house! There was no market among his newer clientele for voluptuous nudes; but his old friends the prosperous saloon keepers vied eagerly for them. Soon his Paris models were posing regularly for the adornment of these walls in the Far West.

Times were good. When the railroad magnates began to build their fine new homes, Gump's mirror and frame business extended up Nob Hill. He had new purchasers for his imported canvases, and the Gump factory on Market Street began to design and gild frames for the enormous oil paintings produced by local artists. Outstanding among these men were two Germans, Charles and Arthur Nahl, who had come to California in the gold rush, recording on canvas the varied experiences they shared.

Their patron was Judge Edwin B. Crocker of Sacramento, the only one of the railroad promoters who did not move to San Francisco. He was a frequent visitor to Gump's because of his interest in art, and one of the first displays in the new Gump showrooms on Sansome street was a huge Nahl painting, resplendent in its Gump-designed gold frame. Art columns of the *Alta* recorded that the Judge had paid Charles Nahl $2000 to carry out this commission.

When Crocker came in to view his purchase he told Gump that he was leaving for Europe to select paintings for the new gallery he was planning to build in the state capitol. Solomon was gratified to know that this man's fortune was being invested in ways that would help to raise the level of public art appreciation. But he was amused when a mutual acquaintance who ran into the California jurist in

Dresden told him later how the Judge did his collecting. According to this friend, Crocker related enthusiastically how a visit to just one gallery accomplished his purpose. He said that the owner started to show him around, explaining in detail the value of the Old Masters he had accumulated, but Crocker saved time and effort by inquiring, "How much will you take for the lot?"

When the Crocker Gallery was assembled, Solomon paid a visit to Sacramento and was pleased to see a few real masterpieces—Rubens' "Moses and the Brazen Serpent"; "Feasting and Dancing in Holland" by Pieter Breughel, the younger; "Landscape with Waterfall" by Salvator Rosa. These and some others equally good were an amazing contribution to the evolving culture of pioneer days; but Solomon, with his knowledge of European art, knew that many others proudly shown to him as masterpieces were not even good copies. Nevertheless, he was too diplomatic a dealer to betray his suspicions to the eminent patron of the arts. Crocker also boasted that the Dresden gallery owner had thrown in a lot of old drawings at very little extra cost. These he had stored in the basement, completely unconscious that among them was an original drawing by Albrecht Dürer, dated 1498!

There were other evidences that the West was waking up to appreciation of good art. In 1871 Solomon became a member of the Art Association formed that year in San Francisco, and was called upon to help in the selection of the canvases by local, eastern, and foreign artists—278 of them—which were exhibited at the association's first public showing in 1872. As yet the association had no settled headquarters. The small museum room of the Mercantile Library served as San Francisco's only "salon d'art." But there was the newly organized Bohemian Club, a group recently founded by journalists, soon augmented by artists and musicians who had found mutual pleasure in the life of the gay young city. Their rooms above the California Market on Pine Street were made available for the annual exhibitions. Later, when the club moved to its own building, those studios became the locale for the School of Design established by the Art Association in 1874. Directing this first school of art was a man of fine training and ability—Virgil Williams, whose background included years of European study.

By the time the Art Association's *Second Annual* was published it listed canvases by local men who were beginning to achieve national recognition. These included Nahl, Albert Bierstadt, Thomas Hill, Jules Tavernier, and a young Scot just then coming into prominence—William Keith.

Solomon had first known Keith as a business neighbor when the artist had operated a small wood-cutting and engraving shop on Clay Street. Here Keith was associated with Durbin Van Vleck, another wood engraver whom he had met when a group of young men originated the Olympic Club in an improvised gymnasium built Turnverein style in the Nahls' backyard. Since Solomon had progressed from the small-business class to become owner of the leading frame and art store in the city, he particularly enjoyed designing for the neighbor who had graduated from craftsman to artist.

By the early seventies San Francisco was becoming a settled metropolis. Home addresses increasingly replaced hotels in the *Social Manual*. Houses were decorated with lavish disregard for cost. Walls of rare woods were hung with rich engravings. Decorous elegance was replacing the garish, and Solomon found increasing demand for better pictures and fine works of art.

Mrs. Milton Latham's open barouche, drawn by two white stallions, often drew up in front of the Gump store. Her footman stepped down from his high seat and ushered the beautiful social leader to the door of the establishment where she could satisfy her desire for elegant furnishings for the palatial country estate the Lathams were building at Menlo Park down the peninsula.

The Gumps were doing well. In their Leavenworth Street home their neighbors were the Dwinelles, the old Judge an early member of the Bohemian Club; the Hall McAllisters; the Lazarus Hoffmans, whose daughter, Fannie, soon became Mrs. Gustave Gump. But this house, too, had become inadequate to the needs of their growing family. Solomon decided to build a "magnificent new home" himself. He was able to negotiate a good real estate deal, exchanging the Leavenworth Street property for a large lot on Geary Street, two blocks beyond Van Ness Avenue.

Friends and neighbors were astonished when they discovered how far out this home was going to be.

"Where *are* the Gumps building?" they asked with raised eyebrows.

"Way out in the dunes!" replied Louisa. "The first house this side of New York, as you come through the Golden Gate."

That remark gave Solomon an idea. Louisa had been a good sport about San Francisco. She deserved a chance to visit her family in New York again. It was time for him to make another buying trip to Europe to satisfy all the fine clients he now had. He invited Louisa to go with him, offering to hire a good nurse to care for the children while they left them with the Livingstons in New York. Louisa could never forget the long seasick voyage to California. No, she would take the family on the luxurious new transcontinental train and wait for him in her old home. They packed great hampers of food and departed on the seven-day trip, leaving Gus to supervise the business, as well as the workmen building the new Geary Street home.

While the family was in New York, the older children enjoyed their weeks among the eastern relatives, especially the horseback rides in Central Park with the Cohn cousins. Part of Henry's fortune had gone to buy the Riding Academy. When the Gump children described the new home they were building in San Francisco, where all the mantels were to be of marble, their cousins replied,

"That's nothing. Even our horses have marble stalls," and the children took their visitors out to the stables of the mansion where they lived out on Fifty-Eighth Street and Fifth Avenue, just to prove their point!

Louisa had a wonderful visit with her twin sister Eliza Bronner, laying plans that would place her among the best-dressed women in San Francisco. Eliza agreed to stand for fittings at their New York dressmaker's and Aunt Minnie Cohn promised that she would send the latest pattern books and samples of materials.

Great emphasis on appearance had been part of Louisa's bringing up. Her mother, Carolyn Bernheimer, was an aristocrat, related to bankers in the Old World and the New. Although Simeon was thrifty beyond all endurance and always roared over bills, large or small, his wife managed to keep peace for longer intervals by purchasing two outfits for each child every time she shopped.

When Solomon returned from Europe, he gathered up his family and they made the return journey in safety. The new house was ready, with its marble mantels, two flights of stairs, and doors of solid walnut. It had cost $7500. Yellow and blue lupin bloomed in profusion in open spaces surrounding it, inviting the children to play and picnic. Across Gough Street was a parklike forest of trees. They were a contented, happy family.

Proud of his European background, Solomon took pains that his children should have every opportunity to improve their minds and tastes. They all went to the Clement Grammar School on Geary Street where the personality of the principal, Madame DuBois, created the atmosphere he desired. Four times a week the girls joined fifteen others from the "best families" at Frau Fritsch's home for lessons in crocheting, sewing, making wax flowers, and German conversation. On Christmas Eve, Frau Fritsch, who was the director of the German Theater in the Baldwin Hotel, gave a great party for all her pupils and the actors. Every Friday night the entire Gump family attended the Tivoli, then run as a German beer garden, where they listened to great singers who included San Francisco on their itinerary.

Her home with its bay window and salon-parlor gave Louisa a sense of pride and security. Now she could entertain in a style consistent with their position in the art and business world. Her salons were held the second and fourth Wednesday and every Thursday night: these dates were duly entered in the *Social Manual*. The great tables were heaped with delectable pastries and other good things, all baked at home under her direction by a skilled Chinese cook who had formerly worked for the editor of the *Argonaut*. Louisa had come a long way since those homesick days in Apalachicola when she had lost face every time she had ventured among the strange black folk in her kitchen to set a spicy raised cake heavy with citron and seeded raisins or bake a juicy apple pie, Connecticut style. Solomon never found her in tears any more.

That Chinese cook had his favorite admirer in Abe, who loved to finger the gorgeous silk banner on the walls of his basement room and listen to tales of ancient China. The long pigtail and the coral knob on the black skull cap intrigued the boy, whose favorite haunt was Chinatown.

While the salon days were of utmost importance to Louisa, the children lived in anticipation of their Sunday drives. At first they used to go in the store wagon with robes over the seats. They would go to Sigie's grave (that little boy had died at an early age) and then to the Cliff House, stopping to pick lupin and poppies along sandy Geary Road where it cost "two bits" at one toll gate, "four bits" at the second. Many a time the children would be required to walk up the hills to save the horses. One such afternoon they met an old friend, David Neustader.

"Gump, you should be ashamed," he exclaimed. "This is no way for a man in your position to take out his family. You should have a carriage."

Long discussion followed this suggestion. They sent east for all the catalogues. Should they buy a coupé or a phaeton? The latter won, and the Gump fringed-top phaeton was the first of its kind to appear in San Francisco. They hired a driver—Frank Dexter, grandson of an old racetrack king.

Despite their social life, Gump spent the greater part of his time supervising the enlarging business of the firm. In 1873 he became interested in a local artist, William Marple, whose landscapes were winning acclaim and prizes at the Mechanics Fairs. To give Marple financial backing, Gump entered into a partnership, whereby he became sole agent for the artist's work, and they opened a studio at 103 Montgomery Street.

Solomon's entry into big business came when S. & G. Gump Company was commissioned to decorate the splendid new Occidental Hotel. Its floor-length mirrors reflected gatherings of the elite of the prosperous city; it soon became the popular rendezvous for California Street speculators, big businessmen, and rich widows. As Solomon and Gus worked in its lobbies, hanging paintings and supervising the installation of mantels and mirrors, they heard the talk of the town and met manipulators of wealth.

The same year Jim Flood and Bill O'Brien, near-by restaurant and saloon keepers, shared in the Big Bonanza on the Comstock. Naturally the Gump brothers were asked to help refurbish Virginia City for its second period of prosperity. They were soon riding over the Sierras to Nevada to measure the walls of The International and to provide fancy back-bars for the saloons.

Solomon, too busy to make his trip to Europe that summer, sent Marple instead, and their Montgomery Street studio was listed in the directory as "Marple and Gump, Importers of Paintings."

S. & G. Gump Company expanded with the fabulous times. As the Bonanza Kings poured new wealth into homes rivaling those of the railroad builders, they looked to these art dealers for their elaboration. The firm needed more display space for the stock of bric-a-

SUNDAY MORNING IN THE MINES

by Charles Christian Nahl

This representation of an early California mining camp was painted from life, for the artist carried his easel along with his pick and shovel into Yuba County in 1851. It now hangs in the Crocker Art Gallery in Sacramento, in a frame typical of the elaborate work of the first S. & G. Gump gilding shop.

(Photograph by Frank van Eckhardt)

brac and gilt furniture, which was crowding in on their mirrors, mantels, and cornices.

In 1874 they rented a four-story building on Market Street at Second. The owner of the building, Jack Cunningham, was fond of the arts and enjoyed visiting the gallery his tenants were setting up on the top floor. One morning Solomon was taking Cunningham for a preview of the exhibit he was planning.

"This is slow service," complained the owner as the elevator climbed haltingly toward the top.

"That is full speed," replied Gump, and forthwith Cunningham ordered new ram elevators for all his tenants.

The Galleries were officially opened in 1875. Engraved invitations and printed catalogues brought frock-coated gentlemen and ladies in rustling silk to view the latest successes of California artists hung beside the European canvases which Solomon had brought from England, France, Germany, Austria and Italy.

Keith had returned from his studies in Germany. His finest canvases were resplendent in frames gilded by Sam Smith and his new assistant, a red-bearded Hollander who had recently arrived via England—I. Magnin by name! Nahl's great "Sunday Morning in the Mines," which Judge Crocker had commissioned him to paint, had a frame especially designed to emphasize its story—a miner's pick and a pan full of nuggets as well as a shaggy bear's head.

A block away from the Market Street store Ralston and Sharon were investing their Comstock millions in San Francisco's imposing new hotels—the Palace and the Grand (connected by a "Bridge of Sighs" across the intervening street). The whole city shared in excited anticipation of the opening of the glittering Palace, epitomizing as it did all the elegance of the era. Only William C. Ralston, who had visioned the great palm-lined court where he would drive his coach and four in a dramatic entrance after galloping up from his suburban home on the Peninsula hills, was not present.

Little Abe Gump, flattening his nose against the window pane

out in the salon-parlor on Geary Street, implanted deep in his mind
the endless procession that formed Ralston's funeral cortege on that
foggy August afternoon in 1875, two months before the great Palace
was finished.

Abe would never forget, either, the wondrous night when his
father took him and his brothers to see the balconied courtyard of
the new hotel. Thousands of gas lights, ignited by electric sparks,
reflected on the thick plate glass roof of the court. The lobbies were
filled with impressive men and women, many of whom greeted his
father and Uncle Gus jovially.

Now that the quaint hotels of mining days—The Original, What
Cheer House, The Oriental—had given way to such luxury, the saloons became sophisticated "bars." Solomon Gump took full advantage of this opportunity to increase their decorative use of oil
paintings. The saloons were becoming the first public galleries of
the West.

Fay and Doyle, proprietors of the Grand Hotel Bar, created a
sensation when they purchased "Cytherea," painted by the French
artist, Lionel Roya. This life-sized Venus descending stairs with
many doves circling about her unclad figure became the toast of the
town; many a wag tossed corn at her feet to lure away the doves.

Solomon even succeeded in raising the artistic standards of the
bars when he brought over some paintings of Normandy fishermen
in their oil sou'westers done by an American artist, Georges Hacquette, working in Paris. When Gump offered these canvases at
auction, Hacquette's cousin, Charlie Hacquette, owner of the aristocrat of San Francisco saloons, the Crystal Palace on Kearny Street,
bid $1500 for one of his cousin's best.

With the prestige that such ownership gave his establishment,
Hacquette soon added other canvases to his gallery, finally paying
$7000 at an auction for one of the earliest paintings brought to San
Francisco from Europe. This huge canvas by Jacob, depicting "Sam-
son and the Philistines," had been among the four hundred paintings

imported in the fifties by John Duncan, proprietor of a waterfront auction house where he sold everything from silverware and diamonds to Japanese curios.

With the acquisition of these paintings Charlie Hacquette's Crystal Palace began to vie with the city's popular amusement park, Woodward's Gardens, where exhibitions consisted mostly of copies of famous pictures plus much weird statuary. Because Hacquette's paintings had real merit, it even became respectable for women's clubs to visit the Crystal Palace on stated days when the nudes and other unsuitable items were relegated to the back bar. And Louisa Gump herself sometimes consented to bring her two girls, Henrietta and Bella, to the Crystal Palace to see the painting of the Normandy fishermen which Papa had brought from Europe.

In the summer of 1876 Solomon sent John Wool to Europe with $20,000 to spend on paintings for the saloons and salons of San Francisco; but by the time his purchases were shipped to their destination, Gump's was caught, like its patrons, in the panic of 1877.

Sound art dealer that he was, Solomon was not so prudent an investor. He had listened to too many high-sounding tips from California Street speculators. Carried along on the surging wave of mad money-making, he was caught, as were many others, when the stock of Consolidated Virginia dropped in a week from $1500 a share to $5. He had to confess to Louisa that they were poorer by $175,000.

The children waited in vain for their Sunday drive that week! All Solomon had left was his business and the nerve which had made him a blockade-runner. He knew how to take losses. When his schooner, plantation, and ship chandlery had been confiscated during the war, he had lost everything except $10,000 which he had brought to New York to restock the chandlery with white goods.

He brought a gambler's spirit to this new land of chance. Money could be made again. Like San Francisco, he was sobered but not de-

jected. In spite of Louisa's downcast face he finally recouped the
loss with the zest of youth.

With San Francisco's recovery from the panic, appreciation of
art was growing. Although the *London Times* of 1878 published
a squib chiding the raw young city for its inability to recognize
"beauty in an intaglio" and saying that "a brilliant is the measure of
its taste," Solomon could have refuted the statement. He was finding many clients to whom music, drama, and good painting were
as essential as bread and mortar.

Gump was not alone in this discovery. In December of that
same year an advertisement appeared in the *Alta* suggesting that
nothing could be more appropriate for Christmas or a wedding present than a fine engraving, rare, and suitable for home decoration.
The notice informed the public that W. K. Vickery of 22 Montgomery Street, opposite Lick House, had just received a fine collection
which his agent had selected in Italy.

Gump knew this young Irishman who had slipped unobtrusively
into town a few months before with a roll of etchings and engravings under his arm. In fact, Vickery had had Gump frame the few
engravings he sold from office to office. Solomon became friendly
with the young salesman who had left the art business in New York
because he had only a few months to live if he remained there.

Vickery found sufficient interest in the art he brought with him
to justify the establishment of his own corner in Doxey's bookstore
under the Palace Hotel. Other dealers were also taking account of
the new culture in San Francisco. Morris and Kennedy opened what
they termed an "Art Depot" on lower Post Street. Snow and May
brought the first piece of fine sculpture to be exhibited in the city—
W. W. Storey's "Lost Pleiad." Gump purchased this firm, with its
Art Agency Gallery frescoed by Nahl and its reputation among the
more discriminating buyers of art.

The young Gump children were growing up in an atmosphere

far better than anything Louisa could have imagined as she dreaded
the move to the "horrid city" Gertrude had described. She reveled
in the prestige afforded by festive Gump Gallery Nights. There her
young people not only became familiar with the best in European
and American art, but they were also hosts to the substantial men
and women who could afford to possess these treasures.

Solomon was just managing to build back his business losses
when Abe ran home to him with the upsetting discovery that he
could not see the school blackboard. Dr. Barkan's prescription of the
dark room brought little relief, and as soon as the insistent boy won
permission to try school again, the shadows deepened.

At the doctor's suggestion, Solomon decided to take Abe to New
York for consultation with Dr. Herman Knapp, world renowned
among eye men.

While Abe remained with the Livingston grandparents so that
he could have the benefit of Dr. Knapp's care for a few months,
Solomon took his oldest son on a buying trip to Europe. He was
preparing Alfred to assume that responsibility as early as possible.

The Livingstons had moved to Fifty-Third Street between Second and Third Avenues. Simeon took his young namesake—who by
now preferred the middle name of Livingston to the first name so
easily abbreviated to Abe—to show him where his grandmother used
to live. The Bernheimer farm at Fortieth Street and Fifth Avenue
boasted the Vanderbilt's brownstone city house. The old man rather
sheepishly admitted his lack of foresight when he had refused to
take his Irish real estate partner's advice and buy on Fifth Avenue
years before.

"Fifth Avenue!" he had exclaimed. "That's only good enough
for goats. I'm buying on Third."

Abe felt very sorry for his grandfather when he told him about
the millions his partner had made, while the elevated had roared in

over Third Avenue and spoiled the value of the homesite where he
was visiting.

When Solomon returned from Europe he learned with grave
concern that Dr. Knapp felt nothing could be done to curb the
glaucoma that would inevitably end in blindness. But there was
consolation in the added remark of the famous specialist.

"Why did you bring the boy way across the continent to me?
Your own Dr. Barkan is equally equipped."

The father knew that he could take his boy home to San Francisco and still have skilled advice as he met this discouraging situation.

The Gump firm was recognized as the leading exponent of art
on the Pacific Coast, both in eastern and European circles, and
young A. Livingston—as Abe now tried to be called—was proud to
participate in the annual Mechanics Fair. The boy, whose love of
San Francisco was rooted in the stories his father had told him of
their part in its early business life, entered into the fairs with the
proprietary feeling of an old timer. His part was humble—handing
out picture postcards, showing Gump's prize-winning displays—
but he listened with swelling chest as he heard visitors exclaim that
Gump could buy such good paintings for them that they did not
have to go to New York, Paris, or Rome for their art, and that workmen right in San Francisco could produce carved mantels, furniture,
and other objects of home decoration worthy of the finest mansion.

The Gump exhibit in 1884 won the gold medal for two mantels
with matching mirrors which the judges declared to form in each
case a "most artistic and beautiful suite." One of them was in
Moorish style, made of polished black walnut, with lofty and lus-
trous mirror surmounted by a carved cap or headpiece, and with
mirror-backed niches at the sides for statuettes, vases or bric-a-brac.
The main shelf was supported by large Corinthian columns, one at

each end. These, as well as the keystone above the fire arch, were skillfully carved.

Their mirror frames, wrought in burnished gold and encrusted with birds and foliage in pale and azure gold and silver, were also worthy of high praise. The judges declared that these reminded them of the "poet's 'apples of gold in pictures of silver.'" A gold frame, with lace work of gold and silver, enclosing the dreamy ethereal portrait of a child caused many an emotional sigh.

Solomon was hailed as a thorough critic in art matters for his careful selections, and he trained his sons to carry on the family tradition. Alfred began to assume the European buying. Although Lafayette was blind, his father relied upon his friendly ways and bright mind to overcome his handicap and succeeded in making a good salesman of him.

Abe, undeterred by Dr. Knapp's dire warning, insisted upon trying to keep up his school. He managed to apply himself so well that he reached high school before Dr. Barkan decreed that the close work of study would accelerate the deterioration of his eyesight and he was taken out. At thirteen he began his apprenticeship in the store.

This was long before the days of typewriters. Every letter, written in laborious Spencerian script, was duplicated by wetting two leaves of tissue paper with a camel's hair brush and placing them, with the letter, between blotters. It was often Abe's task to turn the wheel of the roller that took off the impressions for the "letter books"; but he found the task boring. It was selling that intrigued him.

Currier and Ives prints were his first enthusiasm—a contagion caught from Solomon. His father often told Abe how he had lingered, fascinated, before the window displays of old ship pictures in the original Currier and Ives shop as he walked down Fulton Street to Nassau in New York. One of his first ventures in San Francisco had been to obtain the exclusive agency for these prints in the Far

West. "Yachting" and "Birth of a Nation" especially appealed to Abe. Holding them close to his face, he memorized the details with such success that his boyish zeal later sold many copies. For four dollars apiece customers acquired prints which multiplied to a value as high as $250 within the span of Gump's lifetime.

Not only as a potential salesman, but also in other ways, the partially blind youth was developing. He was fond of boxing. He perfected his skill, surprising opponents by punches well-placed despite dim eyesight. One day he accepted an invitation to a shoemakers' picnic in Marin County, taking as his partner a young Irish girl with more humor than judgment.

When a big bruiser asked her to dance, Abe took offense at a fresh remark and the result was a fight. Not being able to see his opponent, Abe's only recourse was to keep on throwing punches until the other fellow was beaten. The victory was a sensation. On the way home, he and his partner boarded a crowded streetcar after they left the ferry building.

"Have you a knife?" she asked him unexpectedly.

Without asking the purpose of her request, he handed her his penknife. Whereupon the girl ripped the linen duster of the man in front of them from collar to hem. As it flapped suddenly in the wind, the owner turned upon Abe, sputtering in anger. Taken completely by surprise, Gump apologized profusely for the girl and succeeded in pacifying the stranger. They had reached their destination by that time. As they got off the car Abe turned to the girl in consternation, asking what on earth had made her act like a vandal.

"I wanted to see you fight again!" was her only excuse.

CHAPTER TWO ∾ *Art for Salons*

ABE GUMP served apprenticeship as a salesman when art was front page news in San Francisco. The boy, growing up under the guidance of Solomon and Uncle Gus, applied a naturally studious mind to lessons in human nature as well as in art appreciation, and his retentive memory held what he learned.

Love of sport and a well developed sense of humor were added to his grasp of those fundamentals, for in spite of his visual handicap Abe was an excellent runner, a good swimmer, and an enthusiastic amateur yachtsman. He was a member of the Oakland Canoe Club, spending congenial hours on the bay with cronies outside the realm of artists, and thus becoming a part of the community in a way that enlarged the store's clientele.

Some of Abe's intimates were members of the store staff. He was particularly interested in the bookkeeper, Eismann, who was heavyweight champion of the Olympic Club and one of Jim Corbett's first antagonists. On Monday mornings Abe always managed to be where he could hear the latest fight talk between Eismann and one of the store's top salesmen. The boy knew that when training season was over these two made a habit of sleeping off week-end hangovers in an inconspicuous corner of the galleries. One huge canvas, Tojetti's "Elaine," was a favorite screen for the erring salesman. The art critic of the *Alta* used a front-page column to describe Tojetti's genius in portraying the "indescribable refinement with which death glorifies the face of peasant or prince." Some ladies, impressed with this eloquence, came to Gump's Galleries to study "how the artist's art illustrates this fleeting glimpse of heaven's reflected light." Uncle Gus was showing the canvas to his visitors with great solemnity.

Abe, who knew that his friend was sleeping on some furniture pads behind the painting, lingered near with his feather duster. The ladies gazed admiringly at the tragic figure on the barge. Suddenly the corpse seemed to snore! Irate Uncle Gus quickly ushered the bewildered group out of the galleries. Abe disappeared behind the counter, keeping near enough to hear his uncle deliver a masterpiece of invective before handing the offending salesman his time.

"Elaine" was typical of the huge canvases appropriate to the high-ceilinged mansions where Abe was in the habit of going with his father. Solomon insisted upon personal supervision of the hanging of such notable paintings framed in his shop. Soon learning that his personable son was welcome in the homes of his patrons, he often sent Abe along to direct the workmen.

The younger man won deserved praise from his father one afternoon when his ingenuity saved the firm a disappointed customer. Solomon had sold a painting, "Milking Time" by the popular French artist Julian Dupré, to one of his more aristocratic Pacific Avenue patrons. When Abe and his crew arrived to deliver the monstrous decoration they found that the framed painting would not go through the front door. There was nothing to do but return it to the shop, where the canvas was demounted and rolled up carefully. Workmen took the enormous gold frame apart and carried the four straight pieces with the rolled-up canvas back to Pacific Avenue. Laying the pieces on the deep-piled carpet, they skillfully reassembled the frame and restretched the canvas. When the job was completed and the picture hung at one end of the great room, Abe felt as if he could walk straight into the meadow; and he was inwardly amused over the realistic effect of cows being milked in a drawing room.

Critics objected that the maid was milking on the wrong side.

Years later, when Abe made his first trip to Europe, he met Monsieur Dupré in Paris. The young San Franciscan put the question to the artist, asking why he had painted the picture that way.

"Very simple," replied Dupré. "In Normandy, cows are milked from either side."

Merchants and customers were on first-name terms in those days of city-building. As Abe followed his father and uncle into salons where gay banter mingled with artistic lore and business planning, he absorbed a profound respect for the men and women who were laying the foundations of metropolitan San Francisco.

Up on Rincon Hill they took their framed masterpieces to the home of Irving M. Scott, president of the Union Iron Works. Abe listened to Scott's prideful enthusiasm over Keith landscapes, for Scott felt that he had discovered William Keith. Abe learned from his father about the day when Scott had called personally at the Keith-Van Vleck studio, indignant because a publicity cut ordered for the Union Iron Works was long delayed. Instead of apologizing, Keith opened a drawer and showed one of his landscapes to the man who was regarded as a great art patron.

Although Scott was still annoyed over the business delay, he recognized that latent talent was being wasted on commercial tasks. A few days later he met the president of the Oregon Navigation and Railroad Company who was looking for an artist to paint some scenic views of the right-of-way. Scott sent the man to Keith and the artist was soon launched on his distinguished career.

The import of Scott's lenient attitude sunk into Abe's receptive mind. What a satisfaction it must be to know that one's perception of talent had such a reward. In imagination he visioned himself in similar situations. He, too, would discover great artists. He would encourage potential creativeness by making his business an outlet for their productions.

The young man was smart enough to realize that this meant having many and varied contacts. He applied himself to learning from every source he could find. The era in which he was maturing was especially adapted to this purpose. San Francisco was full of self-made men, some of them ruthless, but all of them devoting the vigor of their manhood to the shaping of a city. Because Gump's dealt in the trappings of culture, Abe had an unusual entreé into homes of distinction.

Often he and his father climbed Nob Hill to supervise the hanging of a newly framed picture for the Leland Stanford Gallery. In this environment he saw the world in miniature. The Stanfords were ubiquitous travelers. They had been everywhere—from Rome to Constantinople—and always brought back a bit of atmosphere. The catalogue of their collection of pictures and statuary was kept in a flawless malachite box, only ornament on the onyx top of a table in the Pompeian Room that adjoined the gallery. The table itself was made from a slab that had once been a part of a faulty pillar removed from St. Peter's.

Stanford wealth was expended on all variety of pomp. The Gumps sometimes worked to the accompaniment of opera music from an orchestrion which occupied the wall opposite the entrance; and when the housekeeper touched a button, gay-plumaged birds on the branches of potted plants came to life and sang!

If he stepped into the Chinese Room, which always had a special fascination for him, Abe saw the carved furniture sent by the Empress Dowager to the Centennial at Philadelphia. These had been presented to the former governor of California "in appreciation of fair treatment and protection of the Chinese in California."

Mrs. Stanford's memento of that exposition had a more personal significance. She told the Gumps of the prize-winning Tiffany necklace of diamond solitaires, with its companion crescent brooch and earrings, which her husband had purchased as a gift for her at the Centennial. Then she showed them the still life she had commissioned a Peninsula artist to paint, preserving on canvas the famous jewel collection of which these pieces were the nucleus; and she asked them to design a suitable frame. As Solomon studied the vivid reproduction of this ostentation, he recognized the meticulous work of a San Jose artist named Cooper. He chuckled to himself when he thought of the many copies of nudes which this same artist had painted for the less pretentious saloons. Since Cooper had carried out this commission to the satisfaction of Mrs. Stanford's rigid taste, the artist would now undoubtedly be received in other carefully guarded salons.

The Stanford home with all its ponderous museum atmosphere was not the place which young Gump most enjoyed. He much preferred the informality mixed with grandeur in the new palace built for Claus Spreckels on Van Ness Avenue. The Gump family were all on a friendly footing here. Abe remembered the sugar magnate as the genial host of Ocean House at Aptos on Santa Cruz Bay. The Gumps had made that hundred-mile trip many a time to enjoy a summer vacation at the Spreckels' hotel. One of Abe's earliest memories was of carrying a flag in the Aptos children's parade in 1876 when he and his sisters, wearing big red, white, and blue sashes, had celebrated the centennial of the founding of the United States.

Solomon often reminded Spreckels that he must buy many pictures in return for the money that Solomon spent in taking his large family to enjoy those weeks at Ocean House. Spreckels responded as a good customer. Huge canvases went regularly from the Gump Galleries to fill wall spaces in the sixty-room dwelling where door knobs and bathroom fixtures were of solid silver. Some of the paintings on the Spreckels' walls, like "The Return of General Ambrioco to Genoa after the First Crusade," became textbooks in Abe's art education—as well as examples of the returns from good salesmanship. That particular picture brought $9000!

The young man was learning from experience how to deal with contrasting elements in San Francisco society. His father was at ease with the newly rich who aspired to the most expensive, regardless of fitness. His knowledge of Europe gave Solomon high rating with these customers who often went abroad themselves, buying much that was atrocious but becoming familiar enough with names of Old World artists and sculptors to give superficial tone to their conversation.

Abe, on the other hand, was sensitive to the cultured atmosphere of other Nob Hill homes, such as that of the William T. Colemans. Mrs. Coleman, with Mayflower antecedents, was the daughter of Daniel Dearborn Page, one of the first eastern Lankers to establish a branch in the Far West. In his rare visits to that home, with its inviting library, music room, and fragrant conservatory, Abe saw and benefited from their good taste. One morning the now elderly Coleman (known as the "Lion of the Vigilantes," for his fearless leadership in the lawless period of the late fifties) came into Gump's as Abe was helping to unwrap a shipment of paintings and water colors from Italy. Delighted to find such exquisite selections this side of New York or Boston, Coleman bought over half of them, without waiting for the pictures to be prepared in the frame shop for display.

The Colemans had wealth as well as culture, but Abe realized that many others whose taste exceeded their bank rolls were making large contributions to San Francisco's finer traditions. He knew well enough that most of these customers sought out the smaller stores like Morris and Kennedy or the new one that W. K. Vickery was opening. When he heard the Colemans enthuse over the unique experiment in selling that the idealistic Irishman was trying, he strolled up to the corner of Morton Alley and Grant Avenue—as lower Dupont Street was then called. As he looked down the notorious alley where painted faces peered from iron-grilled windows he speculated drolly as to how the fastidious good ladies who were Vickery's major customers would take the new location.

There was nothing elaborate in the setting of the store itself. One print hung in the window. Inside was a small table with a plate of crackers, evidently all the dealer could afford in the way of hospitality. People were wandering in to ask what was being sold. For those who were really interested either Vickery or his young associate, Bruce Porter, would open a drawer and produce a carefully chosen etching. In a city accustomed to blatant display this was indeed new selling technique! Abe gave thoughtful heed to its implications as he went his way. By this process Vickery was transplanting some of the wiles practiced by subtle old merchants on upper Dupont. There was an important difference, however. If the wise Cantonese did put away their finer pieces of porcelain and ivory for the few buyers who understood real beauty, they also filled their windows with enough cheap stuff to attract the unsuspecting tourist.

Gump's had certain advantages over the newer firms in a community composed of strangely assorted characters. Their roots went deeper into pioneer ground and their diversified stock brought customers of all classes to their store and galleries. They were asked to do strange things by the eccentric as well as the wise. The lowest ebb came one day when the jangling silver bells of a carriage, drawn by matched gray horses, interrupted a conversation Abe was carrying on with one of his most cultured patrons. A woman, whose millions were matched by her avoirdupois, waddled into the store with a white-enameled toilet seat over her richly clad arm. A near-by clerk quick-wittedly drew the dignified customer away as the newcomer hailed Abe by his familiar nickname; but they were still within hearing distance as the intruder loudly commanded the embarrassed young Gump,

"Have your cabinet shop enlarge this opening—five inches wider and ten inches longer—and gild it. I've always wanted to sit on gold."

The next time she came in Abe could not resist the question, "Is the seat satisfactory?"

"A perfect fit," replied his old friend.

Not all the wealth of early San Francisco was in the hands of the respectable. The women who kept their houses in the shunned district which extended from Morton Alley between Geary and Post Streets practically to the door of St. Mary's Church appreciated the beautiful as much as did their neighbors higher up on the hills.

Tessie Wall, one of the refined red light residents, stood entranced before the Geary Street store window. She was looking at a painting of a seventeenth-century salon with gorgeously gowned women under crystal chandeliers.

"How much do you want for that, Willie?" she asked, as the youngest of the Gump sons, now a salesman in his father's store, came by.

"One thousand dollars."

"I'm going to bet on a long shot. If I win, I'll buy it."

He asked the name of the horse and later on rang up Corbett's. Sure enough, her horse won. Sorry that he had not bet himself, Willie phoned Tessie,

"I see your horse won. How about the painting?"

"You know me, Willie. I never break my word," said Tessie. "Bring it over."

She paid him in twenty-dollar gold pieces. But when he returned to the store, his Uncle Gus counted the money.

"You are ten dollars short."

"Oh yes, we celebrated by opening a bottle of champagne."

"You might have opened a smaller bottle," was his uncle's quizzical comment.

Another of Tessie's contemporaries, May Stuart, once owed a long overdue bill upwards of five hundred dollars. Abe was sent to collect it at her house on Stockton between Post and Sutter. A colored maid opened the door and showed him in to Miss Stuart.

"May, I have come for that five hundred dollars."

"Don't worry, you'll get your money. Do you want to know who'll pay it?" she asked, opening the door to a bedroom.

There lay a bachelor acquaintance, scion of one of the old families and also a good patron of the arts. He had been May's guest for some time, as was evidenced by untold empty champagne bottles on the floor. The bill was shortly paid in full.

Friends and clients were quick to sense that Solomon's enthusiastic young son, who was already beginning to show a special talent in recognizing the intrinsically beautiful, was a salesman to be trusted. His very handicap of defective vision seemed to make him more careful. Where the ordinary person took in a painting at a glance, this young man would stand patiently before a canvas, almost rubbing his nose on the paint, as he examined the surface closely and accurately. All the time his mind was fusing the impression into a lasting memory.

Whenever he helped his father uncrate a new shipment of paintings, he would ask questions about the legends depicted on the huge canvases. Then as he stood before them flecking dust from ornate gilt frames he memorized the stories of street scenes in Venice or Bagdad, sunset in Cairo, or cheese making in the Apennines. His enthusiasm was often ahead of his knowledge, and he sometimes got his facts confused.

A visiting actress saw through his bluff one day and called him.

"You should be an actor, not a salesman," she told him.

Complimented, and unconscious of the implied rebuke, Abe answered, "My poor eyesight would be too much of a handicap."

"Far from it," she answered. "That would be an asset. You would not be annoyed by the audience!"

He was, however, exceedingly sensitive to his audience—when he could hear it. And he made good use of his acute hearing, especially at card playing. As long as he could hold the cards close to his face and distinguish spades from clubs he was a good poker player. The controlled muscles of his placid face, and eyes that could not betray his emotions, won him many a hand. He learned that although it was easy for him to maintain a poker face, that was not enough. He had a better secret. He could interpret sighs, nervous fumbling with cards, or tapping on the table with greater accuracy than others could read the meaning of twitching eyes or pursed lips.

Abe Gump cultivated his handicap as others would their talents. His malady was such that he had good and bad days. When the good days came, the fog lifted from his eyes and he could see things that others with normal vision, but busily preoccupied minds, would ignore. Thus he gradually acquired a reputation for perspicacity that caused him to be signaled out among his brothers and the other clerks as a dealer with rare judgment. This opened doors to him that brought new friends and lasting satisfaction.

When the wife of Judge John S. Hager, Collector of Customs, called for Abe at the store in her stylish carriage and asked that he accompany her to the home she had just purchased from the Charles Josselyns, he was highly complimented. The walls of the San Francisco mansion built by Josselyn, a wealthy ship chandler who had moved down the Peninsula to Woodside, had space for many large paintings. The opportunity to select appropriate canvases for Mrs. Hager was one of Abe's first large independent commissions, and Solomon was gratified to find that his confidence in this son's ability was justified in spite of the physical handicap which had seemed to threaten his plans. Mrs. Hager expressed haughty preference for European artists. Abe's patient study of Weisse's Arabian mosques and Edwin Lord Week's pluricolored scenes of India gave authority to his praise whenever he recommended a foreign landscape to this customer.

Another approach was necessary when he dealt with Kate Johnson. This eccentric philanthropist, who spent half her time abroad, liked to consider herself a patron of California artists. Canvases by Toby Rosenthal, William Keith, and others who were painting the California scene hung next to those she had collected on her travels. Because of her diversified interests she was a frequent visitor at Gump's, appreciating the rare objects chosen by Solomon and encouraging the young man whose salesmanship appealed to her. Mrs. Johnson sometimes called Abe to her home to share her pleasure in a special souvenir of a journey. One day she showed him the largest rock crystal elephant he had ever seen.

"If you can lift it, you may have it," she offered. But when he accomplished the feat, she reneged.

Abe had been too young to participate in the assignment of furnishing cornices and mirrors for the fashionable Del Monte Hotel on the Monterey Peninsula, when F. S. Douty, secretary of the Pacific Improvement Company—subsidiary of the Southern Pacific —had come to Solomon in 1880 with that important job. But after the original edifice was destroyed by fire in 1887 Abe had a large part in selecting paintings and other furnishings for the resort, then known throughout the world as the finest vacation spot on the Pacific Coast.

Success in that undertaking brought him into contact with top management in the railroad organization. His understanding of men grew as he served those leaders both in their business enterprise and in their homes. Senator Stanford's secretary, Stephen Gage, became a particularly heroic figure to Abe. Standing six feet, two inches tall, Gage was a typical product of the West, straight as an arrow, his luxuriant beard filling the space left open by his unbuttoned shirt.

A. N. Towne, vice-president of the railroad when Abe first knew him as a customer, was another who represented superlative leadership to the young art dealer. Towne, who had risen from a job as brakeman to his present responsibility, was close to the president, Collis P. Huntington. It was through their friendship that A.L., as he was becoming known in business circles, met the man who taught him to respect most thoroughly the wisdom of a true connoisseur. In 1891, when Huntington decided that the Palace Hotel was too noisy as a San Francisco headquarters and purchased the Nob Hill home of his former associate, the late General David D. Colton, he called upon A.L. to assist in reassembling the art collection which he acquired along with the house.

"What shall we do with these?" Gump questioned as they paused over some paintings which were not up to Huntington's standards.

"Put them in the Mineral Room," answered Huntington, indicating the room where the former president of the California Academy of Sciences had garnered his specimens, "and we'll call it 'Colton Annex.'"

Although relations between Colton and the "Big Four" of the railroad became strained in his last years, he and Huntington had earlier been on friendly terms. Huntington explained that he had chosen some of the canvases which hung in the big wooden house—painted white as a copy of an Italian marble palace. At times Colton, who was his San Francisco representative, had sent him checks as large as $5000 to be spent in the eastern art market. An enormous seascape hanging behind the grand piano became a favorite of young Gump. Painted by Professor Leffler of Vienna, it depicted the battle between the *Bonhomme Richard* and the *Serapis*. When the lights in the crystal chandeliers glowed, the picture seemed to come to life. Abe Gump's imagination transported him into the smoke and flames of that stirring scene on the moonlit sea. He could almost hear the captain of the *Serapis* shout, "Do you strike?" and Captain John Paul Jones' answer, "I have not yet begun to fight."

The same driving force that Huntington put into railroad building went into his art collecting, and his taste was equal to his energy. When Abe made his first sale to Huntington, he discovered how quickly the railroad magnate could recognize a splendid painting.

A strange circumstance preceded that transaction. One morning Alfred handed his younger brother an advertisement from the *Chronicle* saying that an elderly French lady, desiring to return to France, wanted to part with a rare work of art.

Abe set off toward North Beach with his pal, Billy Morrow.

They carried their fishing poles under their arms in case the search should prove fruitless and they should have some time left over for an hour on the wharves.

They climbed up rickety stairs to quarters over a grocery store where a gentlewoman opened the door to them, exclaiming in surprise,

"My dear sir, you are very young. This is a serious matter."

Then, removing a sheet, she revealed a gorgeous painting of the Empress Josephine lying nude on a couch, holding in her hand a miniature of her first husband, General Beauharnais. Above the couch, draperies were clutched in the beak of a great carved eagle.

The picture was signed "Baron Girard." Young as he was, Abe knew that signature. He remembered Alfred's interest in paintings by Pascal de Girard (afterward made baron by Napoleon) from his elder brother's descriptions of his own early visits to the Louvre. The Frenchwoman told him that the painting had come into her possession when her father, a Parisian art dealer, had been ordered to destroy certain works of art at the time of the downfall of the Empire. It was obvious why this one had been included. The old man had reported it as destroyed, but his sense of the beautiful had led him to hide and keep it for his own satisfaction.

Abe may have seemed *very* young to the elderly owner; but he was wise enough to recognize that the painting was a prize worth having. He brought tears of relief to the old lady's eyes as he agreed to pay her the $700 dollars she asked. He and Billy Morrow had no time left over to go fishing that morning! Between them they carried the large painting down the narrow stairs and hailed a cab to take them back to the store. It was noontime when they arrived. Solomon had gone home to lunch; but, as was sometimes his habit, Collis Huntington dropped by to see what was new in the galleries.

His cultivated eye caught sight of the Empress Josephine at once and he asked Abe where he had found such a canvas in San Francisco. Proud of his opportunity to deal with this important customer alone, Abe related his experience of the morning, assuring Mr. Huntington that he had thought at once of offering the painting to him for his collection.

"What are you asking for it?" inquired Huntington.

Abe thought fast. This was his chance to prove to his father that he had learned his lessons in salesmanship well. A thousand per cent profit ought to impress the older dealer.

"Such a masterpiece is well worth $7000," he answered.

"You are right," agreed Huntington. "You may bring it to the house this evening."

Abe waited impatiently for Solomon to return from his leisurely noon meal. Proudly he told his father of the handsome profit he had turned on the morning's deal.

"What did you ask to start with?" inquired Solomon.

"I asked him $7000, and he snapped right back, 'I'll take it!' "

Solomon shook his head. "You made a big mistake. If he took it that quickly, it must have been a bargain."

Crestfallen, Abe spent the rest of the afternoon wondering if he ever could measure up to his father's standards of successful selling.

If it did not bring immediate praise from his father, the deal won Abe continued patronage from Huntington. Thereafter whenever the president of the Southern Pacific had an order to be dispatched with alacrity, he sent for A.L. Sometimes he demanded speed that seemed impossible. The day he asked his young friend to frame, all alike in simple oak, a number of etchings and engravings he had brought from New York and have them ready for a banquet he was giving four days later for the board of directors of the railroad, Abe was afraid he would lose his good standing.

The manager of the frame shop told A.L. that they did not have sufficient quantity of oak molding to make that many frames. There were no finishing mills in California and all their material came from Cincinnati and Chicago in twelve-foot lengths which were cut and polished in the Market Street factory. A.L. was determined to meet Huntington's specifications and he appealed to his co-workers to use their ingenuity. The stock moldings came packed in cases of oak, walnut, and chestnut, usually eagerly seized upon by Gump cabinet makers for their wooden mantels and fine cabinets. Abe scoured around the factory hunting out every piece of oak.

Then he told the frame makers to take out their tools and sand paper. These craftsmen were proud of their ability to apply their hands to such a challenge. Within the four days they had the needed amount of handmade frame material ready for the polishers, who worked many hours overtime. The pictures in their gleaming oak frames were all in place for the banquet.

Huntington was delighted, and the many compliments of his guests, amazed over Gump's feat, were indicative of a widening clientele. Towne was particularly gratified that the young man he had recommended to his chief was able to meet whatever demand Huntington made. His own California Street home with its dignified white marble portals was decorated with many a fine painting selected by A.L., who was well aware of the firm friendship between Towne and Huntington. In the morning as the two drove to their office behind well-groomed horses from the Huntington stables, they would nod in cordial greeting to the young art dealer and often they would spend part of the noon hour together in the galleries. Thus, when Huntington commissioned A.L. to find "the finest modern painting" as a gift for Towne, Abe knew what would be welcome. He chose a spicy picture by Leo Herman, a rival of Vibert, and took it to hang in the Nob Hill mansion, satisfied that Towne would share his pleasure in the realistic portrayal of a rosy-cheeked peasant girl milking her cow to the evident entertainment of a jolly priest standing by admiring her.

When another Southern Pacific executive, William F. Herrin, built his brownstone dwelling in a newer residential district, some distance from his associates on Nob Hill, he bought many canvases from the Gump display. However, Abe hardly expected the large order he received one morning when he made a casual, but very well-timed, call on Herrin at his office.

The busy attorney was opening his morning mail when Gump walked in. Herrin greeted his caller pleasantly as he slit open a long envelope. He stopped and handed Gump a sheet of paper.

"Read this," he directed. "You have made a sale this morning."

"I'm sorry, but I can't read it—my dim eyes, you know," replied Abe, mentally excited, but outwardly cultivating a polite unconcern. "May I ask you to read it to me?"

Herrin drew a check from the envelope and picked up the sheet he had started to hand Gump.

"There is $5000," he said. "Not bad pay for these few words!"

Gump's eyes were not too dim to discern that the legal opinion for which Herrin had been so munificently compensated covered less than a full sheet of foolscap. He was glad that he had followed the hunch that led him to the railroad attorney's office that morning, when Herrin continued,

"The check is yours. I can't think of any better use for it than to buy more paintings—a good Keith or two, perhaps. What do you say?"

Herrin was one of the many who had followed Collis Huntington's often-repeated admonition to "buy Keiths." Solomon was reaping benefits from his continued promotion of the work of his old neighbor, and he had passed on his admiration of Keith to Abe, who was nearing twenty when the artist returned from his second period of study in Europe, this time in Munich. Keith had found the boy whom he had known in the galleries grown into an enthusiastic salesman, overcoming his visual handicap with a mind rich in appreciation and contagious responsiveness to beauty.

Artist-dealer relationship with Keith was unusual, for the artist always insisted that the price in stores was the same as in his studios. This fairness to the men who sold his paintings helped to cement his friendships with them. As A.L. came to be trusted with more and more of the art phase of his father's business he fell heir to the understanding between Solomon and the now famous former wood-cutter.

He also met other men of importance in the art world as he frequented Keith's studios. Among them was George Inness. Although Keith and Inness had developed a friendship by correspondence, it was not until the dean of American landscape artists was in San Francisco in 1891 that the two met personally. The day after they had been formally introduced at a brilliant reception given by Irving Scott in his Rincon Hill home, Gump happened to be in Keith's shabby Kearny Street garret studio. He was watching the progress of a landscape he had commissioned Keith to paint, when Inness walked in. Keith turned to Inness and asked how he liked the effect.

"It's too tight, William," he exclaimed. "Bust it wide open!"

"Suppose you do it yourself," answered the bearded Scot.

Inness slipped into one of Keith's alpaca coats, stared a moment and then tore into it like a mad man. From a conventional forest landscape the canvas suddenly turned into a thing of beauty, the soft hues of twilight creeping over the great trees. They called it "Twilight Hour," the only painting ever worked on jointly by the "Masters" of East and West. Gump immediately purchased the painting, which was later presented to the Keith collection at St. Mary's College in Moraga.

Deals like the Herrin surprise were not common. There were many other times when Gump's Galleries were overstocked or when business depressions slowed up buying. Then they called in the auctioneer. San Franciscans, sport-loving by tradition, flocked to auctions with the avidity of racetrack followers. From his youngest days Abe was fascinated by these events. He thoroughly enjoyed the excitement and the personages who frequented the sales.

He learned from his father how to make them attractive. The

catalogues were prepared with the same effort as those which brought the elite to "Gump Openings." They were well-illustrated with fine photographs and carefully annotated with scholarly notes about the more prominent artists presented in the sale. To conduct the auctions Gumps sent for the experienced auctioneers Louderback and Brother, of New York.

Irving Hall on Post Street, where these gatherings were held, attracted men and women keyed up for the fray. One afternoon stocky Senator James G. Fair strode into the room. He wore his toga lightly, remaining at heart the adventure-loving miner. Spying Solomon's young son he tapped him on the shoulder.

"Sit with me, Abe," he commanded, and proceeded to bid and win every time the young man assured him a painting was of real value.

This personal acquaintance with the Senator enabled A.L. to identify the face on a most unusual portrait of Fair which was offered to Gump's some years later. Painted on the smooth side of a huge slab of coal, it was unsigned, but apparently the work of an itinerant artist of the Virginia City days. A replica of the first locomotive of the Central Pacific Railroad was carved in bold relief on the reverse side of the slab.

The daily papers complimented the Messrs. Gump on the success of these auctions, noting that one sale brought something more than thirty thousand dollars, and expressing the hope that the firm would continue to import first-class European paintings to the city. They even listed the canvases, purchasers and the prices paid, ranging from $40 for "Venice" by Jules Guérin to $2500 which Mrs. Theresa Fair gave for "Trio Champêtre" by Edouard Bernard Debat-Ponsan. This painting, which was exhibited in the Paris Salon in 1889, was reproduced in the new artotype series in the *San Francisco News Letter,* where the reviewer remarked on the careful attention to every detail from the little neckerchief around the neck of the half-grown peasant girl to the frill of her petticoat. The writer injected a bit of philosophy as he added, "She is a barefoot girl, but withal there is something so refined about her that one is inclined to think that the artist desired to give an expression to the sentiment that the outward symbols of gentility could go with people who are born of the peasant class."

Mrs. Fair and Mrs. Count Zimmerman, one of the city's wealthiest women, were indefatigable attendants at the auctions and helped swell the returns to the Gumps by their competitive bidding. At the same sale where Mrs. Fair bought the Debat-Ponsan, Mrs. Zimmerman bought several paintings which were included in the artotype series. "Welcome Comrade" by K. Dery of Munich cost her $1750. When Solomon was enroute home from Europe with this Hungarian drinking scene he had shown a photograph of it to William Walter Phelps, who had immediately offered to exchange the painting for a Defregger, an artist whose canvases were bringing extraordinarily high prices in the eastern art market. Solomon declined the offer, but it bolstered his belief in the value of his own selection.

While most of the Gump prestige came from these European importations, the brothers began to realize that California was developing other successful artists besides Nahl and Keith. When Samuel Marsden Brooks continued to receive gold medals in the Mechanics Fairs for his punctiliously faithful paintings of fish and fowl, Solomon made room on his crowded walls for a few, including the peacock on which Brooks had worked a full year to earn the thousand dollars Mrs. Mark Hopkins had offered when she commissioned him to paint it. The bird looked so natural that she doubled the stipend! When "Califran," the critic of the *Alta,* visited the galleries, he added long adjectives to his praise of Brooks' achievement.

Norton Bush, whose "Mt. Shasta" gave him deserved recognition, brought Gump two contrasting paintings of Sutter's Fort, where James Marshall had taken his gold from Coloma and changed world history. These canvases depicted the fort in all its glory in 1846, and again in 1876, a relic of its former splendor.

Gump sold another canvas of mining days, "The Laboratory of Thomas Price, California's First State Assayer," to the Metropolitan Museum of New York. Solomon pointed out to Abe that the young artist, Henry Alexander, who had died at thirty-two, just at the threshold of a promising career, had displayed almost a Holbein touch in his handling of still life. Through a window behind the assayer scales he had included a glimpse of What Cheer House. Solomon paused to reminisce about the old landmark which had stood only a block from the Hausmann shop at Leidesdorff and Sacramento Streets. He told Abe that a Rhode Islander, Robert Woodward, had built this hotel, just for men. It had been the first place in San Francisco where meals could be had à la carte. Its proprietor also set up a library and bootblack stand in its lobby— both free to the public.

The name Woodward had been associated in Abe's mind only with the famous gardens to which he had ridden so many times on the mule-drawn balloon cars out Mission Street to Fourteenth. Solomon told him that Woodward had devoted the fortune made in his hotel of mining days to building these gardens as a homesite out in the dunes; but when the public first saw them at a charity fete so many people asked to see them again that he turned the estate into a public amusement park.

Many and varied were the wonders Woodward added to keep his visitors entertained. Abe and his young friends had their first nature study in the Zoologican—a revolving platform with stuffed animals against appropriate backgrounds, where Europe, Africa, Asia and the Americas became vividly real for them.

Now, in 1893, this park with its circular boat and its camera obscura, reflecting in miniature the moving panorama of all that was going on below in the gardens, was closing forever. The chutes, scenic railway, and ferris wheels along the beach had eclipsed the gardens.

Golden Gate Park, stretching farther west, anchoring the dunes with deep-rooted green, was undergoing extensive transformation in preparation for the Mid-Winter Fair planned for the following year.

At the same time the Gumps were devoting their energy to preparations for the annual Mechanics Fair, from which prize-winning exhibits would be chosen for the San Francisco contribution to the Columbian Exposition in Chicago. A large section was assigned to them this year and they cooperated by changing displays daily, attracting many visitors to enjoy what was adjudged the finest collection of frames, cabinet work, and ornamental bronzes ever seen by a San Francisco audience. The gold medal awarded for their general collection of art work and the prizes for the best single figure and group in marble brought reward for all the effort involved.

Then, in the midst of prosperity, financial panic turned public attention from fairs to food. By June of 1893 San Francisco was suffering with the rest of the West as Nevada silver mines shut down and hungry unemployed miners by the thousands became a public menace. Mercantile houses, railroads, and banks failed. Luxury dealers like the Gumps were quickly affected. Solomon was forced to call in the Louderbacks again. Once more huge paintings of Arab chieftains and Normandy pastorales were sold to the highest bidders, and the Gumps weathered the financial storm.

Solomon had devoted thirty years to the city which had captured his imagination so long ago. He and Louisa could spend their declining years surrounded by children and grandchildren. Their eldest daughter, Henrietta, now Mrs. William Schwartz, made her home with them and her husband soon became secretary of the firm. Their young son, Sydney, brought new life to the big Geary Street home where he shared a room with his Uncle Abe, his companion in running matches and swimming meets. He, too, was becoming a Keith enthusiast, and on Sydney's thirteenth birthday Solomon presented his first grandson with a splendid example of Keith's early work, "Mount Tamalpais: Golden Morning."

Paintings of that "sleeping lady of the mountain" in the varying moods captured by California artists were always favorites of Solomon, who had never forgotten that first majestic view as his steamer had brought him through the Golden Gate. Sometimes swathed in swirling fog veils, sometimes clear cut against the blue of wind-swept skies, Tamalpais, as well as Marin oaks or the redwood groves at the base in Muir Woods, evoked the artists' highest efforts. All the Gumps treasured Keith's interpretations of those scenes.

When two of the daughters left California for eastern homes, Solomon saw that Keith paintings were part of their doweries. Bella, now married to her cousin, son of Louisa's twin sister, Eliza Bronner, hung hers in New York. Goldina, nearest to Abe in age, when she became Mrs. Lou Swabacher, took hers to West Virginia, along with the splendid linen woven specially for her in the old Heidelberg factory.

The sons of the family still remained bachelors, sharing the family home on Geary Street. Abe often walked the short mile that separated home and store. In so doing he sometimes joined a younger Huntington, Henry, who had come to San Francisco in 1892 to assist his uncle. Huntington was living at the Richelieu Hotel on Van Ness at Geary. One morning as he walked toward town with A.L. he mentioned that he was anxious to purchase a home in San Francisco. Gump recalled that another of their patrons, Herman Heyneman, West Coast distributor for a large tobacco firm, wanted to dispose of his establishment in the fast developing "Western Addition," where some of the sand hills beyond Van Ness Avenue were being reclaimed for the building of homes overlooking the bay and Golden Gate.

Gump told Heyneman about Huntington. A dinner invitation followed. Over sumptuous food and plenty of drink, the home was sold, complete with all its furnishings—the large empty lot next door being thrown in. Huntington did not even have to change the monograms on the linen—HH. Both men were warm in their thanks to Gump for bringing them together.

With this good start, Henry Huntington also became a client of Gump's, finding there many decorative pieces and paintings for his home. Among the Keiths sold by Gump to his new patron was one which Abe always considered his friend's masterpiece—"After the Storm," picturing the sun bursting through brooding clouds hanging over a grove of Marin oaks.

A well known mining engineer, Daniel Jackling, later bought the companion picture, "Breaking of the Storm," and wanted Huntington's landscape, but the latter refused to part with his Keith at any price. A.L. took justifiable pride in the fact that the art patron, whose early purchases he had shepherded, valued ownership of the work, that he, too, held in such high regard.

"Henry," A.L. would always say, looking at the motto on an antique Doulton mug which Keith had sent from Ye Cheshire Cheese in London, "good is not good enough. The best is never too good. Always, when you can, purchase the very finest."

CHAPTER THREE ∽ *Deeper Roots*

THIS FRIENDSHIP for Henry Huntington almost took A. Livingston Gump away from San Francisco. At the turn of the century, Huntington, in a huff with the supervisors of his adopted city, decided to transfer wealth and talents to southern California. Before he left for the south, Huntington called on Gump in the San Francisco store. He told him secretly of his plan to transform that leisurely land of orange groves and tourists to a great industrial home-filled community. He would develop a network of interurban cars and help finance power lines.

"Come with me, Abe," he said. "I'll provide the land and build you the finest art store in the world if you, too, will leave San Francisco."

A.L. spoke to his father that night. When he finished, the older man smiled, patiently. All he said was,

"Yes, son, it's a great opportunity."

The young man, who had always been his father's confidant, sensed the forbearance in those words, a relinquishment of dreams and plans often spoken of between them. Somewhere deep within himself Abe became conscious that his own love of San Francisco was as firmly rooted as his father's. He would stay where he belonged and help build Gump's into an integral part of the city with which it was growing.

Solomon was aging; more of the artistic burden of the business was falling on Abe's shoulders. Alfred was, like Uncle Gus, more concerned with merchandising. Following the pattern of the grand-

50

INTERIOR OF THE S. & G. GUMP STORE IN THE NINETIES

Solomon Gump and his son, William, surrounded by *objets d'art* garnered from the Old World.

father who had gathered the men of that generation into A. Gump and Sons in New York, S. & G. Gump was now a firm in which Alfred, Abe, and the youngest brother, William, were partners. Lafayette, alone, had broken from the fold. His one venture for the firm, a branch store in Portland, had failed. Back in San Francisco, he had established his own furniture factory.

The city to which Abe continued to devote his best efforts had increased in stature as it had grown from the shanties on the mud flats to the castle built by Mark Hopkins on the crest of Nob Hill. Abe often climbed that hill now to look at the work of talented young artists studying under Arthur Matthews. This fine teacher had become the director of the Art Institute after Mrs. Hopkins' legatee, Edwin Searles, willed the mansion to the University of California. Abe was an admirer of Matthews' work; but he realized, too, how privileged those students were to study among the treasures Hopkins had collected in his wide travels through Europe and Asia.

Once in a while A.L. offered to exhibit the works of the best students in the galleries of the new store to which the Gumps had moved in 1892. This was located at 113-115 Geary near Union Square which, with neighboring blocks on Geary, Post, and Grant Avenue, was becoming the fashionable shopping center of the city. George C. Shreve and Company, jewelers with Bostonian antecedents, and high class dry goods firms like the City of Paris and the White House attracted stylish ladies looking for finery. Gump's new headquarters was easily accessible.

A block farther north, on Post Street, Vickery had also moved to a new location. His little shop was a gathering place for intellectuals. Judges, businessmen, students, and school teachers spent leisure hours absorbing the atmosphere created by the quiet man who had found health and brought culture to the boisterous city. Modestly and with great patience Vickery persuaded such people to study the intimate human expression in choice etchings. He displayed Dürers, Rembrandts, Haydens, Whistlers. He brought out the Soulé reproductions of famous "Old Masters" and later stocked the Braun photographs which made art live for people who could not afford to travel.

Lyman Abbott, editor of *The Outlook,* commenting on his San Francisco visit when he returned to New York, spoke in his pages of the national reputation of Vickery's attractive store. Conclusive evidence of the "large cultivated artistic and literary constituency in and about this western city" was furnished by Vickery's, as well as by the adjoining bookstore, which Dr. Abbott described as the most charming establishment of its kind that he had ever seen, East or West, in America or in Europe. The latter housed the stock of Paul Elder, who had formerly been a clerk in Doxey's Bookstore where Vickery had also had his San Francisco start.

In 1900 Elder became associated with Morgan Shepard, a bank clerk with artistic ambitions who designed the unique store now offering competition to both Vickery and Gump, with pictures and decorative objects of pottery and metal added to their books. Elder and Shepard also had begun to import from the Orient, and their back rooms displayed rich brocades, bronzes, and strange curios.

Gump shared with his contemporaries the benefits from the rising level of culture, although he continued to import the showy theatrical canvases demanded by the majority rather than to compete in catering to the few who were more refined and selective. As a concession to a growing interest in American art he stocked more of the John Rogers groups, those small statuettes which had first been introduced to San Francisco by Jones, Wool, and Sutherland. A well decorated parlor needed at least one of these genre, capturing the spirit of home and family, on a marble- or onyx-topped table. Oak-framed chromos, another fad of the era, were turned out by the hundreds by Gump's shop and sold for a few dollars apiece.

San Francisco not only was developing more art appreciation; it was becoming a creative center as well. A group of young men—Bruce Porter, Gelett Burgess, Willis Polk—were editing a gay little magazine, *The Lark,* published by William Doxey, revealing San Francisco to the world as a storehouse of artistic and literary treasure.

A.L. sought out new genius, not only in the Hopkins Art Institute but in the more informal atmosphere of the Pine Street studios where Keith had taken over the commodious rooms formerly occupied by the Bohemian Club. Upstairs above the stalls of the California Market, whence the fragrance of oyster stews and broiling lobsters rose to tempt the hungry, students were carrying on traditions started by Virgil Williams, that artistic aristocrat of earlier days to whom Robert Louis Stevenson dedicated his *Silverado Squatters.* In these small studios A.L. met young men like Maynard Dixon, who spent his daytime hours splashing advertisements on billboards, his slouch hat pulled down over his face to escape recognition as he earned funds to support his art studies.

When Keith opened his large studios so that a selected public could see the first assemblage of his California canvases, Abe Gump —or Abie, as the Scot called his young friend—was a frequent visitor. Here Abe found himself a member of an inner circle gathered around the artist who was rapidly becoming the most successful man of his profession in the West.

Lunching downstairs in a glass-partitioned stall, the young man enjoyed conversations with John Muir, Tom Flynn, editor of *The Wasp,* Edward Robeson Taylor, poet-mayor of San Francisco, and often with eastern visitors of note. As they snapped open tiny California shrimps and waited for sizzling lamb chops or other entrees which were part of these hearty forty-cent meals, he heard Daniel Burnham outline dreams for city planning, and Charles Follen McKim of the New York architectural firm of McKim, Meade, and White, exclaim in delight over the canvases he was taking back to introduce Keith to the eastern art world.

Those lunch hours were sometimes jolly, sometimes grave. In one of their lighter moods, Keith turned to A.L.:

"Read Muir your verses, Abie."

In his best voice A.L. pronounced his philosophy:

> "We live to love,
>   "We love to live;
> "And we live to love to live
>   "And love to live to love."

Muir's deep-set blue eyes twinkled as he exclaimed, "Why, that's the whole psalm of life!"

A.L. was speaking from more personal experience than his lunchtime companions could have guessed. His rhyme was not mere philosophy. He had fallen in love.

Thus far he knew his lady only as a customer with a voice he would never forget. She had avoided his persuasiveness in the selection of a gift a few days before and hurried out of the store; but he was determined to discover her identity.

He did not have to wait long. One noon as he dropped off the street car at the corner of Geary and Franklin Streets he heard his nephew Sydney Schwartz talking with the lady of the lovely voice and a somewhat younger man.

"Who *was* that?" he demanded of Sydney as the two went in together to the Gump home for their midday meal.

"Oh, those are our neighbors, the Lichtensteins—Mabel and her brother," replied his nephew.

"Present me," commanded Abe, in the same decisive way his father had said of Louisa "that is the girl I am going to marry."

It did not take him long to press his suit after Sydney brought them together. Mabel confessed that she had hurried out of the store that first day feeling that "young Mr. Gump was somewhat forward." But she relented when she made sure that his gallant attentions had been honestly motivated by his instinctive response to her charms. She was truly a glamorous young woman, graduate of

Miss Lake's exclusive school, and a favorite of the amateur dramatic set.

They were married on Admission Day—September 9, 1902. Their life together started happily, as Mabel matched with her intelligence the ambitions of her husband, whose book education had been cut short by dimming eyes. In a richly modulated voice, trained to win audiences, she read aloud to the man who craved learning. She shared with him her understanding of literature and history, made more interesting because she had traveled extensively. Abe's retentive mind drank in all the readings until they saturated his every thought. Solomon, too, felt the boon of his new daughter's attentions. She spoke four languages fluently and nothing pleased the older man more than to have her read Goethe in the original.

As Mabel and Abe started housekeeping she was determined that the furnishings of their apartment should express something better than the age of glitter in which they had grown up. She, too, had found a friend in the Pine Street studio groups, a man who knew good furniture and the principles of home decoration. He was a young chemist from the Selby Smelters across the bay—Ed Newell, who used his leisure hours to pursue his own hobbies, collecting examples of early American art and antique furniture.

Mabel and her friends had discovered the studio where Newell worked with his finds when they were looking for stage props. She knew well what interesting pieces he had unearthed as he snooped around old shops south of Market Street. He showed her the old desk where he had found the love letters of John Adams in a secret drawer, and some rare bits of porcelain and pieces of fine teakwood he had dug out of basements in Chinatown. Mabel often came upon Newell taking the black stain off the teakwood and rubbing down the glistening natural surface underneath.

Abe accompanied his wife as they joined friends from other studios for music and a bottle of claret while Newell showed his latest discovery of some remnant of the old-fashioned furniture brought around the Horn by pioneers—men and women who had often forfeited every possession in the hectic days of "boom and bust." While Mabel appreciated the beauty of these old tables or chairs, it was the teakwood that most appealed to A.L.

Their common interest in things Oriental drew the two men together. Abe could not remember when he had not wanted to go to China. He used to cherish a secret fearful hope, when he was playing around the wharves with his fishing pole, that some of the tales he had heard about boys being shanghaied and carried off to sea would have him as a hero. Then he could have all the lichee nuts and candied melon rind he wanted without waiting for the cook to bring the boxes with their strange lettering on Chinese New Year.

As Abe grew older, Chinatown with its pots of pungent lilies, fumes of mysterious incense, and its great fire-spitting dragon was a magnet for his adventure-seeking spirit. He had many cronies among the slippered proprietors of Dupont Street curio shops, where he learned the feel of carved ivory and expertly glazed porcelain.

Except for the Cantonese merchants of Chinatown there were no importers of Chinese wares in San Francisco. After Japan opened her ports to westerners, trade with Nippon began. A.L. always walked to work along the south side of Market Street to see the wondrous things the Australian George Marsh displayed in the windows of the shop he opened under the Palace Hotel in 1876. Marsh made yearly visits to Japan, bringing home bronzes, kakemono, delicately designed ivories, silks, and prints.

As the Gumps became better acquainted with Ed Newell, A.L. sometimes accompanied his new friend on Chinatown treasure hunts, enlarging his own knowledge of fine porcelains and silks.

When Elder and Shepard, as well as Vickery, introduced Japanese wares into their stores, A.L. began to doubt his father's widsom in sticking strictly to the European in his foreign buying. Vickery had recently enlarged his firm, taking into partnership both his nephew, Henry Atkins, who had come from England to keep books for his uncle, and another associate, Fred Torrey. Atkins had grown accustomed to drawing rooms highlighted by colorful Oriental porcelains, for England and France had learned their decorative value as early as the seventeenth century. He was soon introducing the graceful lines into rooms he designed for some of the more discriminating builders of the bay area.

The apartment where Mabel was displaying her teakwood and embroideries was now too small for their accumulation of valued possessions. With the birth of their first son, Robert, in 1903 they determined to build a home of their own. They selected a site on the north side of one of the hills in the Western Addition. Standing there in the fresh breeze they looked across the sparkling bay with its white sails and ferryboats. Tamalpais on its far side beckoned them to the play land of Marin County which they both loved.

A.L. called upon Edgar Matthews, brother of the director of the Hopkins Art Institute, to design a home that would provide the proper setting for Mabel's tasteful furnishings. The Matthews brothers were contributing to the growing grace of the city which reflected their artistic vision in some of its finest homes and public buildings as well as in the achievements of the young artists trained by Arthur.

Confidence in Matthews' skill as an architect was justified and, as the new Gump home neared completion, Mabel paid many visits to Ed Newell's new shop on Sutter Street, The Copper Lantern, to select rehabilitated antiques for her rooms. Newell had found his sideline profitable enough by now to hire someone to run this shop while he was busy at his regular job in the Selby laboratories.

One day Mabel and A.L. dropped by late in the afternoon to talk with their friend about a table he was refinishing for them. They found him excited. Bruce Bonney, one of the three partners in Shreve and Company and another frequent visitor to The Copper

Lantern, had invited Newell to attend a meeting of the board of directors of the jewelry firm.

Newell told the Gumps that George Shreve had turned to him after Bonney's introduction and said,

"Bonney thinks well of you as a judge of art. How would you like to go to Japan as our buyer and select stock for the Oriental department we are planning for the new store?"

That was not all. They had promised a trip to Europe with their regular buyer, Charlie Foster, to come later. A.L. and Mabel congratulated Newell and urged him to accept this opportunity to see the world.

The news that another fine store was going into Oriental art was disturbing to A.L. He was conscious of increasing interest in the artistic contributions of the Far East but he had not been able to convince his father and brothers that they, too, should enter that field.

Vickery, Atkins, and Torrey now were agents for Yamanaka, largest distributors of Japanese art in the world. As they catered to a cultured clientele beginning to understand the hidden symbolism of the Orient through reading and travel, they were attracting San Francisco homemakers from the cluttered aisles of Gump's to the restful atmosphere of Japanese prints, carved ivories, and simple bronzes.

A.L. was more convinced than ever that their own establishment was behind the times as he listened to Newell's enthusiasm over his coming trip. Newell received encouragement from his neighbors the Hydes, whose daughter Hallie was engaged to his friend Will Irwin. The other daughter, Helen, was in Japan—the first American artist to learn the ancient art of making block prints. The Hyde family offered to give Newell a letter of introduction, for they knew that in Helen's Tokyo studio he would meet the leading artists of Japan.

When Mabel and A.L. waved Newell off on his voyage across

the Pacific they were impressed with the passenger list of the vessel on which he sailed. Among those who were journeying to the Orient were Jane Lathrop Stanford, George Ade, Captain John J. Pershing, General Arthur MacArthur. Mrs. Stanford had recently purchased the Baron Ikeda collection of Japanese art. A.L. suggested to Newell that he might discuss some phases of that collection if he could manage to meet her on shipboard.

Letters from the traveler told them that he made good use of every such opportunity, especially after he reached his destination and was introduced to the inner circle of Japanese who had been flattered by Helen Hyde's sympathetic interpretation of their people and customs in her exquisite prints. She had told him that previous to Western interest in these prints they had been considered of little value by their own people. The prints had been used as wrappers for their parcels.

Newell's commission from Shreve was to buy porcelains, which they intended to mount in silver. When he returned he told the Gumps that he had also brought back brocades, silks, bronzes, and many prints. His conversation revealed that his mind was steeped with knowledge derived from intimate glimpses of the way of life in Japanese homes usually well hidden from foreigners. He had found the simplicity of their arrangements and decorations quite satisfying to his own aesthetic sense. In Japan he had enjoyed the change from San Francisco's overfurnished parlors. The charm of a single scroll on an otherwise unadorned wall, one bronze bowl containing a single spray of blossoms on a bamboo stand, groups of white-stockinged people in kimonos seated on clean tatami (straw matting) as they drank ceremonial tea—these were some of the memories Newell shared with his friends.

When the time came for Newell's European buying trip A.L. was more apprehensive about the competition they would have when the careful selections he knew Foster and Newell would make were offered San Francisco purchasers. He was not surprised that Newell included Oriental porcelains and rare cloisonne, which had traveled from China to Paris, along with his purchases of Georgian·silver, chaste white and gold Minton, and gold-mounted petit-point bags that he and Foster brought back to Shreve's. A.L. was beginning to realize more and more that fellow citizens of this city facing the Pacific were appreciating the art that cultivated Europeans had long recognized.

As A.L. and Mabel welcomed Newell to their new Green Street home they sensed how far their friend had advanced in understanding since his old days of snooping into south-of-Market second-hand shops and the basements of old Chinatown. They coveted his knowledge for the future of the Gump's own increasing business.

O NE MONTH after all the treasures from the far places were unpacked and displayed for the Shreve clientele, they were rubble and ashes.

On the morning of April 18, 1906, not one wisp of the soothing sea fog beloved by San Franciscans appeared in the sultry dawn. Suddenly a violent tremor convulsed the city and flames shot into the dead blue sky. Lurching from the shock of the earthquake, which broke her water mains, the proud city of the Gay 'Nineties met impending doom.

Abe Gump, roused from sound sleep, looked out of his high bedroom windows. The floor under him and the street below were heaving like the waves of the ocean. Horses hitched to a milk wagon struggled to keep their balance. One went down but pluckily picked himself up. Chimneys were toppling in every direction. Mabel Gump bent over the crib in which a new baby—Richard—slept undisturbed. Then she joined her husband at the window. Off toward the bay thin gray ribbons of smoke were rising straight upward into the cloudless blue, streaked now with the bright colors of red that showed the intensity of the fires already raging in the commission district.

As they stood, hesitant, another tremor shook the house. This was not an ordinary quake. There was no time to lose. Even as he gathered up two-year-old Robert and his baby brother and hurried with Mabel into the sheltered back garden, Abe's thoughts were on the family art store far downtown. Had falling walls crushed the gilded mirrors, the French porcelains, the Italian marbles? How fast would those threatening fires travel? Could he get there in time to save the great framed pictures that hung in the Gump galleries—that superb portrait of Voltaire in his rich red velvet robes—Paul Veronese's conception of Christ and the mob who would stone the sinful woman—the Renoir nude which his father had picked up on his last trip to the Latin Quarter of Paris? His father! A.L. shuddered with dread as he contemplated what this shock might mean to the aging head of the Gump establishment.

He raced down the steep front stairs, almost colliding with the fleeing Chinese cook as they both stumbled over bricks from the fallen chimney. Wong's usually placid yellow face was almost white as he sped past his employer and on down the street, never to return. Years later the family heard from him in Canton; but that morning he had no good-bys.

A few blocks from home Gump hailed a passing car, a large White Steamer. He offered the driver one hundred dollars rental for the day. The streets were already full of people going in both directions, businessmen such as he hastening to see what could be saved, homeless hordes pouring toward the safe open spaces of the Presidio. It was now after six o'clock. The procession of refugees marched continuously to the west, bedding lashed to sewing machines pushed along on rollers, parrots in cages scolding raucously, while their good-natured owners greeted fellow travelers with the camaraderie that turned disaster to adventure. The earthquake had made neighbors of everyone, and laughter was more frequent than tears, as houses minus walls exposed rooms in all stages of order—and disorder.

But those who were headed townward had no heart for laughter as they came closer to the business district. No sooner had the White Steamer puffed up the first hill than the sight of the Call Building, looking like a great chimney belching smoke and flame as it towered above the skyline, struck terror to Gump's heart. His destination was only two blocks up from that Market Street blaze.

First, however, he must find out how his parents had fared. At Geary Street he ordered the driver to turn west two blocks. To his horror, the two-story family home had toppled off its foundations and was leaning crazily against Judge Louderbach's house next door. The family, white and shaken, were gathered in the yard, miraculously unhurt. Calling to his brother-in-law, William Schwartz, to jump into the car so that he might open the office safe (a feat A.L.'s poor eyesight made impossible for him), he headed toward the burning city.

Soon they neared Union Square. This was full of milling crowds half-demented with fear. A pink-pajamed individual walked barefoot, heel and toe, around and around the Dewey monument. On a bench close by a distinguished-looking gentleman in a long white night shirt continually replaced his monocle in an eye which immediately twitched it out again while his flowing whiskers blew about in the rising wind.

But such kaleidoscopic sights blurred into the disaster which faced them on the block beyond. Crowds were thronging about the wreck of a three-story lodging house crushed beneath the toppled fire wall of an adjoining building. Gump and Schwartz urged the driver to honk his way through the crowd only to draw up in front of a similar catastrophe at their own building. This was intact except for the fire wall which had crushed the frame house next door. Here Frank Desirello had had his flower market, where A.L. was in the habit of buying a fresh carnation for his lapel every morning. Now Desirello's screams pierced the air. He was hopelessly trapped, bed and all, beneath the weight of the fallen wall. A group of men were clawing at the debris, but there seemed no way to release him.

With the moans of the dying man ringing in their ears, Gump and Schwartz fearfully opened their own door. Inside, all was chaos. Small objects were scattered grotesquely over the carpets, beautiful porcelains lay in jagged heaps. Heartsick, they mounted the stairs hardly daring to look at what must have happened to the treasures they had left there the night before. How proudly Solomon had watched his fine pieces as they stood in the elegant display cases he had purchased from Shreve's at the time of their recent move.

Nature had played a weird trick. The two men could hardly believe their eyes as they looked at the perfection of this newly decorated upstairs room. All fixtures were in place. Inside the plate glass doors nothing in the cases was seriously disturbed. French figurines and Italian marbles stood erect on their onyx and antique stone pedestals. Everything was intact.

It was about eight o'clock. They started for the safe, which Schwartz opened readily. He lifted out a ledger and handed it to A.L. Crash! The building shook with the third violent quake. Schwartz slammed the safe shut. They scrambled for the doorway, carrying the one ledger they had been able to remove, but leaving $5,000 in gold leaf still cached.

In the few minutes they had been inside, the White Steamer had disappeared. Seeing them looking frantically up and down the street, a bystander said, "Looking for the Steamer? You're out of luck. A gent rushed out of Marchand's Restaurant and offered the driver $250 for the car—had his lady with him—looked like they were trying to duck a scandal."

The building was still swaying and they feared to re-enter. The street was full of scurrying bewildered people. No vehicles were in sight, no cabs, not even a wagon. The moderate southwest wind which had been gradually rising since the quiet of dawn was blowing harder, but still in a direction carrying the smoke and flames away from them. They hoped that the conflagration, which they could see on the opposite side of broad Market Street, would not jump that barrier and envelop them.

For a brief moment they stopped to take stock of the neighborhood. The worst damage on near-by Grant Avenue seemed to have been caused by broken plate-glass windows, although the new

Shreve Building looked intact except for one large window. Turning toward Market, they found the street filled with jagged glass. Every store appeared to have lost its show windows. Samuel's Lace House; the R. R. Davis millinery and women's-wear store, displaying post-Easter-sale bonnets that were now tattered ribbons waving above splinters of jagged glass; Heller and Frank's Men's Store, and Greenburg's Fancy Goods Store—all were a shambles.

They turned and walked back toward Union Square. The St. Francis Hotel stood undisturbed despite this third severe quake, but its guests were milling about, some carrying suitcases and others with unpacked clothes thrown over their arms. Even here no cab was to be had. The two men commenced the twelve-block walk to the Geary Street home of the senior Gumps, carrying the one heavy ledger they had rescued.

Joining the family, huddled together in front of the tilted house, they trekked on over the hills, Mother Gump supported on the arm of her youngest son, William, to join the increasing group of relatives and friends in the sheltered garden of A.L.'s Green Street home. Abe and Mabel, however, were determined to find a way to reach the summer cottage they had rented in San Rafael. From their front windows they could watch the ferryboats scuttling back and forth across the Golden Gate. They chafed to be on one. Finally late in the afternoon a neighbor was found willing to drive them to the ferry.

They made their way slowly toward the Ferry Building by way of the sea wall. Wharves and buildings along the waterfront were intact, continually drenched with salt water pumped up by the fireboats anchored in the bay; but flames were licking up the narrow streets that led from the sea wall into the congested city. They had almost reached safety when Mabel screamed, "Duck!" . . . and a falling wire grazed A.L.'s head. He might easily have been decapitated. No sooner had he escaped that fate than two men jumped onto the runningboard. Near-sighted A.L. did not see their bandanas, but his wife was already slipping off her diamonds to offer as a bribe to the supposed bandits.

"We have to make this ferry," said A.L., politely urging them to get off the runningboard.

"No use. She's broken a wing," answered the first, but his partner broke in, "He seems to be a decent guy. Let's help him."

With this, the would-be bandits turned samaritan, helped load the grips on the Sausalito ferry and the Gump family was out of danger.

Dusk was enveloping the city as the ferry threaded its way through the harbor full of craft of many kinds, fireboats, navy patrols, private yachts, fishing skiffs, anything that could carry people away from the racing flames. One of the ferry's paddle wheels was crippled (the "broken wing" referred to by their late visitor); but the other churned up a white path through the darkening water as it propelled the vessel haltingly away from the pier. Screeching gulls swooped hungrily across the wake. But there was no bread to waste tonight; there were no merry holiday passengers with their bags of crusts and popcorn to feed the birds.

The setting sun, dropping red into the Golden Gate, was pale in contrast to live flames whipping wildly up the hills of the city that had stood proud and gay above this great landlocked harbor. A.L. leaned on the rail with little Robert by the hand, watching the leaping flames under the dusky mauve of the smoke-filled sky. Every few minutes a muffled roar would drift across the water and another cabbage-head of smoke would rise above the general pall, signaling a new block of buildings dynamited in the frantic effort of waterless fire fighters to check the spreading blaze.

Would any part of the city Abe loved be spared? Not that store where he had seen his treasures secure on marble pedestals that morning. No, he was reconciled to that loss now. But what of the mansions on Nob Hill, the Collis P. Huntington home with its priceless collection of paintings; the Stanford residence—perhaps its wide lawns would save that. The Mark Hopkins home, like a great Norman castle with its granite walls; surely that would not go! Perhaps someone would rip the paintings he had hung in the galleries of these mansions from their heavy gilded frames and carry them to safety. He saw the magnificent new Fairmont Hotel proudly silhouetted against the sky. He hoped that would be spared. Where was his old friend, William Keith? What had happened to those studios over the old California Market on Pine Street? No use thinking about them. He could see that the fire was raging up that hill. The wind, fanned by the fire, was blowing furiously now.

The ferry boat creaked against the Sausalito pier and A.L. hurried his little family off the boat and onto the Northwestern Pacific train for the last lap of their journey. It was nearly dark when they finally arrived at the Lucas cottage in San Rafael. Fallen chimneys warned them not to trust the inside of the house. The night was warm and they pulled sofas into the garden; but even in this haven, with his wife and children safe about him, there was little sleep for the man who watched the red glare of the sky across the bay.

Early next morning he rented a stage coach and started for the city to pick up the many things they would need for the summer but which they had not been able to carry in the hand grips they had brought. Morning had evidently brought no relief to the stricken city. He wondered, as he tried to pierce the smoke pall that hung heavy over the blackened skeletons of familiar buildings, what he would find when the ferry docked. Would he even be able to reach the Green Street home? How would he find his father? He remembered how exhausted the old gentleman had looked as he sank into that garden seat.

The ferry bumped against wet piles. They were back, facing a scene of utter desolation, but the Ferry Building still stood sentinel. The horses neighed and whinnied. The driver cracked his whip and the stage coach creaked as the unwilling animals stepped on to the slippery gang plank.

East Street along which they had reached the ferry yesterday was now blocked to traffic. The only way to avoid the fires and rubble was a roundabout course via old Mission Dolores. Eventually they made their way back across the city—a weird city reverting to its pioneering days. Neighbors were chatting over ham and eggs cooked on stoves pulled onto the sidewalks. In front of one tall mansion the Chinese cook was making doughnuts over a coal-oil stove and serving all comers, unless his wary eye caught someone after seconds. Then he pointed a long finger and called, "You no havee. Clome back twice."

On Green Street, A.L. found only part of his family, just then trekking back from the Presidio where they had all been ordered to spend the night. Reports came from downtown and all of them were discouraging. The business district was gone—all those blocks of stone, brick, and concrete. Now the flames were licking up Chinatown, threatening Nob Hill. A.L. knew that his worst fears had happened. Even if there had been anything to salvage, it would be impossible to get to Geary Street today.

There was nothing more he could do in San Francisco. He loaded up the stage coach with the family's clothes and everything he thought might be most useful during their "exile" in San Rafael, and started the long roundabout trip back across the bay. Returning the following day, he braced himself to face the ruins. Yes, 113-115 Geary had gone with the rest. Everything was gone. All the Currier and Ives prints. All the treasured Keiths—. With sinking heart he ventured among the blackened ruins. There were a few fine old bronzes that had not melted in the terrific furnace. The next day he would hire a wagon and try to salvage these pieces whose value would only be enhanced by the baptism of fire. But the next day was too late. When he drove up with the dray, looters had been ahead of him. Sydney Schwartz had rescued one bronze bear. That was all that remained.

Even the supposedly fireproof safe had melted in the hellish furnace. The ruin was complete, no records, nothing with which to start again.

His father-in-law, Mr. Lichtenstein, had come down with him that morning. He proposed that they walk over to California Street to see if the bank vaults had fared likewise. If not, they could open the safe deposit box and get some securities with which to float a temporary loan. Father Gump had followed his life-long habit of bringing home twice a week enough twenty-dollar gold pieces to run the household. Thus, they had enough cash to tide them over a few days for necessary things, but ready money was growing scarce.

They were in the basement of the half-demolished bank building looking for their safety deposit box when a blast of dynamite in an adjoining ruin sent a plate glass window crashing.

"Let's get out of here and go up to the grocer's instead," suggested A.L. "We can fill our suitcases with provisions."

Food was very scarce. The commission district had burned first of all. Reactions of merchants ran the gamut of human response to disaster. Some wholesale meat dealers on the first day gave away all their stock to passers-by. Others tried to hoard and everything spoiled. Still others, like this grocer, marked everything left on the shelves at double prices.

"This is bad judgment," remarked Abe Gump to the clerk as he noted the prices he was being charged. "It will be an everlasting reflection on your business if you continue to treat your fellow citizens like this."

Nevertheless, he bought what the suitcases would hold and trudged all the way to the Green Street house with his heavy load, pondering with every step if he would not do better to abandon such a seemingly futile business as dealing in art. What these people need is food, he told himself. He even broached the subject when he got home. Perhaps his brothers would join in building a model grocery store.

What a laugh Mabel got out of that!

"Can't you just hear him say, 'Yes, Mrs. Spreckels, this is our finest coffee,' or 'Good morning, Mrs. Flood, the strawberries are superb today!' "

With her best stage presence she tried to ridicule her husband out of that fantasy. But he was in deep earnest. The art business was quite unnecessary in this desperately hungry city. He reminded Mabel of a splendid market they had admired in Santa Barbara. He would get her brother, Milton, to draw plans for one similar to that in San Francisco. A.L. was first a merchant, a man whose business it was to recognize public demand and supply it.

As serious as he was about this proposition, something held him back from discussing it with Solomon. His father's strength seemed to ebb with the shock of the disaster. He dared not suggest this radical change until everyone else agreed. Willie had already found an emergency occupation. In partnership with the driver of the store wagon he was busy day and night in an express and delivery business.

The older brother, Alfred, was in Rome on his honeymoon, with which he was combining a buying trip for the firm. If the wires were working A.L. must send a cable before Alfred spent any more money on nonessentials. He stopped at a temporary Western Union office on Van Ness and cabled: "Gumps destroyed. Cancel everything. Come home." Then he wired his sister in West Virginia: "Store total wreck. House still standing. All well. Send money."

In a few days the answer came from Rome: "Goods en route. Cannot stop orders."

That news, in addition to some cool advice from William Schwartz, made A.L.'s decision for him. Gump's must revive their business. Other firms were setting up make-shift headquarters out beyond Van Ness Avenue where the fire had not reached. The backyard of his father's partially wrecked home on Geary Street just two blocks beyond the blackened rim of the burned area, be-

came the office. As shipments began to arrive the goods were unpacked and stored in the kitchen and washroom. Inverted packing
boxes served as display cases—sardonic contrast to the luxurious ex-
Shreve fixtures, but quite in keeping with the reviving city.

Blueprints for rebuilding were being drawn before ashes cooled.
The dreams A.L. had heard Daniel Burnham unfold in those noon
hours with Keith and Muir had been embodied in an elaborate
survey intended to rectify the haphazard growth of the sprawling
city. Then nature had cruelly leveled it ready for remodeling.
Benjamin Ide Wheeler hailed this "providentially fortunate Burnham plan" and optimistically predicted the conquering of hills and
the widening of streets so that "cable cars will twitch and rattle
no more."

But this rationalizing of disaster could not stay the hands of impatient businessmen when over 160 million dollars in insurance
money poured into San Francisco. Roofs were needed and implements for daily living were immediately in demand. Business leaders rolled up their sleeves and went to work. They could not afford
to delay for dreams to come true, no matter how alluring.

The only concession to change was to re-establish the shopping
center along wide Van Ness Avenue beyond the debris of the former
downtown area. Some of Gump's competitors believed in the per-
manence of this location. Paul Elder, for instance, asked Bernard
Maybeck, a Berkeley architect with revolutionary ideas, to design
an old-English type of store for him at the corner of Bush Street.
His former partner had left for New York and he had persuaded
John Howell to leave a newspaper office and join his staff. Placing
Howell in charge of the new store, Elder went to New York himself with John Henry Nash to carry on temporarily in rented headquarters the Tomoye Press, a sideline undertaken just previous to
the fire.

Vickery took an old barn on California Street and remodeled it
into an attractive setting for the stock his associates had miraculously

rescued. Quick-witted action had salvaged all of Vickery's Oriental
treasure. First they had carried vases, bronzes, and prints to the
Lowry home on Russian Hill. Later, when fire threatened—although it did not destroy—those sightly residences, they had removed all the pieces to Bruce Porter's home at the Presidio Gate,
where they were placed between mattresses used for beds in the
basement. Porter told his associates that he woke the next morning
to find his mother sleeping with a five thousand dollar vase beside
her pillow.

When a generous letter came from Yamanaka to Vickery, Atkins, and Torrey enclosing a receipt for everything on their memo-
randum, they returned it to the Japanese firm with thanks. None
of their Oriental art had been destroyed.

The Gump firm was hardly in a position to hold their own with
these more fortunate dealers. Out of the millions of insurance
dollars which were underwriting the rehabilitation of San Francisco,
they had received only ten thousand. That had come from a small
policy placed with the Home Insurance Company of New York.
All their other policies were placed with German firms—the result
of Solomon's blind loyalty to his native Heidelberg. In contrast
with the record-breaking promptness with which many American
and British companies met their obligations, most of the Germans
procrastinated, withholding payment on the contention that the
earthquake had destroyed the buildings, which were therefore non-
existent before the fire.

Nevertheless, Solomon's sons were equal to the challenge. Although his own fighting spirit was quelled as he lay ill from a
stroke at the San Rafael cottage where A.L. had persuaded his
father and mother to spend the summer of 1906, he rallied to his
son's suggestion that they re-establish themselves in the new retail
center. By the time Alfred returned from Europe they had started
to make over a large low building on California Street between
Van Ness and Polk and were participating in the lavish buying

induced by the rebuilding boom. Homes throughout the city were being constructed and furnished with riotous spending such as only a city brought up on Gold Rush and Bonanza could engender. Alfred had to return to the Old World to splurge on carved pedestals, marble busts, onyx table tops, gilded cabinets, and Venetian lamps for the extravagant public.

The sudden post-earthquake boom was short-lived, however. Nation-wide financial panic struck the bewildered city a new blow in 1907. Ready cash disappeared. Good customers could not pay their bills. Others paid with "Clearing House Certificates," an emergency currency. As matters grew worse, and their own obligations became more pressing, Alfred came out of his office one morning with a worried look.

"What are we going to do, Abe?" the older brother inquired of A.L. "There are several drafts coming due. We haven't enough money on hand or in sight to meet them."

The brothers knew that the firm of S. and G. Gump, with fifty years of established credit, should be able to negotiate a larger loan. Each year it had been their practice to estimate their needs for funds to cover planned buying programs and make suitable arrangements with their bankers, at that time the Anglo-Californian.

A.L. replied with assurance, "Guess I'll go to the bank and increase our loan."

The Anglo-Californian had recently returned to their old building on Pine at Sansome Street, the first floor of which had been reassembled from the post-earthquake ruins. As A.L. entered and walked down the corridor to the farther end of the room, tall handsome Philip Lilienthal looked up from his desk behind the wooden rail.

"Well, A.L., what can I do for you?"

This was an auspicious beginning. He had been right to go directly to his friend, warm-hearted popular Lilienthal, the banker who had pledged name and fortune to persuade New York financial circles that the rebuilding of San Francisco was a safe risk for their money. Lilienthal was known, too, for his generosity. No one in need ever left his office empty handed. It might have been different if Abe had encountered the other partner first, stern Ignatz Steinhart. He would have been afraid to speak with confidence as he now did.

"I am here to borrow some additional funds. We will need about $25,000 more than we have arranged."

In more normal days Lilienthal would have extended his hand cordially and said, "That's fine, A.L., we are always glad to co-operate."

But the bank manager did not even rise from his chair. In fact, there was a sharp edge in his usually smooth inflection as he shot back,

"Nothing doing. This bank needs all its funds for much more important commitments at this critical time!"

"But we *have* to have it," persisted Gump, waiting a moment and then backing away with a sense of utter defeat and humiliation. Lilienthal made no reply. He merely shook his head regretfully and bent over his desk full of papers, without so much as a spoken good-by.

A.L. turned, walking slowly toward the door. His mind turned back to that April morning when he had first looked at the rubbled mass of broken porcelain and charred paintings. The misgivings that had lurked in his inner mind welled up from the subconscious where he had valiantly submerged them with the enthusiasm of the reconstruction period. What place did an art dealer have in a city still so full of scars? Yes, A.L., he told himself, face facts. Hard-headed bankers considered art a useless business.

Perhaps he should not have let Mabel mock him out of the grocery store idea. Men still had to eat. He had better go back to his brothers and make some realistic plans. The good will represented by the Gump name was an asset. There would surely be a use for it in an essential business. Then he thought again of the beautiful objects still arriving from far ports. Was life in this western city really too elemental for the more gracious touch of the artist? Were the only tangible assets stocks of necessities?

His dim-sighted eyes further clouded by these broodings, he almost walked headlong into the man he feared most to meet.

"Well, A.L., why so glum?" Steinhart did not smile, but there was reassurance in his tone.

Gump poured out his story.

"Come on back. Let's talk this over," said the banker. Gump, astonished, followed him back down the corridor, waiting nervously as Steinhart opened the gate to the desk area and sat a few minutes in earnest conversation with Lilienthal. He did not have to wonder long. Steinhart came over to the rail, clasped his hand, and said,

"It is all arranged. If you need more, you can have it."

Abraham Livingston Gump breathed deeply as he left the bank, intrigued and yet puzzled by what had just happened. What had induced the tough-minded Steinhart to see merit in Gump's claim to share in the precious money so jealously guarded by the other usually more affable partner? He was still wondering as he lifted his foot to the low step of the California Street cable car and swung himself into a corner of the outside seat next to the gripman.

The car jerked on up the hill through the ruins of his beloved Chinatown, where the bells of Old St. Mary's hung ghostlike above the blackened shops of Chinatown—those shops whence his old friends among the Cantonese merchants had often produced their cherished finer porcelains and ivories for his appreciative touch when he and Newell had penetrated back of the show windows.

Up and up the little care jolted, past the wreckage of Nob Hill. How it hurt to recall the irreplaceable works of art that had perished in those lavish mansions! He gazed through the broken masonry of the Huntington home and saw in memory that great canvas which had so stirred his youth—the flaming ocean battle of John

Paul Jones. Then he thought again of the fragile French lady and her "Empress Josephine"—that carefully guarded treasure must have gone up in the relentless flames.

What tragedy that so few paintings had been cut from their frames and carried to safety, as someone had managed to do with Mrs. Huntington's prized "Carthage" and Mrs. William H. Crocker's "Man with the Hoe" by Millet, and Corot's "Dance of the Nymphs."

As the car neared broad Van Ness Avenue Abe looked toward the gutted Spreckels' "Palace," and thought of the boast of its owner that it was "absolutely fireproof." It was not surprising that a careless maid had left a third-floor window open in the panic of sudden exit, but what havoc had been wrought when curtains, ignited by the flaming wind, had sucked in fire to lick those walls he had helped to cover with huge paintings from master hands.

The car jerked to a stop. Gump dropped off the rear, almost opposite the barnlike store. His reveries had somehow seemed to reaffirm his faith in himself and in his business. Culture was, after all, the permanent link between generations—indeed, between nations. His life purpose was becoming clear. The creative artist must have his patron. Someone must bring them together. He began to understand why Steinhart, the far-sighted man of finance, had acceded to his request while Lilienthal, engrossed in the anxieties of the chaotic present, had refused. Practical Ignatz Steinhart knew that the business of an art dealer was far from "useless." Properly managed, it could bring lasting fame to any city. The banker had evidenced his confidence both in the business and in A.L. The art dealer vowed that he would use these funds to keep a tryst with the creators and purchasers of the best that could be found.

Great works, like the one the old Parisian had risked his life to save, were now destroyed. It would be his responsibility to find others and see that they were preserved more carefully. By training and inheritance he could judge and select the best. Moreover, he realized that he had the ability to pass on his own love of beautiful objects to those who had the means to possess them.

Even if these thoughts were not consciously formulated, the experience of that morning had a profound effect on all of A.L.'s life. Never again would he question the usefulness of the business handed down by Solomon Gump to his sons.

to the Orient

T HE GUMPS had reached one other important decision during that chaotic year. Abe finally convinced the rest of the family that future profit would come from across the Pacific. Only a short month after the fire he had encountered Ed Newell on the Sausalito Ferry as the two stood watching the sun drop into the Golden Gate.

"What are you doing with yourself these days?" A.L. inquired. "We are thinking of starting an Oriental department. How about coming with us?"

"When do you start?" queried Newell, with no effort to conceal his eagerness.

"October fifteenth—I hope."

Newell frankly admitted that he was without a job. After the earthquake had shattered the treasures he had garnered for Shreve and Company in Japan, that conservative firm had concluded that the art business—at least the Oriental phase—was "useless" for them. They had the agency for Rookwood pottery and Tiffany glass, the only American objects of art then fashionable. They would stick to their jewelry and silverware, plus these sidelines. They did not need to turn to the Orient to satisfy their clientele. Naturally, this had meant the end of their use for an Oriental art buyer.

A.L. could understand what disappointment that decision had

brought to Newell, who had left his dependable job as a chemist to indulge his dreams for so short a time. Newell told A.L. that he had been offered an opportunity to go into the furniture business of Charles M. Plum and Company, who were already preparing to decorate the many new homes planned in the bay area for people left without shelter by the recent disaster. But he told A.L. that the appeal of Oriental art was too strong; his taste of travel had spoiled him for work in plain surroundings. What he wanted most to do was to continue his quest of the exotic.

The months between May and October would be lean; but A.L.'s offer was too tempting to refuse, in spite of the question of family cooperation which Gump confided was the reason for his qualifying "I hope." Newell explained that he was temporarily driving a truck in Oakland, and that this could supply the necessities until the Gump project crystalized. A few days later a friend of Mabel's— Mrs. Michael Stein, whose husband was president of one of the street railways—hunted up Newell. She had brought back some rare antique jewelry from her last trip to Paris. Would he care to sell it for her?

Other friends offered a "rent-free home" on their Napa ranch for the summer. With that and the commissions from the jewelry sale, Newell managed to eke out a living and hold himself in readiness for the Gump opening.

A.L. kept in touch with him during the intervening months. Whenever the three enthusiasts—Mabel, Newell, and A.L.—conferred they visioned the complete transformation of the barnlike store on California Street. Never again, if they could help it, would Gump shelves be crammed with the conglomeration of bizarre statuary, French gilt clocks, and bronze busts, nor would the walls be hung with framed chromos and the huge oil paintings which had covered every inch of the Geary Street space.

The men who had founded the business were no longer directing it. Uncle Gus was dead. He had succumbed to a heart attack before the earthquake and fire—had collapsed at the store after overexertion from climbing the steps of the Catholic Cathedral, where he was supervising the installation of an altar built in the Gump factory. Their father, lingering between strokes, had relinquished the management to his three sons, Alfred, Abe, and William.

The brothers were not, however, of one mind concerning the Oriental venture. Alfred and William, alert and practical merchants, still gravely questioned the profit possibilities of the plans A.L. was making. The reputation their father and uncle had established had given the firm pre-eminence in certain lines. Why experiment, especially in a field distasteful to a large portion of a public saturated with anti-Oriental prejudice?

A.L. was determined. As his semi-blindness caused him to withdraw more and more from normal pursuits, he could give free play to his imagination, visioning things he could not see. The spell of Far Cathay drew his thoughts to the unknown across the Pacific. With psychic perception he foresaw Gump's future in Oriental trade.

Mabel alone, of all the family, was sympathetic to her husband's enthusiasm for the new venture. A few years before, Professor Ernest Fenelosa, formerly of the University of Tokyo, had begun an American lecture tour by addressing universities and art and women's clubs in the San Francisco bay area. Mabel had listened with constructive intent. She realized why Bostonians, privileged to learn first-hand from the Fenelosa Oriental collection bought for their museum in 1886, were among the few Americans with any true appreciation of this field of art. They had learned from Fenelosa himself when he came home from Japan in 1890 to direct the Boston Museum's new Oriental Division. His insight had awakened the Japanese people to the importance of their own art and saved them from casting it aside in the first flush of westernization.

The imprint of Fenelosa's lectures had remained with Mabel. Now opportunity was within reach for her to contribute to a more general understanding of the art then interpreted by this exponent of the deep significance of Far Eastern culture. She shared with her husband the conviction that the time had come for them to help make the West as conscious of the culture across the Pacific as was faraway Boston.

When night came and Abe returned to the quiet of their San Rafael cottage, wearied by the constant argument over what should go into the nearly completed store, Mabel would lay down the Goethe she had been reading to Solomon and turn to Oriental lore. They delved into the few books they could find on Oriental art. Then, relaxing in the descriptive prose of Lafcadio Hearn, the Gumps learned the legends of the kakemono. "Miracles of drawing and of color" Hearn called these scrolls, in his book *Glimpses of Unfamiliar Japan*. As they read of the "soft blue light of a Japanese day" and "earth-crust souls descending, flitting all white through inky darkness," Mabel and her husband began to sense what these silk-mounted scrolls could do in replacing the garish decorations that had covered American walls.

October finally came. A.L. had won his brothers to compromise. The temporary store would be divided into two sections. Two-thirds would be kept for European imports. The remaining third was converted into an Oriental Room, where a few choice pieces were displayed on an altar secured by Newell from the ruins of a Buddhist Temple in Chinatown. This setting evoked a sarcastic question from one of the brothers, who inquired from Abe as he looked at the austere high-legged teakwood altar,

"Since when has Gump's gone into the counter business?"

Newell had been fortunate in purchasing some exceptionally fine pieces from private collectors. A Japanese Room on the second floor held stock which compared favorably with Yamanaka merchandise displayed in Vickery, Atkins, and Torrey's near-by windows. Almost as soon as the Oriental Room was in order, George Crocker walked in with Captain A. Cheeseborough. Both were connoisseurs.

A.L. proudly produced the choicest porcelains and embroidered brocades they had hidden away behind the altar. When the men gave him a substantial order, he could point out to his brothers that the strategy of Chinese merchants in withholding finer selections for the discerning was profitable. From then on that became Gump policy.

Crocker carried word of his discovery to others with money to spend. Thus, although the Gumps were still waiting for their own insurance returns, they profited from the luxury spending of this "easy come, easy go" period. Shreve was selling more diamonds than ever before. The department stores specialized in silk shirts. Only the wary old merchants of Chinatown failed to catch the spirit of extravagant spending. Sing Fat and other proprietors of fabulous pre-fire shops were fearful of reinvesting in wares of real value. They filled the windows of their temporary stores with lures for souvenir hunters—cheap merchandise made for foreign trade like chop suey in their restaurants, palatable only to those unfamiliar with viands served at Chinese banquets.

A.L. realized that connoisseurs, accustomed to the finer porcelains, lacquer, and teakwood that proprietors of pre-fire Chinatown shops used to produce from their back-store hiding places, would be disappointed in the newer Grant Avenue shops. He was quick to take advantage of the hesitancy of these merchants to restock the better articles.

Newell's Shreve-buying experience in Japan had made him conscious of the tricks of Oriental trade. On that trip he had had unusual opportunity to learn from Japanese collectors and artists how to recognize goods made for export and how to judge the genuine. For instance, they had shown him the rich red-brown of native teakwood, explaining that the blackwood sold in Canton was stained to imitate ebony, the wood most prized by the English gentlemen who were major customers in the old treaty ports of China. In some of Tokyo's better homes Newell had seen the natural glow of fine teakwood. With the experience of his studio days he scraped black stain off furniture shipped from Canton, and men of taste were surprised by the beautiful pieces displayed in Gump's.

Soon their stock was increased from an unexpected source. Soldiers and marines, returning from tours of duty in China, came into the Gump store with treasure secured during the Boxer uprising. There were solid gold boxes, set with uncut jewels, gorgeous embroideries, and other finery indicative of luxury almost beyond the comprehension of practical Americans. Neither their temporary owners nor the purchasers had any idea of the real value; but their very strangeness lured San Franciscans with their suddenly well-filled purses.

These samples of China's magnificence intrigued the imaginative A.L. and Mabel. Now home on Green Street after the summer in San Rafael, they looked out on the bay and dreamed of travel across the Pacific to the land whence this mysterious beauty had come. But their turn to go did not come immediately. First they sent Newell on a second voyage to the Orient. This time he went as a buyer for the Gump Oriental Department, which even the skeptical brothers were beginning to recognize as a source of new revenue.

When Newell reached Japan he made use of his earlier contacts. Most foreign buyers bought from jobbers in the ports of Kobe and Yokohama, now filled with merchandise contrived for export trade. Searching out rare pieces valued by cultured Japanese meant trips into remote towns and villages. This required time and effort, but Newell was willing to invest both. He knew his way because he had made a thorough tour of Japan on his previous trip. At that time one of his Japanese acquaintances, a Harvard graduate and scion of a leading family, had obtained a letter from the Premier for Newell and an American war correspondent (this was during the Russo-Japanese War), giving them entree into homes all over the Island Kingdom. It was from the aristocratic Japanese met on this tour that Newell had acquired most of the knowledge of Oriental art he now had to guide him in his purchases for the new Gump department. This time he made his way again into remote villages, even undertaking a disagreeable boat trip to Satsuma. Here he saw descendants of the first Korean immigrants, still wearing little topknot hats, men who were entirely unfamiliar with the outside world.

Artists and craftsmen in all these outlying districts were uncontaminated by western commercialism. Newell admired an exceptional bronze in Kyoto.

"What is the price?" he asked.

"Ten yen," replied the maker.

"I'll take it, but I could use several dozen like it. How would you sell them by the dozen?"

Out came the abacus. The Japanese and his wife worked over the beads. Finally they said, "One hundred and fifty yen a dozen."

"Wait a minute," protested Newell. "Twelve times ten is only one hundred and twenty."

"Yes, I know," calmly replied the artist, "but if I make one, that is a pleasure; if twelve, I get tired—lose interest. Anyway, if you want them that bad you should be willing to pay more for them."

Newell appreciated the viewpoint. For he had a Japanese friend in San Francisco whose father had long been an art dealer. One day Newell asked the son, "How old is your father?"

"Eighty-four years."

"He does not seem that old."

"Oh, yes," answered the son, "people in the art business live to be very old. They always have something to think about besides themselves."

Newell was a man who used his creative faculties. He knew from experience the relative unimportance of passing years to anyone so employed. Recalling his own leisure hours poking around incense-filled rooms back of Chinatown's shops where he had first seen Oriental art, he now appreciated the opportunity for first-hand study of the methods used by these obscure Japanese artisans. He lingered in ark-shaped houses where paper-screened partitions gave privacy to men fashioning beautiful objects with an unhurried attention to detail.

He found that these people did not take business too seriously. They were overjoyed when a foreigner made the effort to visit them in their simple homes. He stopped in one small town noted for its brasses. The entire population poured out hospitality. Every night he was entertained lavishly in the tea houses, with lovely geisha girls as hostesses. His only complaint was that his hosts woke him too early in the morning to ask how he fared after his nights of pleasure. As this was a trial trip in which he was purchasing in experimental quantities, his whole order amounted to only about seven hundred yen. His interpreter told him the village had spent fully that amount in entertainment! But they had had a good time, and that seemed to be all that mattered.

Among the collections made on that trip were many rectangular priest robes bought in Kyoto. These were made of gorgeous brocades, cut into small squares and sewed together. At first Newell could not understand why they would mutilate such fabrics. Then he discovered a strange Oriental twist of mind. The priests were supposed to live in poverty. By making patchwork of their robes they were clad in rags—but what rags!

Newell bought all the good pieces of brocade he could find. He visited several pawnshops and found wonderful kimonos and haori (outside coats) as well as startlingly beautiful obi, or sashes. Those worn by women were twelve inches wide and three and a half yards long. Wound round and round plain silk kimonos, their bright colors furnished the only adornment. Astonished at the high price demanded by the pawn shop for unredeemed obi, Newell checked with a large shop where he discovered many of them to be worth two thousand yen apiece.

In contrast to the great value Japanese placed on bronzes and silks, Newell found that he could still buy wood block prints at a reasonable price. Although aesthetic Japanese paid little attention to these colorful representations of everyday life, he realized that, as Currier and Ives had caught the spirit of early America, so these prints, expressed the indigenous artistry of Japan. He knew that their influence on the foreign art world was far-reaching. Even Whistler had felt the influence of the "blue mystery that veils the world from dusk to dawn" in the color prints of the great Hiroshige. As he adapted Japanese moods to his own form of expression in painting his "Nocturnes" he told his friends that he translated Japanese art, or "carried on the tradition."

No art dealer presuming to enter the Oriental field could do without a stock of the wood block prints. Newell's letter of introduction to Helen Hyde came in very usefully here, for she was well acquainted with the local artists specializing in prints. Under her tutelage, he could make a wise selection for the Gump galleries.

While Japanese connoisseurs cared little about these prints, they considered Chinese paintings as the pinnacle of art. Newell saw a Sung Dynasty painting in Tokyo priced at five thousand yen ($2500). He began to understand the Oriental concept of art as a stable form of wealth.

By the time he was ready to carry out his promise to A.L. that he would visit China, Newell had learned from his Japanese associates where to go and what to select from across the China Sea. Like most foreign buyers he went first to Canton. Until recent years this had been the only port with an extensive export trade. Newell sought teakwood as his first venture. He thought he knew something about this phase of the business, but he was surprised to see how greatly the real Chinese furniture differed from the familiar blackwood. The native pieces were much simpler in design than the elaborate dragon-decorated chests and chairs he had known in San Francisco's Chinatown. He found that Chinese tables and other pieces were easy to take apart and could be shipped in knocked-down state. They were compactly crated, each piece numbered so that the furniture could be reassembled in the Gump workshop. This native-style furniture would serve a double purpose—a floor display unusual in San Francisco and a demonstration of their own designers of the importance of simple lines.

Among other Cantonese purchases Newell bought much hand-embroidered linen and many Spanish shawls elaborately worked and intended for the Manila market. With great roses on soft tan or white silk and long strands of knotted fringe, these were so perfectly fashioned that it was hard to distinguish right from wrong side.

There were hundreds of badly worn Mandarin wedding skirts in the Canton market. Newell bought about a hundred small mats cut from their panels, writing A.L. that these exquisite bits of gold-thread embroidery could be mounted under glass to make small decorative trays with brass handles.

Newell realized that when it came to buying porcelains he would have to choose very carefully. The Cantonese merchants on Grant Avenue had stocked up profusely with what was known as "Canton ware"—porcelain actually manufactured in Kingtehchen, south of the Yangtze River, much nearer to Shanghai, but sold via Canton because of the foreign trade. In San Francisco this ware was offered at low prices since the Chinese undervalued their imports for customs purposes. Newell would have to declare full value and he knew Gump's would not be able to compete except by virtue of better quality.

In Shanghai, where he next stopped, Newell had his introduction to the value the Chinese placed on jade. He was offered several small strings of matched jade beads for which the dealers wanted $1500 apiece. He knew that he could not sell them at home for $50. The value of jade was unknown outside the Orient. The only jade seen in San Francisco had been green stones from Canton, mounted locally in 24-carat gold rings. Newell refrained from hazarding any of his available funds in the Shanghai jade and turned his attention to the beautiful hand-loomed silks and satins. He bought a few dozen bolts superior in color and quality to anything he had ever seen.

Then he was ready to undertake the difficult and tiresome journey to Peking, becoming one of the first buyers from the West Coast to penetrate the hitherto unknown northern provinces. Here he learned that Chinese art had many facets. He found that he had reached in Peking the center of ancient Chinese culture. Cantonese commercialism and the lush decoration of South China, influenced as it was by contact with the semitropical regions of India and Indo-China, were lacking in the capital. Grandeur was there, but it was expressed in simple lines and magnificent color. Peking, originally Yenching, a small fortified town on the great Chili plain, had buried in dignified isolation the splendid art developed through the centuries by a curious compound of militant Tartarism and the mild philosophic culture of Cathay.

As the nomads constantly foraged into northern China, their blood became infused into the being of these ancient peoples and the influence of Khitans, Arabs, and Mongols produced art and architecture austere, except in color, in comparison with the gaudiness of the south. Newell had judged Chinese art only by what had been available in San Francisco, Japan, and Canton. He was awed by what he saw in Peking. Sunlit yellow-roofed vermilion palaces and massive woodwork were enlivened with blues and greens unlike any shade he had known before. The golden lattice work on windows reflected Persian and Arab design. Roofs were like giant tents.

In strange curiosity shops where thick Korean paper over windows shed an eerie light he found lamps of lacquered wood, cups of jade, and bronzes more beautiful than any he had ever seen.

Newell thought of the people he had left in money-mad San Francisco. What, if any, of these relics of age-old magnificence would they comprehend? Would it be possible to carry home to them any fragment of the splendor spread before his own astonished eyes?

He was inexperienced and bewildered, scarcely knowing how or what to buy. He found, too, that business to Chinese of the older generation was a kind of contest, a game. In south China there had developed stability of trade, through long dealing with English and European agents; but here in the north the ignorant and unsuspecting were quite generally shorn clean. Nevertheless, these men of ancient China exhibited a kindly feeling toward Ed Newell. He had a frank admiration for their art; he approached those venerable experts as a pupil would a teacher. That put upon them an obligation (for did not Confucius in his five relationships stress the mutual responsibility of student and teacher?). They respected his lack of cunning and intrigue. He fared well.

Still Newell was unwilling to risk too much of his firm's cash until he knew how the public would receive the new venture. He dared not bid high enough and as a consequence he was never shown the finest pieces. Instead he was offered what the underground of Peking termed "mixed cargo." He bought a good many brasses, some Mandarin coats, and a few old porcelains, not allowing himself to take anything valued at over one hundred dollars.

Before he left China Newell established himself with the Belgian Trading Company in Tientsin. The Belgians had asked no extraterritorial rights in China and thus stood well with the Chinese. The head of the company was the son of a Chinese princess and a Belgian exporter. Newell felt that he could safely entrust Gump's Oriental interests to such a well-connected person.

He stopped over in Tokyo on the return trip and arrived in San Francisco to find A.L. enthusiastic over the first shipments from Japan and Canton which had preceded him. The shop was already busy making the trays he had suggested, and they sold as quickly as they were put on display. He had to write back to Canton for more pieces of wedding skirts.

When word came that the north China shipment had arrived, A.L. put all other business aside and joined Newell in the receiving room. His eagerness was like a small boy's on Christmas Eve. At last he would have his own possessions from the mythical land beyond the Great Wall of China! He trembled with excitement as the workmen raised the lid from the first crate. Out came a jumbled mass of broken porcelain—almost as complete a loss as the rubble he had seen in the ruins of the Geary Street store a little over a year before!

Newell was frantic. He had hired professional Japanese packers in Peking, known as the most careful packers in the world; but he had forgotten one admonition. His Peking purchases had been opened for customs inspection in Tientsin—to collect a two and a half per cent duty levied on goods from the interior. He had failed to arrange for personal supervision of their shipment through that port. The inspectors had gone through the entire lot and tossed the pieces back into the crates without any attention to the protective wrappings. Every other piece was broken.

There was despair in the Gump establishment as they surveyed the debris. Then, while they were still separating the pieces that could be salvaged, Mrs. Francis Carolan paid them a visit. A daughter of the Pullman magnate, she knew Chinese art from her many years in Paris. Her delight in finding examples of the art of north China in her home city of San Francisco was expressed in a sizable purchase, including the best of the unharmed pieces. Luck had favored the Gumps again; the Oriental Department was assured.

A.L. proceeded to increase and diversify his new stock. Occasional large sales to customers such as the Crockers, Mrs. Carolan, and other wealthy clientele were encouraging; but the turnover of the stock as a whole was disappointingly slow. Eastern tourists who might have recognized the importance of this art rarely came to San Francisco. A.L. often thought that Huntington had probably been right in insisting that the kind of store he wanted to build up would do better in southern California among the winter visitors.

Discussing this problem one morning with a member of his staff, his associate remarked,

"What we need is better-informed salesmen on the floor."

This led to an introduction to Edward Wheeler and his brother Joe, two devotees of Oriental art, who had begun their careers among the carefully selected Japanese collections in George Marsh's exclusive shop.

A.L. took the brothers to lunch at the Concordia Club. Then he brought them on a tour of inspection through his new Oriental rooms. He took a bronze incense burner from the shelf and handed it to Edward.

"Why doesn't a piece like this sell?"

Wheeler turned it over and looked at the price.

"Not at that price!" he exclaimed. "People who know Oriental art will wonder what's wrong with it. Mark it high enough to denote its value and I'll sell it quickly."

A.L. forthwith engaged the services of both men.

Edward Wheeler was not only one of San Francisco's recognized critics of Oriental art; he also made a fine art of selling. He realized that most of his fellow citizens were not students. They would have no way of knowing the intrinsic worth of a fine porcelain. But he had his own way of encouraging pretentious spenders. As he discussed the bronze or porcelain with his patron he shared his own knowledge in such a way that the new owner went away unconsciously bolstered in his self-esteem as a collector who could meet an authority on common ground.

A.L. leaned heavily upon their advice in that early experiment in Oriental trade. He was still learning the values of his new possessions when Ed Wheeler called him into the Treasure Room to introduce a Mr. Wiltsee of Denver. A.L. hardly expected this tall sombreroed man in typical miner's outfit to be a connoisseur of fine art. But Ernest A. Wiltsee knew Chinese porcelains. He selected an Oxblood, a fine Hawthorne, and several other equally rare pieces.

When he had finished his buying he gave Gump a $25,000 check on his Denver bank, saying,

"You needn't ship the things until the check has cleared."

Turning to Wheeler, A.L. said, "Edward have these things on their way as soon as they can be packed." Wiltsee was so pleased that he became one of Gump's most consistent patrons.

Not long after this incident Ed Wheeler died suddenly, following an attack of inflammatory rheumatism. His death was a major misfortune to A.L., for Wheeler had shared his knowledge with his employer with unsparing exactitude. Much of the later reputation Gump acquired for his understanding of Oriental art was traceable to the careful authority with which this man explained each new acquisition.

The Gump brothers had invested some thirty thousand dollars in the temporary building that housed their business out on California Street, relying on agreement with the property owners that they would be reimbursed for their expenditures when the time came to return to the downtown business center. The verbal agreement had been that the Gumps would receive back one-half of the appraised value of the modernized building when the lease expired. What happened when that day came was a disillusioning experience to these sons of Solomon Gump who had started business at a time when a man's word was his bond. The agreement had never been put in writing, and their thirty-thousand dollars dwindled to a thousand in the end.

Nevertheless, the Gumps were ready to participate in the exodus to Union Square again as soon as business moved in that direction—in the summer of 1909.

Vickery, Atkins, and Torrey had torn down the ruins of two small houses on Sutter beyond the former downtown area. They were building their galleries and showrooms behind iron grilled gates leading into a garden. The Gumps were therefore able to lease a ninety-foot frontage, including the site where the Vickery and the Elder and Shepard stores had been on Post Street, less than half a block above the Shreve corner. Here they undertook the remodeling of a two-story building, adding small manufacturing shops on the roof.

Before blueprints for the new building were approved, A.L. had to cope again with the remonstrances of his more dogmatic brothers. They finally agreed to stock the new store in the same ratio of traditional and Oriental merchandise they had had on California Street. In the third of the floor space allotted to him, A.L. proposed to carry out dreams secretly cherished since the tempting Huntington offer.

The Gumps were determined to avoid any suggestion of a "Chinese Bazaar." Architect Clinton Day shared A.L.'s insistence upon authenticity in carrying out the Oriental theme. They engaged skilled Japanese carpenters, giving them only one specification—to make it original and to devise ways of keeping the best things out of sight. It was impossible to blueprint the interior of this part of the store. The clever carpenters evolved their plan as they worked. Two-thirds of the way back they erected a torii, or temple gate. Gnarled pieces of mahogany-colored madrone wood were brought down from the hills to form divisions in the irregularly shaped shelves. Sometimes a small tree trunk would become a bracket. In these unusual settings Newell arranged the modern less expensive bronzes and ivories chosen to catch the eye of the casual visitor. Dwarf trees and flowers arranged with the symbolism which every Japanese homemaker must learn gave the entire place an entirely noncommercial atmosphere.

Winding stairs led to the second floor. On the walls above the landing, portraits of the founders looked down on scenes neither of them could have imagined. There was Solomon, sketched in pen-and-ink by the Bohemian Club artist, Fred Yates, and an oil of Gustave by S. W. Shaw, California artist-historian who painted many portraits of early-day Masons and Pioneers. The remaining second-floor space was converted into Oriental rooms that created a sensation in San Francisco.

Under Newell's supervision carpenters partitioned that part into four rooms, separated by shogi, or sliding doors. Across the front, behind rice-paper windows which shut out everything except soft yellow light, a typical Japanese home was represented. Thick tatami floors, the traditional Tokonoma or household shrine at one end with its kakemono and single bowl holding a branch of flowers— these would give the visitor a sense of being in the land of the silks and brocades displayed. He and A.L. planned that kimono-clad Oriental maids would serve tea to honored callers in this room.

Next was the Kimono Room, built as a replica of a room in a Kyoto temple. Adjoining this, the Blue and Gold Chinese Room was Newell's personal design. Behind panels brilliant with color and carved in simple Chinese style, they kept the choicest embroideries and old porcelains. A curving Oriental Court led into the galleries. Beyond that was another small Japanese Room filled with decorative hangings, priest robes, and cut velvets.

While all this was being built, A.L. sent Newell to the Orient again. He provided him generously with letters of credit and assured him that he would back his decisions in the purchase of whatever unusual pieces he could find in Japan and China. There was only one other great dealer in general Oriental art in the United States—Van Tine in New York. A.L. was ambitious to outstrip his reputation by making San Francisco pre-eminent in the field.

Newell had more courage as a buyer this time. He knew that the public would appreciate what he chose when it was properly exhibited. His Belgian associate introduced him to a Chinese in Peking by the name of Liu, a man who had the respect of his countrymen not only in matters of art but also as a student of Chinese history. Liu became his comprador, or "go-between," in all his future dealings. There were no books on the art of northern China at that time and Newell took careful note of the stories Liu told him.

When Newell returned, all this information was passed on to Gump. In the same way that he had memorized paintings in early days, A.L. made the stories his own, sharing them with irresistible enthusiasm wherever he found an audience.

His lifetime habit of reaching the store early meant that his office work was out of the way before doors were open to customers. Then A.L. started on his daily rounds, stopping to chat with each member of the sales force, asking questions about the previous day's sales and passing on whatever new information he had acquired about the merchandise in that department. In this way he was often on hand during the process of an important sale. He would be introduced as the member of the firm responsible for the beauty and originality of the Oriental rooms. Picking up whatever object was involved in the sale, he would explain its history and symbolism.

Customers, flattered by this individual attention, told their friends not only to visit the beautiful rooms but "to be *sure* to see Mr. Gump." A.L. became an apostle of Chinese culture, and the San Francisco treasure house began to be known far and wide. Van Tine could no longer compete. That house was still emphasizing the Japanese. Their buyers had not penetrated into northern China as Newell had done.

In spite of his Chinese discoveries, Newell had not neglected his own Japanese contacts. He brought back an enormous red lacquer Buddha, the largest ever taken out of the country. This and several other show pieces were selected to give atmosphere to the Oriental Court, with no idea of offering them for sale. He was astounded, therefore, when he returned from a subsequent trip to find that an enthusiastic visitor from Iowa, a chiropractor by the name of Dr. Palmer, had bought them all. When A.L. handed him a letter from the new owner describing the museum he had opened as a successful side line displaying the Gump purchases, Newell realized that he would have to search for another Buddha on his next trip. He found one—even larger and older—in bronze.

The Kimono Room was a mecca for most tourists. The exquisite garments displayed here were made to order in Japan. On every trip Newell spent long hours with their Yokohama designer, choosing with his inherent color sense every hue to be used. The heavy silk was then farmed out to small home shops throughout the country. The results were works of art.

While women's kimonos were variegated and bright, those for men were black, unornamented except for a small crest on the back. John Drew happened to be in the Silk Room when Gump's first shipment of these black haori coats was unpacked.

"Try one on," urged A.L., inviting him to step into the Blue and Gold Room.

The actor slipped into the austere garment, its white Tokogawa crest reflected in the great mirror—framed in carved teakwood and guarded by two stone Foo dogs.

"Most distinguished!" beamed A.L. "It becomes your dignity."

"How many of these have you?" asked Drew.

"Just six," A.L. replied.

"I'll have them all," exclaimed the actor. "I'll have something no one else will have—for a while, anyway."

Newell also brought home bolts of heavy silks from Peking. Gump's began to make kimonos to order in their own work rooms. Now they encountered real competition in San Francisco. Tourists in Chinatown were attracted by windows full of showy garments at far lower prices. In order to demonstrate that Gump kimonos were actually worth the difference, Newell purchased a dozen of the less expensive quality from the Canton shop which supplied San Francisco's Chinese merchants. If a customer demurred at the high prices in the Kimono Room these were brought out. The visitor was invited to compare the weight and quality of silk, or urged to check for himself in Chinatown.

Customers who could afford the better garments rarely left without one or more of these luxurious robes. Men on business trips to San Francisco took kimonos home to wives and daughters in the East. Hundreds were sold for prices between $75 and $100 apiece, and the Gump name became known in new circles.

Occasionally A.L. was hard pressed to live up to his everwidening repute. Clients sometimes expected more specialized information than he was prepared to give. Nor could Newell and Joe Wheeler be every place at once. About six weeks after the opening of the Post Street store Gump was chatting with a chance visitor who introduced himself as Gustave Liljestrom, a former teacher at the Chicago Art Institute. Liljestrom said he was en route to China and, having stopped over in San Francisco for a few days, had dropped in to see the Gump Oriental Department. Their conversation was interrupted when A.L. was called to the telephone.

He came back saying,

"Mr. Liljestrom, would you consider joining our staff temporarily? I have a client in Hillsborough who wants us to arrange and catalogue an Oriental room. If you will take on this job I'm sure I can rearrange your transportation. You can go to China later."

Liljestrom consented, and his trip to the Orient was postponed indefinitely. He became an integral part of the Gump organization, and was soon preoccupied in designing harmonious furnishings for homes of clients who had been won to the Oriental motif.

Rivalry between the two older Gump brothers became more intense and the volume of business grew. Alfred, carried along in the postearthquake boom, had insisted upon increasing the inventory of glass, chinaware, and European decorative objects far beyond his allotted amount. A.L., relying on the promised reimbursement from the California Street property owners and hoping for settlement of the German insurance claims, had spent more in the beautification of his Oriental rooms than current income justified.

Before the end of 1909 he was forced to make another call on his bankers. The Anglo-Californian had merged with the London, Paris and American Bank to become Anglo, London and Paris National. At its head was Sigmund Greenebaum, who had married a daughter of Henry Cohn. Learning that the bank president was ill, Abe presented his problem to Greenebaum's son-in-law, Herbert Fleishhacker, a man whose avocation was art collecting. This interview was much less trying than his conference with Lilienthal and Steinhart two years before. When A.L. met with immediate acquiescence to his request for the funds, he realized that he had justified Steinhart's confidence in art as a business essential to the development of a cultural community. This loan carried them over until the tardy compromise payment finally brought a small share of the overdue insurance.

It was fortunate that Gump finances were in a state that made it possible to take advantage of the unheard-of opportunities presented to Newell on his next trip. He was in China in the dramatic year of 1911 when the Nationalists of the south won their victory over the Manchus. Sun Yat-sen's followers were concerned only with the monetary value of treasures hoarded for centuries in the Imperial Palaces of Peking. Things of beauty hitherto undreamed of by Occidentals came out of hiding with the plundering of these palaces.

The Empress Dowager had held many foreign audiences, but even those officials who had been in her presence had seen only the audience rooms. No one had any conception of what artisans of the court had wrought during the centuries of absolute monarchy. Tribute silks of fantastic beauty, Coromandel screens set with precious and semiprecious stones, lacquer and teakwood more wonderful than any Newell had ever seen, bronzes, porcelains, jades and ivories, embroidery so fine that stitches could be detected only through a magnifying glass, plates that were supposed to change color if anything poisonous were served on them—these were just a few of the treasures suddenly available to Newell in the loot offered in the Peking market.

In roadside camps and back-street shops he found rugs that had never been trod by the feet of common man. In all his trips he had never come across anything to compare with them. Once, in 1908, he had bought a small Chinese rug of strange design on the back of a mule; but until now he had had no real conception of the beauty woven by the ancient Chinese into their Palace floor coverings. On his first large rug-buying engagement he had to think fast. Liu had told him that the Yamanaka agents were due in half an hour. Rugs were not included in the Gump agenda; could they count on another Mrs. Carolan to recognize the worth of these unprecedented decorations plundered from Imperial floors as their Hillsborough client had done with their finest Chinese porcelains? Even in Paris, with its porcelains and silks, or in Boston, where captains of Clipper ships had brought home fans and shawls along with tea and chinaware, no one had ever seen an Imperial Chinese rug.

Newell made a quick decision, grateful for A.L.'s unlimited confidence—and his sizable letter of credit! With Liu's guidance he was able to place the winning bid. Gump's had the satisfaction of introducing these rugs, prized by generations of haughty Manchus, to the amazed western world. Opportunity soon same to realize handsome profits. Mrs. Frank Havens, wife of one of the Oakland pioneers, bought the pick of the shipment to cover the floors of a "palace" she was building on the East Bay hills—a palace contrived with rare woods imported from the land of the Maharajahs. Louis Tiffany of New York bought a runner in yellow tones, more regal than any of the others.

Importation of these rugs opened new vistas to the imaginative mind of A.L. Gump. Mabel read aloud everything they could find about the ancient art of rugmaking. They studied about Persia and the Mongols, following on the map the trek of camel caravans. As they read they pictured how the art of rugmaking had been brought "over the top of the world" to China.

They realized that few customers could afford the Imperial rugs. They knew, too, that there were not many to be had. Why not adapt the ancient patterns to new conditions and create their own coverings for the floors of the homes their decorators were planning? They would sponsor rugmaking. Liljestrom and his staff of designers went to work in the San Francisco studios. Water-color copies of the finest Imperial rugs were sent back to China. There skilled artisans set up their looms and began supplying America with rugs of deep Chinese blues and soft tans which soon set a new standard of taste.

Gump's idea of custom-made Oriental furnishings brought a dramatic change in San Francisco's decor. Where the homes of the 'nineties had had their gilt cornices, gold-framed mirrors and marble statuary, the early nineteen-hundreds saw Japanese screens embroidered to blend with individual color schemes, Chinese rugs on the floor, Japanese and Chinese prints on the walls. Displayed on teakwood stands were small ivories or fine bronzes modeled by creative Japanese artists from animals in the Tokyo zoo. Pianos were draped with mandarin coats from China, a priest robe from Japan, or a "Spanish shawl" from Canton. Framed sleeve bands from coats so old they were falling to pieces, or the attractive trays made from embroidered mats, added an Oriental touch to the simplest living room.

Demand for the native teakwood furniture introduced after Newell's first trip inspired Gump designers to adapt that wood to their customers' needs. Along with the water colors of the rugs they began to send drawings for custom-made furniture, to be fashioned by skilled Chinese hands. Sometimes they were surprised by the results. Oriental artisans were not accustomed to Western methods; but a chair with a back twice as high as the designer intended proved to be one of the best sellers.

Newell brought home other relics of China's antiquity more important to the student of Oriental art than the magnificent Palace loot. A.L. listened with rapt attention as Newell told him about these tomb pieces, which he said Liu had showed him with half-hearted interest when a few clay horses and figurines had filtered into the Peking market. Liu said that they were recently unearthed burial pieces from the T'ang dynasty, dug up less than a year before when engineers building the Lao-Tung railroad had uncovered a tomb filled with these clay objects. Camels, dogs, horses, and human figurines had spilled out on the dusty right-of-way. Frightened coolies refused to touch them. Then a few with the bravado of iconoclasts set them on hillocks as targets for their stones.

Both A.L. and Newell were familiar with stories of grave robberies which had gone on for a thousand years in spite of a death penalty for those who were caught at it; but Liu explained that Chinese collectors had no interest in objects buried as recently as the T'ang dynasty (A.D. 618 to 907). Grave robbers of the past had sought only early bronzes of the Chou and Han dynasties, sacred objects in which sacrifices were made to heaven and the spirits of the departed. The pieces shown to Newell had no religious significance. They represented family aggrandizement, demonstrating by the number and the amount of gold used in their decoration the wealth of the deceased. They were considered unimportant by Chinese connoisseurs; but a few of these recently unearthed objects had attracted the eyes of foreigners and Liu thought Gump's might find purchasers.

A.L.'s curiosity alerted his active mind. He wanted to know the secrets of a mysterious past so rudely disclosed by industrial progress. He asked Newell to tell him everything he had learned from Liu concerning Chinese burial customs. Newell traced the story as Liu had described it to him, back to a period before the time of Confucius when human servants were buried with their masters. This practice, he said, was discontinued by the time of the Han Dynasty (206 B.C. to A.D. 220), an era when the Chinese Empire reached

across Asia and touched that of the Romans. At that time clay
figurines began to be substituted for the living, and a great variety
of objects were provided for the use of the departed in the hereafter.

With the advent of the Golden Age of China (the T'ang dynasty) elaborate entombment and pretentious funeral processions
marked the wealth of the deceased. Finally the burden upon the living became so great that imperial orders brought an end to the
practice.

The western world knew little of those strange relics of antiquity
when Newell chanced upon his first purchase of tomb pieces. There
were only a few examples in Peking, but some of them reminded
him of Tanagra statuettes from Greece which adorned all European
galleries. He concluded that they were worth a gamble. He bought
a couple of priest figures, about three feet high, a few horses, a camel
and some miscellaneous small pieces. They certainly were different
from anything else he had seen in China.

He told A.L. that the investment did not represent much outlay.
They might prove of real value, or they could be tossed into the ash
can! The figurines arrived without much breakage, and A.L. ordered that they be put on display in the Oriental Court.

One of the first visitors to share his interest in the new acquisitions happened to be Otto Kahn, president of the Metropolitan
Museum of New York. His purchase of a large T'ang priest confirmed Newell's choice as fine art. Kahn told them that the famous
collector of Chinese art, George Eumorfopoulos, a Greek ship-owner
living in London, had noted several specimens of these T'ang tomb
pieces at the Burlington Art Club during their annual exhibit the
preceding summer. When this exhibit had first opened, in May,
1910, no one had ever heard of these clay figures; but a few weeks
later the first specimens had arrived, sent back to London by the
British engineer whose railroad gang had so unexpectedly dug into
the past. A new display case was added to the exhibit, revealing for

the first time to the Occidental art world the rhythmic lines of the figurines that had so appealed to Newell.

A.L. was elated to learn that he was the first dealer to introduce this important phase of Chinese art to the American public. Word went back to Liu to watch for every good tomb piece he could lay his hands on.

As the world began to realize that the shrieking locomotives had not only pierced the burial mounds of China but had also rent the veil which shrouded her long past, the carefully wielded spade of the archeologist followed the ruthless path of the railroad. Amusement turned to amazement, and wonderment to awe as the work of anonymous sculptors was unearthed. Bronze, wrought with skill unexcelled by ancient or modern artists, came from the hands of these long forgotten men of Asia.

Liu responded to Gump's instructions, sending shipments representative of many dynasties even older than the T'ang. The glaze on Han dynasty bronzes, affected by their long burial in the damp earth, was iridescent, adding more beauty to the ancient pieces.

A traffic in grave robberies began to fill dealers' shops in Shanghai and Peking, as the demand for these antiquities increased. With rising values, the temptation to take part in the systematic looting reached beyond adventurers to merchants and war lords. On his next trip Newell heard the tale of a dealer who risked life and reputation in his feverish search, stealing to the grave in the dead of night with a gang who worked in silence. As one half of the group stood guard the dealer, disguised as a coolie, dug in with the others in frenzied stealth. But he was apprehended. His life was saved by the forfeit of half his fortune. He felt he could no longer appear as the devout Buddhist he had been. He abandoned his disciplined life, bought a half interest in a sing-song girl, and disappeared from his daily haunts. Although he continued to deal in ancient treasure he let others bring it to him, with no questions asked.

Newell bought every good tomb piece he could find. Gump's

was building a new reputation with collectors and museum directors. Even people who were not otherwise interested in Oriental art were fascinated by the sculptural perfection of these lovely figurines. With all the expansiveness of his world-circling mind, A. Livingston Gump proudly elaborated Newell's tales of the retrieving of these relics as he escorted famous visitors through his treasure rooms. Mary Garden almost missed her opportunity. She was interested in two Italian marble bird baths on the first floor and refused Newell's invitation to go upstairs to the Oriental rooms.

"I hate Oriental junk," she told him.

The next day Miss Garden's sister was in the store and Newell arranged a meeting with A.L. After a fascinating hour she left, determined that Mary should share that pleasure. When they did return together, A.L. was in the Oriental Court.

"Oh, Mr. Gump," exclaimed the opera singer, stopping before a prancing T'ang horse, "I *must* have this. I'm leaving in a day or two for Paris to play *Salome;* but I want the horse to go everywhere I go. Can you make me a packing box that will protect it?"

"You shall have a personally designed container that will make it possible for you to carry your horse anywhere safely without danger to body or limb," declared A.L. as he picked up the realistic clay steed and started toward the upstairs shop.

In a few weeks a letter came from Paris.

"I have your T'ang horse on a Louis XV table in my room. I love it better than anything I possess," wrote Mary Garden.

CHAPTER SIX ∽ *A Wider Circumference*

AS THE REVIVED CITY of St.
Francis matured into metropolitan stature, the pioneer era was passing. With that era, too, the carefree basis on which all comers to this cosmopolitan port had been accepted was also disappearing. Newcomers became, in a sense, intruders.

Population had congealed into distinctive strata, each jealous of encroachment from the unqualified. "The Society of Pioneers" would not admit anyone whose family had arrived later than 1849; the "South of Market Boys" were as individual in their traditions as were the proud residents of Nob Hill. Even the shopping districts were dissimilar. Those who found their bargains in "The Mission" scorned the "extravagant" black-suited ladies who paraded Post Street.

Chinatown was huddled closely in the few blocks between Stockton, Kearny, California, and Pacific Streets. "Little Italy" had taken possession of North Beach. Between the two was the Barbary Coast, which had absorbed the brothels crowded out of the downtown alleys when lower Dupont Street was dignified as Grant Avenue.

Potrero Hill belonged to the bearded Russians who had emigrated from Siberia via the sugar plantations of Hawaii, as well as via the Caucasus and Martinique, to California. Now they had selected this most sunny part of San Francisco to gather in their Molokan Church and plot together in their crowded flats about the great day when the peasants should rise against the czar and establish their socialistic state.

Families who had moved down the Peninsula or across the bay to Oakland, Berkeley, or Marin County at the time of the great fire remained in these outlying communities to build up suburban areas.

For many of these, ferryboat commuting became part of that leisurely era. On these craft with their stubby noses and churning paddle wheels many lifelong friendships were formed between men who watched with possessive pride the rising skyline of the city founded by their pioneering fathers. They had the individualist's scorn for the promoter spirit that was drawing a heterogeneous population to that sprawling city in southern California—Los Angeles.

Yet when men like Bernard Maybeck, prophet of modern architecture, paced the decks of the ferryboats, dreaming aloud among friends of the progress their city should make, there came an urge to invite the world to celebrate San Francisco's rebirth. Then they realized the implication of the approaching completion of the Panama Canal. On days when the Farallone Islands were silhouetted against skies clear of fog, these San Franciscans looked beyond the far horizon and sensed that a new day was dawning in world relations. They realized that as the great canal would split apart jungle barriers between two halves of the western world, commerce would be rerouted. Their city, with its magnificent harbor, would share handsomely in the increased trade.

As the epoch-making event drew closer, it became an obsession with San Francisco leaders to plan a celebration worthy of this triumph over nature.

In the same way that his father had responded to the excitement of Bonanza days and plans for the Mid-Winter Fair, A.L. perceived the opportunities that lay in exposition planning. He joined with other enthusiastic citizens at a great mass meeting on April 28, 1910, and subscribed his share of the four million dollars in exposition stock auctioned off that morning.

Then, imbued with enthusiasm for the prospective influx of world visitors, Gump felt the need of a more diversified stock to meet the varying tastes of the notable men and women who would be coming to San Francisco. That Gump's should be prepared to cater to their cosmopolitan desires he determined to follow treasure trails to Europe. His success in selling Oriental art had made him many friends throughout the country. He wanted to add to his personal knowledge of the art goods sold in his store by going to the sources of supply himself. Alfred was involved with the more utilitarian phases of the business and was ready to share the European buying with his brother; but he realized that Abe's poor eyesight would be a serious handicap in traveling and selecting merchandise. Mabel was too busy to go with her husband as they had a three-year-old daughter—Marcella, born in 1909. Alfred suggested that Charles Hass, head of the chinaware department, accompany A.L. Accordingly, in the spring of 1912, the two embarked on the liner *Olympic,* bound for the trade centers of Europe.

It was an exciting voyage, interrupted in mid-ocean by a wireless message: s o s. TITANIC CALLING. WE HAVE STRUCK ICE AND REQUIRE IMMEDIATE ASSISTANCE. Their ship turned back in a great semicircle and proceeded at full speed toward the location radioed by the sister ship. But when they had covered the fourteen hundred miles there was nothing for them to do. The few survivors had already been picked up by nearer vessels. A.L. and Hass settled back in the cabins they had willingly surrendered in preparation for taking on rescued women and children. A.L. listened sympathetically to discussions among *Olympic* crew members whose friends had been transferred to help man the proud new ship and had gone down with the rest.

This was a first European voyage for both men, but Abe's mental picture of the continent, etched by his study of paintings in the Gump galleries, his father's vivid tales, and all that Mabel had read and told him about her many trips, was so accurate that he found himself speaking with the assurance of one on familiar ground. In England and Spain, Paris and Vienna, he trod on soil made famous in history and art, surprising his companion by his ability to select fine paintings and delicate porcelains. Hass did the routine buying, but subject to A.L.'s scrutiny—a long and tedious process which involved standing by the hour before great canvases or testing with sensitive fingers the shape and quality of the china and glass offered them in dealers' showrooms.

Samson in Paris, famed for his inimitable copies of old Chinese porcelains, challenged the San Francisco dealer.

"I'll bet you a thousand francs I can tell the difference," asserted Gump. "Bring out your wares and let me see."

"I won't bet on a sure thing," declared Samson, well aware of his visitor's handicap as he spread out his copies and originals, promiscuously intermingled. Being color conscious himself, he could not believe that anyone with defective vision could possibly have a basis for deciding between them. As true pitch depends upon acute hearing, so Samson knew that color tones were discernible only to good eyes. He was confident that his glazes matched perfectly the subtle hues of the original Chinese pieces.

A.L. lifted each sample, feeling it carefully with his long sensitive fingers, as a bank teller seeks to detect counterfeit money. He was correct in his verdict every time.

"You forgot the weight and feel of the material," he explained to the astonished Samson.

The Parisian dealer thanked Gump and assured him that he would be guided by this advice. Later when Samson "copies" found their way into the Gump shop as bases for artistic lamps, A.L. was gratified to note that his precepts had been well followed.

On another Parisian contact that same year, A.L. learned the hard way that he should have trusted his gambling instinct as he did his fingers. In the Paris salon his attention was called to a painting by Paul Chabas. He stood before it a long time, absorbing in his peculiar way the subtle glow over the whole scene, the rosy pearl-like water, and agreeing with Hass that the exquisite nude figure surpassed any that his father had ever brought from Paris on the old trips. Impulse told him to place a high bid; but the canvas was exceptionally large—twelve feet high, and the figure life size. He hesitated. While he pondered the possibility of finding a purchaser for such a spectacular painting among his now more conservative clientele, his commissionaire came to the hotel in great excitement.

"Your indecision has cost you *the* painting of the year!" he said. "It has taken the Grand Prix and goes to the Luxembourg!"

A.L. returned to America and began to hear of the sensation caused by that painting—"September Morn"—and the millions of reproductions sold as its popular appeal made it the most talked-about canvas of the period. There was meager consolation in the realization that he had recognized its unique appeal instinctively.

Soon after A.L. returned from this European trip the firm started plans for extensive enlargement, in preparation for the expected influx of exposition visitors. Now that they had buyers combing the world they needed more space to display their treasures to advantage. The building next to them belonged to the Board of Education but its two lofts were so badly built during the immediate postfire rehabilitation that it had never been occupied. The Gumps secured part of the building on a long-term lease and A.L. called Newell and Liljestrom into his office.

Together they mapped out plans for Oriental rooms even more elaborate than the ones in the existing store. A.L. decided to give free rein to his gambling instinct this time. Money would be no consideration in perfecting the setting for the superb collections he was accumulating from Newell's Oriental trips.

Liljestrom designed a Jade Room with deep recessed show cases behind carved panels—a room where their richest treasure would

be guarded as though behind the Great Wall of China. Tomb pieces
and gorgeous scrolls would make the adjoining Treasure Room
suggestive of old Peking; while the Red Lacquer, Lotus, and Porcelain Rooms opening off a much enlarged Oriental Court would provide ample space for every variety of valued possession. Ivories
would have a separate showroom and the far end of the court would
open into a room to be designated the Garden.

A.L. did not put all his thought into these Oriental rooms. The
street floor provided space where he planned to display antique
furniture and splendid iron-grilled gates from Spanish palaces,
which had been among the trophies of his European treasure hunt.

A third floor offered the first opportunity to recognize the importance of the new phase of his increasing business. With the
introduction of individually designed Chinese rugs and custombuilt Oriental furniture, the firm had begun to acquire a reputation
as decorators. In fact, the Gump touch in homes furnished in this
style had led them into a new field just as casually as Solomon's
chance use of European bric-a-brac had transformed his mirror and
frame shop into a distributor of objets d'art for the salons of the
'seventies.

Now A.L. turned to Mabel's brother, Milton, one of the city's
successful architects, asking him to design a series of period rooms
where appropriate furniture and harmonizing decoration could be
presented.

The plans grew in elaboration. A.L. was constantly in an expansive mood; but he could not stand attention to detail. Newell
came into the office one day with a contract involving the expendi-
ture of $50,000 in preparation for work on the Oriental rooms, the
first step in the new program. A.L. listened for a while as his associate read the long legal pages. Then he interrupted Newell
abruptly:

"I have to see Malley about a teakwood stand. Be sure you are
right, and then go ahead," he tossed over his shoulder, as he felt

his way toward the door and headed for the upstairs shop where in his daily calls on Fred Malley, head of the repair department, he kept in touch with other details that interested him more.

There was real cooperation within the Gump organization as the venture began to shape up. The brothers were no longer skeptical. They knew what word-of-mouth advertising had meant to Gump's since the public had discovered the artistic rooms in the original building. This time obstacles appeared from the outside. When the carpenters' union discovered Oriental workmen on the remodeling job, A.L. was faced with a threatened strike. Resourceful as always, he took his problem to top authority. Former mayor P. H. McCarthy, president of the Building Trades Council, was an old acquaintance.

With persuasive enthusiasm A.L. described to McCarthy the attraction his project would offer Panama-Pacific visitors. He pointed out that in a year of international cultural cooperation an obstructive attitude on the part of California workers was quite out of keeping. McCarthy listened with understanding and promised to use his influence in finding a solution. But the carpenters were obdurate; they flatly refused to work side by side with "Japs."

Finally A.L. suggested a compromise plan which McCarthy was able to sell to the workers: The store had two entrances; the inside connecting doors between the two halves were boarded up, and the union reluctantly agreed that there were then two separate jobs. Their members proceeded with necessary readjustment in the old building; the visiting artisans installed the carved panels and latticed doorways that transformed the new portion into a glimpse of the mysterious Orient.

Chiura Obata, famed Japanese artist and later faculty member of the University of California, designed and painted the mural ceiling of the Lotus Room. Although A.L. could not clearly see the results of Obata's expert brush strokes as the artist spent hours lying on his back on the scaffolding, he took pride in knowing that the best available talent contributed to perfecting every detail of this undertaking.

The progress of his building plans absorbed A.L.'s major attention through the early months of 1914; but that sixth sense which often led him to quick decisions in augmenting his staff penetrated his preoccupation when a young German came in to apply for a job.

The man introduced himself as William K. Drewes, telling Gump that he had recently arrived in San Francisco from China with his Russian wife and two small children. He said that owing to an unfortunate chain of circumstances he had found himself stranded on a bench in Union Square, his last dime spent for a cup of coffee. Realizing that he must find work to ward off starvation he had walked down Post Street, pausing for a moment before the familiar Oriental beauty displayed in the Gump windows.

His English was halting, but he showed Gump the pocket dictionary which had enabled him to make out the meaning of the sign in the window—"Packer Wanted." He told A.L. that he *must* find a job—he would do any kind of work, if only he could remain in this fascinating place among things he understood and appreciated.

A.L. listened sympathetically but did not engage Drewes. Some hours after the young man had gone, he turned to his secretary and dictated a card asking Drewes to return the next day. A.L. had sensed a kindred spirit in his eager caller.

When Drewes came, post card in hand, the older man said,

"You are not a packer, but I think I can make a salesman of you."

He called in Ed Newell, introduced them, and said, "Take this young man to a bookstore and buy him a *good* German-American dictionary and the best works on Chinese art."

A.L. had an apt pupil in his new employee. Many a morning as he made the rounds of the establishment Gump came on Drewes studying ancient Korean pottery in the Gold Room, or cataloguing Chinese paintings kept in cabinets back of the altar which had been moved from the California Street setting. Drewes lingered near with unconcealed interest as A.L. or Ed Newell explained the significance of the great rugs that Drewes took out of cabinets for them to show to special customers. Imperial rugs, particularly the one with blue Ho birds on a soft yellow background, became so deeply impressed in his mind that he never would forget their details. Under A.L.'s guidance and with methodical inheritance from a professor father, Drewes began a life-time habit of setting aside three hours for daily study in some branch of art. With the patience of a true student he took time to emulate his mentor in the early morning hours before the store was officially open, sitting with closed eyes and trying to distinguish by the touch of his fingers the different glazes of the porcelains he had seen A.L. fondle as they had discussed the history these bowls and jars represented.

A.L. personalized every transaction. After his first European buying trip he realized that it was easier to sell objects that he could identify with their actual setting. He reminded Alfred that their father had always made it a practice to supervise the display and sale of paintings and *objets d'art* which he had chosen personally in Europe. Alfred agreed that it might be a good idea to alternate buying trips so that each should be in the store the year following his search. Sales talk would then have the vigor of personal persuasion.

A.L.'s turn to go came again in the spring of 1914. This time Mabel found it possible to accompany her husband and Hass. She left the children with competent help at home and shared with Abe her background and experience that made this return pleasant and fruitful for both.

In Paris, Mabel's fluent French afforded them many a wayside contact, one of which proved valuable for years to come. As they strolled through the Latin Quarter, thinking of the times Solomon had gone on similar quests, they paused to watch an artist who had set up his easel on the curb. In her friendly way Mabel questioned him about his paintings. Thus they came to know Edouard Cortes, whose Paris street scenes became favorites with Gump patrons.

Again, as they stood admiring a picture in a Paris gallery exhibition, A.L. whispered to Mabel to ask the artist if he had ever painted in San Francisco. She hesitated, wondering how her near-sighted husband could have seen enough to have a glimmer of recognition. He insisted and she said in French, quite apologetically,

"My husband sometimes gets queer ideas. He thinks he has seen your pictures in San Francisco."

"But surely," answered the flattered artist. "I was there in 1895 to paint the portrait of Monsieur le President de l'Orpheum!"

A.L. had recognized the brush stroke in the same way that experts judge handwriting. In spite of his handicap he had his own way of looking at a painting, a method that seemed to implant a deeper image in his mind than the usual cursory look from eyes too eager to pass to the next object. If the canvas was large, he would step close, examine it minutely, but in sections. His mind would then bring the whole picture into focus, each portion vividly impressed and blended until it was as if he himself had created the thought behind the picture. If the painting was small enough to handle he would hold it close and to the side, where it seemed easier to bring it into focus with his eyes than if he held it straight in front.

Paintings were not the sole object of their buying trip. They went to Austria to select fine leather goods, Coldscheider pottery, and terra cotta ware in Vienna, to Haida for Bohemian glass, and on to Italy in search of Venetian glass, rare marbles, fine mosaics.

One afternoon as they were driving through the Italian Alps A.L. was not in a buying mood. Mabel was looking for rare old laces and they stopped in a small village. Relaxing in the car, A.L. was enjoying a quiet smoke when a little boy ran out of the shop, motioning him to "come in." Mabel was standing by the counter looking up at an immense Genoese collar hanging on the wall. She pointed to it, calling A.L.'s attention to the remarkable soft-hued

FROM CHINA'S ANCIENT PAST

This bronze ceremonial bowl, thirty centuries old, was unearthed at An-yang, capital of ancient China. The bowl is twelve and three-quarters inches in diameter.

(Photograph by Frank van Eckhardt)

velvet edged with pure gold galloon, and to the bronze-gold bells at the ends of the points.

"*Quanta costa?*" ventured Gump to the shopkeeper.

"Fifteen hundred lira," replied the man.

"I'll give you 150," offered A.L. as a starter, fully expecting a round of bargaining.

"Very well," answered the man.

They put the collar in the trunk of the car and continued on to Florence, pleased with their discovery but not fully aware of the value of their chance purchase until they took it to an appraiser. Then they found they had an authentic collar once used by the Medici to dress up their white oxen on festival days.

Hoping to add more unexpected booty for their museum collectors at home, they crossed into Spain. Mabel looked forward especially to gay Madrid; but they had gone only as far as Barcelona when A.L. woke one morning and turned to her.

"Let's beat it for home!" he exclaimed.

That inner voice which had guided all the important decisions in his life, from card playing to choice of friends and staff, had warned him of growing unrest in Europe.

Despite her disappointment at their interrupted trip, and her feeling that he was unduly alarmed, Mabel had learned long ago that when her husband had a hunch it was well to act. Reluctantly she helped reorganize their plans and they reached England ahead of the frantic tourists who were caught in the general exodus a few weeks later.

The Gumps reached their San Francisco home in August, 1914. The city was in a furore of preparation for the coming exposition, while the peaceful Europe they had enjoyed so short a time before flamed with sparks from the anvil of Mars. San Francisco, the cosmopolitan city whose population stemmed from varied European ancestry, was more concerned with this conflict than most American communities. Yet trouble in the Balkans was thousands of miles away. If the Kaiser felt compelled to conquer those tempestuous little countries and become the ruler of Europe, there was nothing Californians could do about it. They went ahead with their plans for the great fair.

With its batteries of searchlights playing on the sparkling Tower of Jewels, the exposition opened in a blaze of splendor on February 16, 1915, its gay participants far removed in mood from the conflagration in Europe.

Although A.L. could see little of the phantasmagoria by the Golden Gate, he shared civic pride in the major emphasis on art, for he knew that its directors had spared no expense or effort in engaging the best talent in America to beautify its courts and halls. When sunlight emphasized the vibrant symbolism of Robert Aitken's "Fountain of Life," or searchlight beams played over walls of soft pastel shades conceived by Jules Guérin, color director, practical Americans dropped the chains of business and found themselves in fairyland.

Treasures from all the world were housed in the Palace of Fine Arts, embodying the fulfillment of those visions Bernard Maybeck had dreamed on the decks of slow-moving ferries. A.L. applauded the director of fine arts, John E. D. Trask, whose planning had started most exhibits toward San Francisco before war disrupted the world. Even Germany was included in what proved to be the most representative collection of paintings and sculpture that any Westerner, except the few who had traveled extensively, had ever seen.

Although the Kaiser, evidently pooling all resources for the secretly contemplated war, had declined San Francisco's invitation to exhibit, Trask had been fortunate in securing a group of fine German paintings which had been on exhibit at the Carnegie Institute in Pittsburgh early in the summer of 1914. When war broke out these pictures were en route back to Germany on a ship captured by a British cruiser. The captain, recognizing the extra-national character of such art, had returned the collection to neutral United States instead of proceeding to England with his prize.

A.L. often joined the holiday throngs who were coming to appreciate the unparalleled assemblage of contemporary American sculpture embodying in bronze and stone the spirit of their national life. He realized that this exposition would pay dividends for years to come to men like him who dealt in the permanent expression of artistic dreams. Here for the first time many of the uninitiated were coming face to face with great art.

The small gallery assigned to Keith had poignant attraction. A.L. looked at the brooding landscapes, thinking sadly of the day only four years before when he had served as pall bearer for his friend. How unfortunate, he mused, that the artist who had brought most fame to his state could not have lived to share in this exposition! He realized how much he had gained from proximity to Keith in his last years when the aged artist had established his studio in the same block as the Gump store on Post Street.

As he escorted special visitors through the exposition galleries, A.L. often explained the two categories of Keith's work. He told them that the first expressed the rugged Scot who had climbed mountains with John Muir and recorded faithfully on canvas the majesty of the California Sierras. Then, as the influence of the Swedenborgian minister, Joseph Worcester, had penetrated Keith's being, his painting became metaphysical. A.L. recalled that when Keith had first expressed the poetic belief that he could trace thought waves to the reverberations of bronze gongs in his studio, Newell had located for A.L. an old Japanese temple gong which became the artist's favorite. How often in Keith's last years A.L. had stood quietly out of sight in his friend's studio, sensing that Keith was struggling to match the mellifluous sounds from that gong in flowing tone and color.

When the renown of the exposition grew, Gump's shared in the attention of visitors from afar—as A.L. had always prophesied it

would. Their unique rooms became in a way an adjunct to the
Oriental displays in the curving galleries of the Palace of Fine Arts.
These rooms had been ready for tourists arriving early for the open-
ing of the fair.

The Gump annex, formally presented immediately after Christmas in 1914, had indeed given San Franciscans a foretaste of what
they would find at the exposition. Having seen a few examples in
the Post Street store, visitors were better able to comprehend the
gorgeous screens—pictures embroidered on silk, wood block prints
and sculptured wooden figures which came from ancient Japan,
and the scrolls and porcelains in the Chinese exhibit.

The displays from these two Asiatic countries, as well as the
unusual rooms presided over by an intelligent little Filipino woman
in embroidered piña cloth, demonstrated to the American public
for the first time, outside of commercial shops and private collections, what generations of culture had produced in countries
across the Pacific.

Throughout the exposition year A.L. insisted that the Post Street
store should be gala with fresh-cut flowers, and each member of
his staff prepared to escort every caller with the cordiality of a
personal host. Visitors began to divide their time between the
exposition and Post Street. Then they wrote home about their discovery of the Gumps' Treasure House. Emily Post was one of the
most outspoken in her praise. She had come West with an assignment from her publisher to describe the details of a unique adventure—making a continental tour by automobile.

Mrs. Post's San Francisco hostess had difficulty in persuading
her to take time away from the exposition to visit what she termed
"a downtown store with the unpromising name of 'Gump'"; but
once she had been convinced that she should make the call, she
lingered long in the Oriental Court, the Jade and Porcelain Rooms.
She drank tea from eggshell cups while she feasted her eyes on
Japanese brocades and tribute silks from Peking. She saw the Ming

dynasty cloisonné ice cooler, and listened to the story of the poison plates. When she returned to the East and recorded her experiences in her book *By Motor to the Golden Gate,* she introduced the beauty she had found in Gump's to a widespread circle of readers.

Men like T. B. Walker of Minneapolis came to San Francisco to see the exposition, and returned home with treasures from Gump's. The wealthy lumberman's interest in old Chinese porcelains first brought him to the store, and his intensive search among the blue and white, ox blood, apple-green and peach bloom vases of the Porcelain Room kept Joe Wheeler busy many a long evening. Walker made a practice of dropping in about five o'clock and staying on until seven or later, utterly oblivious of closing time.

A.L. nearly overdid his informative selling one night when he took Walker to see a pair of jars just unpacked from the latest Chinese shipment.

"Look at these, T.B.," he said in the familiar tone he used with his eminent customers. "They are five hundred years old—superb specimens of the Ming dynasty."

Walker was looking, with a quizzical smile. He had dealt with A.L. long enough to understand his visual handicap and at the same time he knew porcelains. He lifted one jar and looked at the store marker on the bottom.

"But Mr. Gump," he protested, "they are clearly marked two hundred and fifty years old."

"That's right," rejoined A.L., refusing to be defeated in an argument, "but you see, there are two of them!"

Walker was considerate but he continued to rely on Joe Wheeler's more prudent salesmanship. The selections he finally took home to adorn the Walker Galleries, his gift to the city of Minneapolis, reflected discriminating taste, both of buyer and seller.

Years later when Walker was escorting a lady from San Francisco through the galleries she lingered before a case filled with jade, rose, and amethyst quartz.

"This makes me homesick for my native city," she remarked. "I might think I was back in Gump's."

"You are right," exclaimed her host. "All these pieces came from your Gump store."

Thus, as famous collectors took Gump-selected treasure to all parts of the world, the name of the San Francisco art dealer began to be familiar beyond the circumference of his immediate associates. A.L. became, like the city he served, a host with an international guest list.

THE LIGHTS of the exposition were switched off for the last time at midnight on December 4, 1915, but understanding of art and the people who created it burned on in the memories of San Franciscans. This art consciousness brought far more gain to dealers than any of them anticipated. Gump's became agents for the little bronze babies by Edith Parsons, Edward Berge, and Jeanette Scudder. These statuettes that had beguiled exposition visitors along the paths of the lagoon around the Palace of Fine Arts served as symbolic reminders in many a San Francisco and bay area garden. And the Gumps sold other outstanding works, such as Weiman's "Night" and "Morning," casts of which went to San Simeon to form part of the collection of William Randolph Hearst.

Hearst's mother, whose art purchases had encouraged struggling genius in the days when her spacious and hospitable Pleasanton home had received many a delivery from the older Gump store, loaned her collection of paintings, tapestries, and fine porcelains to the Art Association. Displayed in the Palace of Fine Arts for several years, this collection helped to prolong awakened public interest.

In that immediate postexposition period new galleries began to vie with Gump's and Vickery's. Marsh found himself competing with Nathan Bentz. Since the exposition had revealed the attractions of the northern California metropolis, winter visitors now included San Francisco on their itineraries and the Bentz Oriental shops in Santa Barbara and Pasadena branched into the north. Businesslike

Japanese were crowding into upper Grant Avenue, displaying in their shops much that had been admired in the galleries of the fair.

In spite of the magnetic atmosphere of Gump's Oriental rooms, with their windows of translucent porcelain and floors covered with Japanese tatami and rugs of the magnificent Ch'ing dynasty, A.L. realized that this competition was making inroads on Gump's trade. He determined to implement his secondary knowledge by going himself to the source of the art he was fostering. With Ed Newell he sailed for the Far East aboard the *Empress of Russia* in 1917.

A.L. was fascinated by his first, and only, excursion into the mysterious Orient. Because of Newell's familiarity with the unusual, they did not tarry long in the ports and cities known to tourists. In the out-of-the-way places to which his companion took him, Gump met native artisans. He began to acquire an understanding of their philosophy and habits, which enabled him to interpret better the works of art from their hands. They spent some time in Miyanoshita, above Lake Hakoni, one of the most beautiful places he had ever seen. Here A.L. slept in the native portion of the hotel, on floors of tatami, with shoji (sliding doors) between the rooms. He was hardly prepared for the silent entrance of the maid the first morning when he stood in fur slippers, but otherwise unclad, to prepare to dress. He was embarrassed, but not she, as she looked him over from head to foot.

"Master, you very strong," she commented as she casually handed him a kimono. As his travels progressed, he learned that this experience was common to all travelers.

Continuing the trip via Seoul in Korea, A.L. found opportunity to procure some unusual treasures. Among them was a remarkable Kwan Yin (goddess of mercy) cut from marble, and a collection of old Korean chests. These were carved by native craftsmen from selected rare woods; their brass mountings were etched by skilled artists. These chests represented the work of a culture then hardly known to Western minds.

Native Korean amber was another addition to his collections. A.L. concluded that the brilliant clear resin, shining like yellow diamonds, must have resulted from some peculiarity in the trees of that ancient country, for he was told that no other land produces any amber comparable to that of Korea.

The ultimate quarry sought by these hunters, however, was not amber but jade—even more cherished by cultured Chinese than diamonds. These two men from California were well prepared to undertake such a quest, for San Francisco had been the first American city to understand the value of jade as a rare jewel. Abe's old merchant friends on Dupont Street always had some jade tucked away—simple green jade rings, carved beads or bracelets, tomb amulets treasured as heirlooms. He realized that jade meant to Chinese women what pearls signified to the European or American. Ownership of at least one jade ornament was the hope of every Chinese girl. Many a collector fell under the spell of this ancient stone "of many virtues" as he poked around Chinatown's fascinating shops. A.L. was one of these; Ed Newell was another.

As they journeyed together, Newell had acquainted A.L. with the intricacies of jade-hunting in China, describing the characteristics of each market. Canton, he said, with its seven jade houses, was the jewel market. In Peking, civilizations apart from Canton, they would find wise and cultivated dealers who had accumulated the finer new jades and the hereditary pieces from the Manchu and earlier dynasties. This was the ornament market. The two men planned to stop first in the intermediate market of Shanghai, the New York of the Orient, where pieces from both markets dribbled in.

In Shanghai A.L. was introduced to Chinese sales methods. They were met by their comprador—a man as important to the seeker of jade as the guide on an African big game hunt. Gump found that although jade hunting was not fraught with the physical danger of stalking wild beasts, it was equally thrilling. Roaming

China as hunters, their "weapons" were bits of jade of known quality. Newell's was a ring, appraised and valued by a connoisseur. When he dealt with men whose knowledge of jade flowed in their veins, a heritage from generations of wise forbears, he could compare what they offered with the cabochon he wore.

A.L. found a ready welcome in this land and its people, already so real to him through books and acquaintances. Newell's earlier associations assured a cordial introduction; soon the sensitivity of Gump's seeing fingers won respect and admiration from the Chinese to whom the feel of jade is more eloquent than the look. This man who handled their revered stone with such perceptive touch was at home among them.

But before he was completely accepted by the knowing dealers, A.L. was put to the test. On their first day in China the comprador asked if he might introduce an honorable merchant, distinguished for his rare good taste. This merchant wanted to show the visitor from America some of his priceless possessions. Gump felt certain that his Chinese guide either wanted to repay some obligation, or that he was trying to build up face by inviting a man of such outstanding reputation to meet his American patron.

At the appointed time the merchant arrived, his silk robes and velvet waistcoat indicating the dignity of the visit. Behind him walked two servants carrying between them a carved teak chest. They set this before Gump, and opened it to reveal a smaller even more elaborate box. Out of this was lifted a porcelain vase gently wound with soft silk. A.L. waited somewhat puzzled, for a few minutes. Then he turned to the comprador.

"What does he ask for this?"

The two merchants talked together, the measured cadence of their strange syllables giving no hint of their mood. Then, with immobile face, the comprador said, "He wants five thousand gold American dollars."

A.L. asked if he might examine it. He felt it with his sensitive fingers. Then he held it to the light, looking at it with the gesture so familiar to those who had watched him judge paintings and other works of art.

"Tell him," he said with equal solemnity, "that it is worth forty dollars."

Again the two merchants talked together. Then the comprador laughed as he turned to A.L. "He says that you are perfectly right. He just wanted to see if you knew your business. Now he will bring out his jade."

As Gump and his agents perfected their technique of jade hunting, they came to know and respect the wisdom and psychology of Oriental merchants. Newell had learned early that it was better to pursue ones' quarry in the regular channels. On one of his previous trips he had made a dangerous and tiresome journey to the borders of Tibet where he had heard that there were some remarkable rugs. To his amazement he found prices two or three times as high as he had been asked for examples of equal merit in the Peking market. When he returned with nothing to show for his pains, his Chinese friends explained,

"Those dealers thought that if you traveled so far and endured so much, these silk rugs must be worth a great deal to you. Thus they doubled their prices."

A.L. was impatient to get to Canton, where he could visit the jade auction houses and feel for himself the blocks of raw stone quarried in the Burmese mountains and the boulders and pebbles retrieved from the muddy streams feeding into the upper reaches of the Irrawaddy River. Eager as he always was to know the facts about any object he handled, he asked questions wherever he went. Stories of the Burma mines, the only commercial source of fine jadeite, filled him with curiosity. As a jade hunter himself he wished he could venture into the wilds of the Kachin country. That was impossible of course. Even the miners could work only three months

of the year, approximately from March to May. During the six
months monsoon season the open pits were flooded and it took three
more months to pump out the water with primitive long bamboo
pipes and lever hoists using kerosene cans as buckets.

He was told that the Chinese regarded the river boulders as of
finer quality, and that this had been the primitive method of gathering jade. Descriptions of the jade-bearing river of Khotan, quoted
from ancient T'ang lore, intrigued him. These tales said that people
used to discover the valued stone by observing spots in the stream
where the reflection of the moonlight was strongest. Accounts of
Mohammedan jade fishers who recognized the stone when their
bare feet touched it had personal appeal for A.L., who understood
so well the infallibility of acute sensory nerves. The legend of this
method explained that every time the man in the stream stooped to
retrieve his stone a soldier on the bank struck a gong and an official
chalked a red mark against the worker's name, holding him responsible for as many pieces of jade as there were marks.

That tale concerned the ancient nephrite of Chinese Turkestan.
What A.L. saw when they reached Canton was jadeite. The comprador explained to him that even scientists had recognized the
difference between the tougher and more translucent jadeite and
the amorphous waxlike and slightly less dense nephrite for less
than a hundred years.

As they mingled with the buyers in the auction houses, A.L.
discovered that there could be no more uncertain gamble than trading in raw jade. Many of the boulders from the river beds were
about the size of watermelons covered with a brown rind—or crust
—resulting from millenniums of immersion. Like purchasers of
melons in California fruit markets, jade bidders insisted upon "plug-
ging." A small groove, approximately one-half inch in width by
about two inches long was cut to a depth of one-quarter inch. If
that revealed a bright green color the buyer hoped that somewhere
within the calcareous matrix might be hidden an area so translucent

and so brilliant that it could be compared with an emerald. Chemical analysis had shown the finest of such jades to be colored with a trace of chromium, the element that also gives color to the precious emerald whose name has been borrowed to designate the color of jadeite most sought by jewelers. The Chinese, to whom all jade is Yü-stone, have even more picturesque terms for their translation of the character that designates the rarest Burmese stone. To them it is "the green in the tail of the peacock," or "the color of young paddy [rice] shoots."

But the plug from the boulder may be deceptive the same as the mouth-watering red of the melon plug may hide a heart that is pithy and unedible. A.L. heard of one man who lost $90,000 when he chanced his all on an eighteen-inch square of brilliant green. The color proved to be only a thin band, while the rest of the piece was white of little value. Another buyer made a profit of over $200,000 from a boulder which contained a huge field of rare "emerald" green.

As A.L. watched the Chinese fondle their pocket pieces and caressed the surfaces of the jades with his own sensitive fingers, he understood what they meant by describing it as "jun" (soft like morning dew or gentle rain) or "wen" (warm and soft like the flesh of a little child). He began to understand, too, why jadeite and nephrite, durable for all time, were the chosen media of China's greatest artisans, both ancient and modern.

With fascinated attention he lingered in the shops where Cantonese lapidaries toiled ceaselessly at their foot-pedal lathes. Taut wire on a wooden bow, drawn through damp gem sand from ruby or sapphire mines, cut the tough stone to specified shape. The cutting was done by the abrasive, not the wire. Then the jade carver, having both hands free, held the object in his left hand, while with his right he slapped on the gem dust mixed with gum from native trees. On lap wheels varying in size from fourteen and one-half inches in diameter to that of a pin head and in thickness from a quarter to a few thousandth of an inch he shaped the fibrous jade into objects of rare beauty. A.L. watched every stage of the work. His own fetish for perfection gave him rapport with the polishers who meticulously produced the final finish by rubbing their jade objects on dry bamboo, ox leather, or gourd skin smeared with emery or ruby dust, fine sand, or pulverized garnets.

The men he saw here were fashioning jewelry of various kinds —carved beads, earrings, brooches. One string of matched green beads, he was told, had taken thirty years to perfect. He could well understand why it was worth $40,000. For his purpose, however, A.L. was more interested in such decorative objects as Newell had previously brought from Peking.

They moved northward to the old capital. Here they were met by Mr. Liu, who seemed pleased to greet in person the man for whom he had been spokesman during the past eight years.

A.L.'s initial impression of their comprador was not reassuring. On their first day together he was disturbed when he saw Liu selling "amber necklaces" in his Wagons-Lit hotel shop to some American customers. A.L. recognized the beads at once as a variety of bakelite made in Germany; but he heard Liu extol them to his customers as "genuinely Chinese." That evening as they lingered over dinner he turned to Liu and chided him.

"Why do you sell these fake necklaces for amber? All these people are nice. When they get home they will discover the fraud."

"No maskie [no matter]," Liu shrugged his shoulders. "They one-time pid-gins—never see again."

"You would not do a thing like that to us, I hope. I would not like to have you treat my buyers that way."

Liu's intelligent eyes lighted with amusement, "Ah," he smiled, "you not stupid. You all-time pid-gin."

Then he showed A.L. a stack of letters three inches high. "All about you," he said. "Everything you do in Shanghai and Canton."

"Who wrote them?" queried the astonished traveler.

"My friends," answered Liu. "They know you deal with me. They write all you do."

Newell had learned long ago that there are eyes and ears behind every silken curtain in China. What one does in a private room in Shanghai speeds by bamboo wireless to any other Chinese interested in the mission in hand. Now A.L. found out for himself that his every act was observed. He also learned that in spite of his friendliness his comprador was alert to every opportunity to line his own pockets.

Liu showed him a pair of jade birds, encrusted with mold and earth, undoubtedly old tomb pieces. He said he would let Gump have them for two hundred dollars after he had cleaned them. But once the dirt was off and the softly rounded birds looked poised for flight, he wanted three hundred.

"Yesterday you quoted two hundred," protested A.L.

"All right," answered the Chinese, "now five hundred."

They compromised and Gump paid two hundred and fifty—to save face for both.

To pay the asking price means loss of face in China, and Liu reminded Newell of the time he had paid the first price asked for a fine jade bowl that had appealed to him on their initial buying trip together. That transaction had almost cost Gump's their comprador, for Liu felt that they both had lost face. As their friend and host, he lost face with his principals.

Newell also recalled an incident on his second expedition to Peking—the time when Mr. Liu had won his lasting confidence. One of the greatest collections of ancient treasure ever offered to the public, including rugs, bronzes and jade, had come into the market. Liu was greatly pleased that his friend had arrived so opportunely. He proposed that they go immediately to see the collection of Imperial rugs owned by a syndicate composed of an art dealer, a war lord, and a banker. Newell recognized at once that he was in the presence of some exeedingly rare loot. He knew, too, that he would have to make a high offer to get the rugs. At the same time, he had learned enough of Oriental ways to realize that too high an offer would register him as an easy mark and handicap his future dealings throughout China. He thought hard. Finally he offered what seemed high to him.

Days passed with no response concerning the rugs. In the meantime the syndicate invited him to see a second collection. This time it was mainly ancient bronzes. Liu instructed him to make a similar high offer. Again, no response. But as they waited, they heard that the *pièce de résistance* owned by the syndicate was an assortment of jade, of fabulous beauty and worth. He dared not chance delay on these. Ascertaining the syndicate's price, he bought the collection outright.

When the treasure was delivered, he turned to Liu.

"What happened to our offer on the rugs?"

"I did not transmit that offer," replied the wise Chinese. "If I had, you would never have seen the bronzes or jade. They would have felt that you did not appreciate the really fine things. From then on, you would have seen only inferior objects."

"What about the bronzes?"

Liu sent for his boy, telling him to bring in some boxes and open them. There were all the ancient bronzes.

"So—they did accept that offer," exclaimed the delighted Newell.

"No," said Mr. Liu simply, "they accepted mine. Yours was too low."

Then Newell found out what a Chinese who really respects his friend will do to save face. Liu had mortgaged his home and brought himself to the verge of poverty to secure these bronzes. Yet, had he not been asked about them, he would never have mentioned them again. Unquestioningly, the bronzes became the possession of Gump's and Liu knew that he was dealing with "all-time pid-gins."

Now as the two men pursued their treasure hunt in Peking, A.L. discovered for himself how his comprador worked. They found three jade cabochons of exceptional quality, which he learned had formerly been owned by a Manchu prince. Two of the stones were resplendent, the other not quite so outstanding. The owner wanted $30,000 for them. That seemed too much. As they left, Liu ventured the thought that *he* could probably get them for twenty-five thousand.

"He has two prices—one for foreigners, one for Chinese," he explained.

Liu did buy the jades and generously offered them to his American patron at cost. Impressed by this generosity, A.L. offered him a 5 per cent commission. The next day Liu wanted the commission doubled. For several days the two were deadlocked in their transaction. Finally Liu agreed to sell the two large stones for twenty-two thousand dollars and keep the third for himself. That seemed to save face.

A.L. also learned, early in his experience as a buyer of Oriental art, that a dealer must be prepared at times to buy what he sees, on the spot. Once Liu brought into the compound a vendor with a great mass of textiles, mandarin coats, tribute silks, needle work. Nothing was particularly exciting until he showed a set of four eighteenth-century Kossu tapestries, their turquoise blue backgrounds showing a decided French influence.

"Superb!" exclaimed A.L. under his breath. Turning to Newell he told him to "take over at once," even though the dealer was asking 25 per cent more than the general run of tapestries. But Newell was cautious.

"We must not pay his asking price," he replied. A.L. would not be put off. He told Liu that he wanted the tapestries even at the asked price.

"Don't worry," the comprador assured him. "I'll get them." But he allowed the vendor to leave. This time the comprador failed in his promise. They never saw the vendor or his wares again. It was a serious loss to Gump's, for the tapestries were unique.

A.L.'s open admiration of the things that he liked presented a problem to Newell and Liu. Newell had learned years before to be cautious in expressing his reactions when he was trading. He thought he was maintaining a poker face, but he soon found that everything he liked was kept at a high price. Then some one reminded him that the Chinese are skilled at reading the expression in the eye. He bought a pair of amethyst glasses; but he had not thought it necessary to warn A.L., whose expressionless eyes could not betray him.

No one could have foreseen, however, the warmth of pleasure that suffused A.L.'s face when the dealers began to bring out their fine jade pieces. Newell had never thought much of Gump's paraded ability to judge porcelains by deciphering the difference in glaze, but he realized then that the waxy feel and rhythmic carving of jade communicated something to A.L.'s inner being that could not be denied. He would bargain over purchases of lesser value, but when they dealt in jade his ambition to become the world's greatest commercial collector betrayed his enthusiasm.

Gump's very appearance accentuated his eagerness. With his well-tailored clothes and immaculate grooming he looked the part of a wealthy American connoisseur rather than the shrewd trader Newell, in old clothes and dilapidated hat, had trained himself to appear. Liu was amused.

"Mr. Gump," he remonstrated one day, "you look too much rich."

Liu taught him many things about the Chinese attitude toward their jade, bronze, and paintings. He began to understand that the place of art in the culture of this race was different from that for the Japanese, who dealt in art as a tradable commodity. As A.L. was introduced to scholars and collectors in northern China he found that they valued their ancestral possessions as a form of wealth practically untouchable. His comprador told him that in the past only the direst need would force a Chinese gentleman to part with his hoarded treasures; but, as the old order was changing, the infection of western commercialism was lowering this resistance.

A.L. discovered in his transactions that syndicates, often composed of dealers, bankers and war lords, were wheedling magnificent pieces from old mandarins who had little other capital. He acquired the technique of dealing with these syndicates, instructing his agents to hold out Gump dollars for the finest jades whenever he heard that such a group, needing American money, had a corner on some ancient collection of art.

Liu was wise in the secrets of his countrymen. He managed to show A.L. some of the finest pieces produced during the reign of Emperor Ch'ien Lung, greatest of jade collectors. One of these—an ornament of emerald-hued jade—measuring about 2 by 1½ inches, was as thin as parchment; yet it was like lace on one side, designed in peonies, butterflies, and birds. On the reverse a scroll represented the Buddhist unending knot of happiness. He saw precious and semiprecious gems combined with flowers of jade—narcissus, lotus blossoms of rose quartz with jade leaves five or six inches wide, grape arbors where real amethysts hung in bunches among graceful green jade leaves. Liu told him that during the cold winters of northern China when palace gardens were bleak and frozen, the Emperor had commanded his court artists to copy nature in minute detail. These delicately carved blooms, in their pots of jade, silver gilt, and cloisonné, were breath-taking to the Californian whose love of living flowers was so deeply ingrained that he had until now always resented imitation.

As A.L. felt and studied these exquisite examples of the work of unknown craftsmen, he seemed to absorb the significance of Confucius' description: "it is not because jade is rare that it is so highly valued. It is because, ever since the olden days, wise men have seen in jade all the different virtues. It is soft, smooth and shining, like kindness; it is hard, fine and strong, like intelligence; its edges seem sharp but do not cut, like justice; it hangs down to the ground, like humility; when struck it gives a clear, ringing sound, like music; the stains in it, which are not hidden and which add to its beauty, are like truthfulness; its brightness is like Heaven, while its firm substance, born of the mountains and the waters, is like the Earth. The Book of Poetry says, 'When I think of a wise man, he seems like jade.' That is why wise men love jade."

After five months in the Orient, A.L. and Newell prepared to return to San Francisco. He left instructions with Liu and his other agents to watch for every authentic piece of Ch'ien Lung jade, as well as for any available examples from the collection of the late Empress Dowager, whose Yü-stones were second only to those accumulated during the sixty-year reign of the aesthetic Ch'ien Lung.

When he reached his San Francisco storehouse A.L. had a new respect for the contents of his Jade Room. Family and friends, business associates and customers became his converts as he expounded the virtues of the ancient stone. He had a light installed outside the Jade Room door which flashed a signal to call the president of the firm every time an important visitor showed an interest in the treasure.

The hushed tone of his voice as he described the intricate work of some anonymous artist of the court working with infinite patience to satisfy the perfectionist Emperor seemed to add human value to the carved stone. A.L. could tell his listener how the very life of the artisan depended upon satisfaction of Ch'ien Lung's minute requirements, for he had learned in China that it had not only meant honor but life itself to accomplish the impossible for the sake of the Emperor.

A.L. convinced himself that by opening a new clientele for these jade objects he could compete with ancient nobility in fostering a new era of production; he bent himself to the task of cultivating a taste for art that had flourished in the past only under the patronage of kings and emperors.

Achievement of this ambition was postponed as America's entrance into world war interrupted all extraneous undertakings. There was little that a firm so wholly in a luxury line could do in the way of war effort. The Interior Decorating Department, however, had a well-equipped factory, built in the heart of Chinatown immediately after the exposition. Here there were woodworking machines of various kinds. A.L. pointed out that these could readily be adapted to the manufacture of war necessities ranging from rifle butts to canteen chairs. The Gumps offered this building with all its equipment to the government without charge; but no reply was received. When that gesture had passed unappreciated, A.L. took stock of its present usefulness.

He found that during their absence in the Orient, the department manager had become involved in a confusion of projects some of which were beyond his ability to carry through. Among other assignments he had undertaken the decorating of a large home in Beverly Hills in Southern California. A.L. was chagrined to discover how poorly his staff had managed this job, and dispatched Newell to bring order, later making him manager of that department.

Consequently, when peace returned and it was possible to commence foreign buying again, Newell was too busy in his new position to return to the Orient. Joe Wheeler became the Far Eastern buyer, carrying on in his quiet, patient way the accumulation of treasure. By 1919 when Wheeler arrived in China, tomb pieces more ancient than any Newell had ever been shown were available. He began to send back bronzes from the Chou and Han dynasties and mortuary figures of great value—discoveries that rapidly increased the number of discriminating collectors who came to investigate the Gump storehouse.

Then in the early twenties China felt the repercussion of international extravagance. There was a renewed interest in jade. As prices for Old Masters in Europe rose with American tourist trade, so the Far East was combed for its art. Prospectors braved the dangers of bandits and jungle to search for more jade desposits in Burma. Jade hunting attracted more adventurers than ever before. The Canton auction houses were filled with speculators. Jade dynamited from the hills did not have the quality of the old hand-hewn pieces, and carvers often worked with modern carborundum in place of the pulverized gems. Wheeler found at least fifteen hundred artists and apprentices employed in fashioning elaborate modern pieces. Some of these were patterned after those retrieved from the palaces and tombs of the ancients, and others were designed as the carvers worked. Such artisans found not only that "the pure essence of hill and water had become solidified into precious jade" as their philosopher, T'ang Jung-tso, had written in the olden time, but that nature by the distributions of the veins of color had literally stamped the pattern to be shaped out of the many-hued stone. When Wheeler shipped samples of these jades to San Francisco, A.L. cabled instructions to "buy every good piece."

During this period of revived interest their Peking comprador, son of old Mr. Liu, received word that one of the most important groups of Ch'ien Lung jade yet discovered was in the control of a syndicate with whom he often dealt. A.L. authorized Wheeler to stay in China until he could get this collection of large vases, jars, bowls, and wine pots "for the right price." For three long years Wheeler worked, matching Chinese patience with his own unhurried diligence. Coded cables crossed and recrossed the Pacific; but negotiations did not progress. A.L. was participating at close range in spite of the ocean between. He was following, too, via news reports the advancing Chinese People's Army (Kuomingtang) as it slowly penetrated farther north. The moment headlines flashed word of the sacking of Nanking Gump was ready with his strategy. He understood Chinese psychology well enough to realize that the syndicate in Peking would fear that a similar fate there would mean the loss of their precious collections. He cabled another offer—the lowest figure he had yet indicated.

He was right. The syndicate would rather have in its possession an easily concealed draft on an American bank than the bulky objects that made up this jade garniture. The offer was snapped up; the magnificent jade jars, each several feet high, the ceremonial bowls and ladles, and the graceful wine pots became the property of Gump's.

A.L. knew how to protect his valuable acquisitions. He instructed Wheeler to have them transferred to the American embassy compound. Here the Marines guarded them along with all the valuables belonging to United States citizens then in Peking. When the conquering army reached Peking this precaution proved unnecessary, for the lesson learned through unpopularity following the pillage of Nanking turned the army into disciplined troops and no depredation occurred. The Ch'ien Lung jade was safely shipped to San Francisco.

Wheeler learned in the meantime that there were several pieces of the original garniture not in the group he had purchased and he queried A.L. for instruction. Guided by his answer, and with Liu's cooperation, he commissioned agents all over the country to scour China for the remainder. Constantly seeking clues to this secret horde, Wheeler did not miss any lead. As he followed each one, even though disappointed in his search for the jade, he came across many other objects of interest. Among these were some huge stone figures which had formerly guarded the entrance to the tomb of a nobleman buried in the latter part of the Ming dynasty.

By now Wheeler was familiar enough with Chinese transactions to be successful in his bid for these antiquarian pieces. Then the problem of shipping the stone warriors, rams, and camels proved almost baffling. It became necessary to saw two of the figures in half before they could be moved. Finally, however, they were crated and shipped across the Pacific; but when they reached San Francisco, warehousemen were afraid that the floors of the storage rooms would not be strong enough to hold them.

When news came that the shipment was parked in a storage yard south of Market Street, A.L. was escorting Dr. Richard Fuller, president and director of the Seattle Museum of Art, and his mother, Mrs. Margaret Fuller, through the store. A.L. showed them photographs of the figures, and proposed that they go down to the lot with him to watch the uncrating. The Fullers shared his eagerness to see the relics. When they found workmen ripping off the protecting boards, both men climbed onto the boxes. Not since the post-fire days in his father's backyard had A.L. done business from the top of a packing crate. Dr. Fuller only needed to look into the half-opened containers before he consummated the deal that meant nailing up the boards again. The ancient figures were re-loaded onto flat cars for the trip to Seattle, where Dr. Fuller planned to use them at spaced intervals on the wide stairs leading into the museum.

The Ming dynasty tomb pieces were sensational; but it had been the arrival of the Ch'ien Lung jades that brought the most unique renown to the San Francisco art firm. With this acquisition A.L. was beginning to achieve his ambition to own the world's greatest commercial aggregation of jade. He took pride in the fact that he was the first American to acquire directly any large portion of the famous Emperor's personal collection.

Although examples of Ch'ien Lung's art had gone out as gifts to contemporary rulers throughout the world, dealers heretofore had been able to secure only occasional pieces in the Tokyo market. Queen Maria I of Portugal accumulated, in the Pena Palace at Sintra, a room full of tokens from this faraway monarch—priceless jade, porcelain, and an ivory pagoda five feet in height; but the rulers of Nippon received the greatest number of the Emperor's gifts—sometimes parting with a fine piece or two when the Imperial Exchequer needed replenishing.

As the jade hunts brought to his storehouse more fabulous treasure than most monarchs could have possessed, A.L. claimed for San Francisco a distinction no other city outside the Orient had at that time. He knew from personal experience that even in New York the value of the finest jade was practically unrecognized. Mabel took a necklace he had brought from China to Tiffany's to be restrung. The beads were so translucent and such a brilliant green that the repair man sent for their gemologist, Dr. George Kunz. That expert was fascinated and thought at first that they could not be jade, as he had never seen their equal.

The western world became more jade conscious; New York, London and Paris developed as famous markets; but the Oriental dealers of San Francisco—Marsh, Bentz, Shiota, as well as the better shops of Chinatown—continued to contribute to San Francisco's preeminence. And A. Livingston Gump became known to all connoisseurs as the premier jade hunter of them all.

No part of his business experience meant more to him than to escort important guests through his Jade Room. As they stood beside the palace screen beyond the heavy entrance doors, A.L. would tell his visitors that its jade panels were of a variety known as "moss entangled in ice." Then panel after panel would be unlocked, revealing floodlighted objects in rainbow colors, carved with infinite skill and patience and in an astounding variety of forms—birds, flowers, gods and goddesses, vases, bowls, seals, and scepters.

Translucent green like the emerald of a forest-lined lake, or white like flecks of cloud seen through windows of a speeding plane —these are the usual connotations of the word "jade." But through years of patient collecting Gump buyers filled shelves with jade of many hues—fei-ts'ui (kingfisher-feather green); hua-hsuah-tai-tsoa (moss entangled in snow), white jade with green veins; sulphur yellow, milk white, bright apple green, mutton fat (white with vermilion streaks) beeswax and butter-yellow, spinach-green, reds, blues, lavenders, brown, even black—all of these with their innumerable shadings intrigued artists through the ages to immortalize beauty in the eternal stone.

One day A.L.'s guest in the Jade Room was the wife of a leading local Chinese publisher. She had brought a distinguished visitor from Peking to meet the jade collector. As A.L. lifted the teak cover from a set of jade tablets, he explained,

"These are the ancestral tablets of the first Manchu emperor, written in gold in Manchu and Chinese. They are dated 1648."

The stranger gasped, "Why, these are our jade treasures, part of the precious heritage of my country! They were looted from the Imperial Museum in Peking . . ."

"Yes," replied her American-born hostess, "but think how safe they are here!"

No tribute carried more meaning to A.L. than these words from a woman who knew both countries. He reconsidered the significance of her reply every time he lifted the precious objects from their accustomed niches. Long after his physical sight was gone he recognized each piece through appraising fingers, and he described to many beauty lovers the quest which had brought these objects safely away from further looting by avaricious war lords.

He liked to think that every time Ed Newell or Joe Wheeler unlocked the lighted cabinets, they were not only displaying the multi-colored stone; they were illuminating the minds of visitors with better understanding of great civilizations from which these masterpieces were mute ambassadors.

ANY VISITORS to the Jade
Room who forgot time in this contemplation of antiquity were invited, like privileged callers admitted to a palace, to sign the guest
book. The record of these signatures, bound in a series of brocade-
covered volumes, was counted by A. Livingston Gump among his
most cherished possessions—equal if not superior in value to his
whitest jade or his finest Keiths.

This distinguished log, kept from the day the new Oriental
rooms were opened in 1908, recorded the visits of an increasing number of world-famous people who came to know this Post Street shop
as one of San Francisco's essential attractions. They inscribed their
names with unique and varied modes of appreciation. Arturo Tos-
canini concluded his ecstatic tour of the Gump wonderland in quiet
reverie, meditating on the timeless beauty of the Jade Room. Then
he took his pen and filled a page with his name and a bar of music—
a theme from a Beethoven symphony.

"That is the way your store has affected me, Mr. Gump," he told
his host.

Madame Schumann Heink borrowed a line from Wagner to express her feelings:

"Gepreist sei der Gott, der uns den Früling und die Musik
erschuf!"

The warm-hearted singer, who loved to exchange anecdotes with
A.L., was typical of the visitors who caused him to remark, "The
parade of famous stars always has a matinee at Gump's." One of the

earliest enthusiasts was Sarah Bernhardt. She departed, enchanted
with a tiny articulated iron snake by Mio Chin, Japanese artist of the
seventeenth century, telling A.L. she would use the snake in her role
as Cleopatra.

Lily Langtry implanted her appreciation on A.L.'s cheek instead
of in the guest book. She was admiring jade goddesses when A.L.
came into the sanctum with a string of the first rock crystals received
from China. Miss Langtry took the long necklace from his hands to
examine it closely. Throwing the string of sparkling beads over her
head in two loops, one short, one long, she exclaimed,

"I'll have to have this, and I'll give you a kiss for bringing me
such a lovely thing!" Quite unmindful of Joe Wheeler's presence,
she planted the kiss firmly on A.L.'s beaming face.

That sale was indicative of the personal touch A.L. gave to the
distribution of his finest pieces. He had a phrase that usually proved
irresistible. "Now I really want *you* to have this," he would say as
he discoursed on the appropriateness of a jade ring to a charming
woman, a rare porcelain to a connoisseur, or an antique desk to a ty-
coon. But experience taught him to follow through adroitly with
more sales talk after one visiting actress, a really good customer, took
him literally when he asked her to pose before the mirror wearing a
beautiful jade necklace—"so perfect for you," he said, "I had you in
mind when I first laid eyes on it. I really want you to have it."

"Thank you kindly, Mr. Gump," she replied, with the gracious
air of one accustomed to expensive gifts from admirers. "It will always be a reminder of your friendship." And she walked out of the
store resplendent with her costly token.

This approach was not always successful. A.L. was accompanying one of his saleswomen and an eastern client through the Jade
Room when the man stopped to admire a slender apple green vase,
exquisitely carved.

"I like this very much, Mr. Gump," he said, handing the vase to

A.L. for his approval. "You know my collection. I believe this would fit in well."

"Oh, indeed," agreed the dealer. "It is just what I wanted for you. The price is $2900."

As A.L. carressed the jade with approving touch the visitor opened his wallet and offered Miss Shand, the saleswoman, twenty-five one-hundred-dollar bills.

"Mr. Gump, the gentleman has offered me $2500," she exclaimed.

A.L. turned to his caller with hurt dignity,

"Obviously you do not appreciate fine jade, Mr. B—," he said as he returned the vase to its niche.

The incident was not closed, however. A.L. knew his clients and their associates. He waited his chance until one day he had a visitor from the same eastern city.

"Mr. J—, you are from Detroit, I believe. Do you know Mr. B—?" he asked. "He is a good patron of mine. Let me show you a piece he admired, but failed to buy," and quite deliberately A.L. sold the $2900 vase to his neighbor for its set price, realizing very well how it would irk the former visitor to be overshadowed in his collection because he had tried to haggle.

A.L. had a standing rule that he should always be called when a visitor of importance was in the store. One day Miss Shand sent for him saying that a Mr. Brady was in her department and could not decide between the ivories she was showing him. A.L. recognized voices as others would faces.

"Jim," he said as he approached the counter, "I am glad to see you here again. Miss Shand, I am surprised that you did not recognize 'Diamond Jim.' I am sure that he does not need to decide between these superb pieces," adding as he turned to his visitor, "You certainly can use them all!"

The sale ran into large figures. "Diamond Jim" Brady was so pleased with his purchase and the attention he received that he kept

a promise to come next day decked out in his famous diamonds—
cuff links, studs, even glittering buttons on his spats.

Although A.L.'s feel for the drama was second only to his art
appreciation he did not have to go to the theater to satisfy his crav-
ing. His store became a stage, as his growing acquaintance with the
men and women of the entertainment world brought more celebri-
ties to sip tea in the Kimono Room or to express their delight in
flowery phrases in the Jade Room guest books. The three young
Gump children grew up listening to tales about visits from such
personalities as Nat Goodwin, Chauncey Olcott, Ellen Terry, Eugene O'Neill and his famous playwright son, whose wife, Carlotta
Monterey, never failed to include Gump's in her leisure hours in
San Francisco. Lillian Russell wore many a silk robe designed for
her in the Gump shop, and May Yohe, former wife of Lord Hope
of diamond fame, was a constant visitor. May's last visit to Gump's
came several years after divorce had forced her back into vaudeville.
She was playing in San Francisco when she came to A.L. to dispose
of some Oriental pieces which had been given her by a maharajah,
pieces so exceptional that Gump lost no time in acquiring them.
In their conversation about the days of her glamorous youth, May
repeated a story of her early married years which deeply grieved
the man who reverenced beauty, animate or inanimate. In anger
over a reprimand from Lord Hope, who had overheard her rebuke
a maid, she took in her hand a priceless peachbloom vase. In her
rage she dashed the Hope heirloom onto the stones of the hearth,
breaking it into a hundred pieces.

Perhaps it was the memory of that story of an irreplaceable loss
that led A.L. to ask the impossible of his friend, Fred Malley, in his
own repair shop. One day he found in his office a grape basket full
of fragments of a Ming vase with a gift card from Daniel C. Jackling, one of his valued patrons. Whether it had been left as a gift
or a challenge made no difference to A.L. He had it carried to
Malley's work bench. Day after day he visited the shop on his

routine tour of all departments, joking with Fred as the latter matched wits with the ancient artisan who had created the graceful vase. At last the day came when Malley had cemented the last fragment of the intricate jigsaw puzzle. They stood it on the shelf and A.L. called in various members of the staff to pass judgment. If they could not detect the repairs at a distance of six feet, the vase would go back to Jackling with his compliments. Otherwise, Malley would be in disgrace. The cracks were quite indistinguishable. Like all who worked for A.L., his foreman had met the challenge and accomplished what was expected by the man who demanded the best in every phase of art.

As one connoisseur told another about the collections garnered by A.L., the pages of the Jade Room guest books bespoke acclaim from all the world.

During the years of World War I Americans, cut off from travel abroad, had learned to know the treasure trove of their own country, including this surprising accumulation of jade and ivory. When peace returned they brought or sent friends to share their pleasure.

One of these travelers, Editor Frank Crowninshield wrote in the Jade book: "A footsore and weary New Yorker, journeying afar in the wildest West, found beauty at last and color and fancy and the most consummate art in the studios of A. Livingston Gump, artist, collector and man of taste."

But A. Livingston was not nearly so famous as another Gump known to newspaper readers all over the country. In August of 1924 front-page headlines and pictures heralded the visit of Andy Gump's son Chester, en route to Australia to visit Uncle Bim. While the mayor was on hand to welcome him and he was tendered a banquet at the Palace Hotel, it was in the Jade Room that his sponsor, Sidney Smith, left his lasting signature. The visit was recorded in words coming from the mouth of a swiftly inked sketch of the famous chinless character of the funnies, "From one Gump to another; may they reign forever," and across the bottom of the picture, "Best wishes to A.L. Gump from Andy Gump."

A.L. had a habit of rehearsing his lines before he greeted a visitor. One afternoon a staff member passing the office heard him muttering to himself: "Mr. Jolson! I am glad to see you, Al. I was just thinking of you when I put away this antique jade bracelet. It would make a delightful birthday gift for your wife." But A.L. was not quite so well prepared when Jolson suggested a reduced price— "from one old friend to another." Jolson entered his name in the guest book with a mock dialogue: " 'Our motto—one price to all,' Mr. Gump. My motto, 'Don't pay it.' " Nevertheless, Mrs. Jolson got the bracelet.

There was another visitor who had the strength to resist overbuying. One of A.L.'s San Francisco acquaintances sent Andrew Mellon to call at Gump's with a card reading, "Dear Abe: You can sell him the whole show." Strangely enough, at the time A.L. did not recognize the name. Mr. Mellon bought his daughter one of the finest jade necklaces in the collection, but when she cast longing eyes on other pieces in the Jade Room he said firmly, "My dear, that is enough for today."

A. L. had better luck with another customer. Sir Phillip Sassoon, whose brother, Sir Victor, later changed the skyline of Shanghai, called on Gump one day saying that he had promised some friends to pick up a good jade necklace. His time was very limited and A.L. asked Joe Wheeler to bring out some of their best jade. Sassoon's secretary made some notes and then Sir Phillip said,

"Mr. Gump, I can't decide this now. I'm on my way to China. I may see something there which will appeal to me more. I will be back in ninety days."

A. L. offered to reserve the selections but Sassoon insisted that would not be fair. In exactly ninety days he came back to the store. His secretary referred to his notes and they requested the clerk to

A TREASURY OF JADE

The jade screen from Gump's Jade Room (described on page 109), to-gether with a variety of jade colors suggestive of the infinite sculptured forms which have been created in this "stone of many virtues" by the artists of China.

(Photograph by Frank van Eckhardt)

show them numbers "so-and-so," two of the finest jade necklaces in Gump's collection.

"Have them shipped right away," Sassoon asked. "We saw nothing in China we liked as well."

When the Crown Prince and Princess of Sweden came to San Francisco, A.L. was proud to welcome to his store a world-famed collector of Chinese art. The Swedish consul general arranged the visit, calling to ask when the royal couple might "have the freedom of Gump's." Once in the Jade Room, His Highness forgot all other engagements. His host for the day, William H. Crocker, began to look nervously from watch to guest as the hour for a welcoming luncheon at the Fairmont Hotel approached.

Finally A.L. said, "Your Highness, we would deem it an honor if you took home some work of art in remembrance of your visit to Gump's."

As the art dealer spoke, he opened the doors to one of the large cabinets containing period porcelain. With the judgment of a connoisseur the Crown Prince selected two pale blue bowls—Claire de Lune of the Yung Ching period. It was a delighted couple who were torn away at last to attend the Fairmont luncheon. The bowls later became part of the royal menage in Stockholm—symbol of the hospitality that made "Gump's in San Francisco" well worth the official call.

Shortly after the royal couple left, A.L. discovered that not only the Oriental rooms had attracted Crown Prince Gustaf Adolf. Members of the Swedish-American Society of San Francisco came into purchase a painting the visitor had admired as he lingered in the Gump galleries. Pleased with his admiration for something so typical of their adopted state, the group sent this gift to hang in the corridors of the palace in Stockholm.

The canvas entitled "October, Point Lobos" was from the brush of Charles Bradford Hudson, an artist whose warmly colored scenes of mountain and desert had brought many enthusiasts to the Gump galleries. A.L. was flattered by the choice of a Hudson canvas for his famous Swedish visitor. Gump had felt a strong personal liking for Hudson from the beginning of their acquaintance. He particularly admired the scientific approach of this former Smithsonian Institution staff member, who had come west at the behest of Dr. David Starr Jordan, president of Stanford University.

A.L.'s own fact-finding mind had followed Hudson's methodical preparations for the assignment which gave the artist his major local fame—painting the background for many of the animal groups for the new Academy of Sciences in Gold Gate Park. When Hudson undertook a long camping trip on a barren island in the middle of Pyramid Lake, Nevada, to study the native habitat of white pelicans, Gump was fascinated. As he sold Hudson paintings, A.L. interjected his own enthusiasm for the personality of the man who could reproduce so faithfully the peculiar atmosphere of a desert sunrise or the exquisite blend of pink lavender in the dusk of sunset.

Vacationing near Clear Lake one summer A.L. met another artist who had a similar approach. Her name was also Hudson—Grace—although no relation to Charles Bradford. In her painting of Indian child life A.L. recognized a valuable contribution to the historical record of California's first citizens. He invited her to exhibit at Gump's. When her canvases were hung he enjoyed relating to visitors how Grace Hudson was able to portray her subjects so naturally because, as the only white woman ever admitted to the local tribe, she had intimate first-hand knowledge of these natives.

It had taken the 1915 exposition to waken the Gumps to a realization that there was public demand for the work of artists like the Hudsons who were depicting the California scene. Other galleries, notably Vickery's, had opened their doors wider to the men and women who were picturing flower-filled valleys, majestic trees, and mountain crags. In the past, European canvases in the Gump galleries had rarely been flanked by examples of western talent, with the exception of Keith and a few other less important artists. In this category, those that seemed to sell most readily were seascapes by N. Hagerup and small landscapes by Jonnevold, an artist whose scenes reminded the brothers of the Dutch masters.

The Gumps soon succumbed to popular trend and began to diversify their showings. They invited Frank Van Sloun, whose exposition murals had won him honor, and Maynard Dixon, Newell's friend from Pine Street studio days, to exhibit.

When Gump galleries were brightened by Dixon's colorful westerns, Newell recalled the night he and Dixon had knocked at the stage door to show Nance O'Neill some posters the aspiring signboard artist had painted with her as the central figure. It had taken great persuasion on Newell's part to drag his neighbor out of the studio; but when Miss O'Neill, highly pleased with the posters, commissioned Dixon to paint her portrait, his career was assured. It was then no longer necessary to use his talent splashing advertisements on billboards.

As Newell had been his ally in achieving fame through Oriental art collections, so now A.L. had a helpful associate in the director of his galleries, Matthew Ansbro. This genteel dealer had joined the force in 1910, not only bringing with him some fine prints and etchings salvaged when the 1906 fire had destroyed his small gallery, but also contributing a clientele of discerning patrons.

Ordinarily their gallery director could lead his public in their choices, but he missed his guess in 1915 when he filled a gallery with Charles Marion Russell's cowboy paintings. Ansbro's reputation with his employer suffered when exposition visitors scoffed at prices of $1500 attached to canvases by this unfamiliar artist. Not until a few years later, when Russell's prestige rose with the patronage of Will Rogers and the Prince of Wales (and his minimum price became $3000) did A.L. admit that Ansbro was a good judge of cowboys.

The next experiment was an attempt by Ansbro to interest A.L. in the California scenes painted by Will Sparks, former editor of the little magazine *Philopolis,* issued by Arthur Matthews, John Zeile, and other city planners immediately after the fire. Gump was unimpressed until one day when Sparks came into the store and stopped the art dealer on the mezzanine landing.

"I hear there is a movement on foot to restore the California missions," he said. "It might be a good idea to paint a series of them as they are today, mellowed, as well as ravaged, by time."

The idea appealed to A.L., both as a business deal and a proper contribution to history. He underwrote the project, and Sparks trekked off with easel and brushes, reversing the footsteps of the padres along El Camino Real, from Sonoma to San Diego. As these historic paintings were sold through Gump's, A.L. made an excellent return on his investment in Sparks' ability.

Thaddeus Welch was another landscape artist with whom A.L. enjoyed a long association. Gump regarded Welch as "one of the most original and memorable artists California ever produced." Although some critics objected to the artist's exaggeration of sunlight, the warm brightness of his portrayal of Marin County appealed to Gump in his half-shadowy world. Many a prospective purchaser of a Welch landscape heard A.L.'s favorite summary: "Sorolla y Bastido was supposed to be the great painter of sunlight, but Welch in his own inimitable style is equally good."

In his last years, after he moved to Santa Barbara, Welch would paint only for Gump's. He was a strange person, oblivious to routine, to such an extent that the bookkeeper of Gump's complained because Welch failed to cash his checks. On a visit to the artist's home A.L. reminded Welch of this, and together they unearthed several checks from the pigeon holes of an old roll-top desk.

Like his checks, Welch kept his sketches hidden away—in a small cement block house which he had built especially for them in his garden. On his last visit, A.L. purchased all the paintings that were finished, including one which the artist did not live to sign.

After A.L. returned to San Francisco, he was supervising the

hanging of one of Welch's outstanding canvases, a large picture of
Mt. Tamalpais, when Louis Sloss, a director of the Alaska Commercial Company and an ardent patron of the arts, came in. Sloss
admired the picture greatly, and almost bought it. That very day
word came that Welch had died. Early the next morning Sloss was
in the store and said that he and a group of other friends would
purchase the mountain painting to hang in the Family Club.

Another artist whose mellow-toned landscapes began to appear
in Gump's and other local exhibitions was Percy Gray. A.L. was
interested to learn that Gray's artistic career had begun, like Dixon's,
humbly. Shortly before the fire of 1906 he had left his job as illustra-
tor for a local newspaper and gone to New York to work on one
of the metropolitan dailies. When the fantastic tales of San Francisco's "complete obliteration" began to click off the wires, Gray's
accurate memory had enabled him to sketch familiar streets and
buildings. Deserved recognition of his ability to express his own
emotion was quickly won.

Then the creator of the sketches felt impelled to see the stricken
city again. Once back in California he began to make use of more
lasting media. Year after year Bohemian Club exhibits displayed
water colors and oils by this artist. The San Francisco public grew
fond of paintings that seemed to bring the scent of wind tearing
strips from eucalyptus or that seemed to invite rest under a spreading
gray-green oak.

Gump's also received descriptive canvases from Gray's San An-
selmo studio, under the lee of the "Sleeping Mountain" whose
legends and varying moods became a favorite subject for him as
they were for so many other artists.

Francis McComas, a popular water colorist of the period, was
not a regular Gump exhibitor; but his first transaction with A.L.
laid the foundation for a friendship. One day he happened into the
store as Newell and Abe were examining a shipment of small

antique rugs. Their exquisite color and weave were tempting to him.

"I can't afford to buy them," he said, turning to Gump excitedly, "but would you take some of my water colors in exchange?"

A.L. told him to make his choice. He selected eight of the rugs and paid with some charming studies.

The pleasant outcome of this barter encouraged A.L. a few years later to call at the New York studio of another highly successful artist of old San Francisco. This man had a long-standing debt to the Gump firm for some frames they had made for him just before the fire of 1906.

In those days the artist·had been struggling for recognition. Solomon Gump had taken an almost paternal interest in his plans for a tour across Canada with an exhibition of his California canvases. The artist had been very exacting about the frames he had ordered for these paintings. He wanted brilliant gold leaf, highly burnished in the French style. He had even gone into the shop to stand over the gilders and make sure they burnished both flat and hollow, to achieve the desired effect.

Solomon and A.L. had started him off with their blessings. The bill, amounting to about $1200, was to be paid from the proceeds of his future sales.

Then the fire came, destroying all the store records. His San Francisco backers had never thought of doubting his honesty, but the years went by with no word from him.

When A.L. talked to him on this New York trip he suggested that Gump's would be pleased to accept two canvases in payment of the old debt—a still life and a marine. The artist agreed gratefully, and Gump waited impatiently for the paintings to arrive. Instead, they received a letter from an attorney a few months later, disclaiming all obligations on the part of the artist on the grounds that the statute of limitations had run out.

About the same time Gump had to return some insurance

money. When he had made his trip to Europe just before the outbreak of the war he had purchased three paintings by a German artist well known in European circles—Herman Rudisuhli. Of course, after hostilities commenced the pictures did not arrive in San Francisco. A.L. had been able to convince his insurance agents that they had probably gone down on a torpedoed ship. Suddenly one day from the customs office in San Francisco came a notice that the paintings had arrived. A.L. discovered that they had been kept in storage in Holland for five years.

Those canvases from Germany brought back to Gump's some of the prewar atmosphere; but 1919 was hardly the time to expect the American public to be receptive to paintings from so recent an enemy. That purchase, received five years too late, rated heavily on the debit side of the ledger.

But the credit side had a boost—not in dollars, for the Gumps refused a commission, but in good will and patriotic gesture when their friend, Dr. Morris Hertzstein, came to the Gump brothers with a request. San Franciscans, like most Americans, grateful for the return of peace, were concerned with war memorials. Dr. Hertzstein, one of the Pacific Coast's eminent physicians, had decided to make a gift to the city—a statue honoring General Pershing. Hertzstein came to Alfred Gump first. Did he know a sculptor capable of executing in bronze the deep feeling fellow citizens had for this tall soldier who had shouldered the responsibility of leading the world against Prussian threats to liberty? Pershing was more than a wartime hero to San Franciscans. He was their neighbor, with whom all had suffered on that tragic night—during his Mexican border command—when fire swept through the frame house in the officers' quarters at Ft. Winfield Scott in the San Francisco Presidio, taking the lives of his wife and three little daughters.

The choice of an artist who could create a proper statue for Golden Gate Park was a great responsibility. Alfred called Abe into consultation, and together they decided that Haig Patigian, then president of the Bohemian Club, was the man to carry out this commission. It was a good choice. San Francisco respected Patigian for his Lincoln at the approach to the City Hall and for his numerous contributions to courts and galleries of the 1915 fair. The sculptor had known Pershing since the days when the young officer had first served at the Presidio. Thus, as he worked from photographs to model the figure of the General, then far away, his mind focused on remembered reality.

Consultations on such important additions to the permanent art of the community were indicative of public deference to Gump advice; but the fame of his own galleries achieved international status through the chance handling of two important canvases which impressed critics and appreciative visitors more dramatically than any others A.L. ever exhibited.

The first of these—Whistler's "Gold Scab"—came to him through a barter deal. He had been showing Chinese porcelains to a mining engineer, T. C. Crawford, a former Californian who now made his home in London. When Crawford completed his selections, he turned to Gump, saying,

"I would like to pay you for these with an original Whistler painting."

As he spoke, the visitor drew out his pocket notebook and made a rough sketch of the famous spite picture Whistler had painted of his erstwhile friend and patron, Frederick R. Leyland, head of the English steamship line bearing that name. He handed the sheet to A.L., asking if he knew the story of the quarrel over the painting of the Peacock Room in the London mansion of the Leylands.

A.L. held the sheet close to his eyes, exclaiming in amazement,

"Why, that's the 'Gold Scab'! How did you ever get hold of it? I always understood that Jacomb-Hood owned it and would never part with it."

Crawford explained that after Whistler's death he had purchased the painting from the artist's former neighbor and contemporary, but that he did not feel free to exhibit it in London because of his own personal friendship for the Leyland family.

A.L. was quick to seize this opportunity to own the renowned caricature of one of England's wealthiest and most cultured gentlemen of the late nineteenth century. When the Mephistophelian portrait reached the Gump galleries, critics crowded to see the brilliant satire. In this painting Whistler's venom against the man who had argued over the lavish use of gold leaf in the decoration of the Peacock Room had produced a masterpiece. Gump wrote in haste to Charles N. Freer, for he had recently purchased the Peacock Room itself for $100,000 and brought it to the Freer Galleries in Washington, D.C.

What later proved a post office error thwarted that hope for a sale, but Ansbro soon found a purchaser in Mrs. Adolph Spreckels, who paid $25,000 for the Whistler panel.

Better luck in the mail attended A.L.'s efforts to place another world-famous masterpiece which became his to sell a few years later. This painting—Heinrich Hoffmann's "Christ in Gethsemane" —had been in San Francisco since 1887, when it was purchased directly from Hoffmann in his Dresden studio by the Zeiles, pioneers in the San Francisco Art Association. It had even survived the fire of 1906 when John Zeile had ripped it from the frame in his mother's room and carried it to safety. For many years after her death it was kept in storage until one day Zeile came into Gump's and sought out his old friend.

"Abe, how would you like my 'Gethsemane' for your Easter window?"

That offer, readily accepted, led to one of Abe Gump's most cherished experiences. Zeile not only left the great painting during the significant week he had suggested, but he allowed A.L. to hang it in a small gallery upstairs, a gallery which for many years became "The Shrine" for hundreds of Gump visitors. Eventually Zeile came in to say,

"If you want that painting, I am willing to sell it."

Satisfactory terms were reached and for five years the painting remained Gump's most significant possession.

Then a customer, Mrs. Elise Drexler, came in to arrange with the new director of the galleries, Charles Sexton James, to have two other Hoffmann masterpieces packed and shipped to New York. She had sold one of these—"Christ and the Rich Young Ruler"—to John D. Rockefeller, Jr., for permanent placement in Riverside Church, and had presented the other—"The Image of Christ"—to the church.

At A.L.'s request, Mrs. Drexler allowed these paintings and one other—a copy of 'The Boy Christ," which had been painted in the Dresden studio under Hoffmann's personal direction—to be exhibited with the "Gethsemane" in "the shrine" for two weeks before they left San Francisco.

As the other large canvases were prepared for shipment he remembered that Mr. Rockefeller had visited Gump's the year that John Zeile had first loaned the "Gethsemane." A letter was quickly dispatched to New York assuring the philanthropist that only the knowledge that the painting would thereby have a larger audience would induce him to part with it.

A letter containing Mr. Rockefeller's order came by return mail, and the "Gethsemane," soon followed by "The Boy Christ"—also sold through Gump's—left San Francisco to carry inspiration to throngs streaming through the towering church on the Hudson.

CHAPTER NINE ⌒ *Passports to Adventure*

ONE BY ONE the Gump family became familiar with the Orient. In 1922 it was Mabel who felt the urge to see for herself the fascinating people and countries which had become so real to her as she read aloud to her husband. From her early youth she had known Europe; she spoke three of its languages. But the Pacific-bordering lands were still mysterious.

Her husband, now president of the firm, was involved with the increased pressure of business resulting from the growing fame of the establishment. He could not be induced to start on new journeys.

One morning when the strong March wind whipped the waters of the bay into beckoning white caps, she telephoned their older son Robert, calling him out of a biology lab down at Stanford.

"Robert, would you like to go to China tomorrow?"

He, too, was an adventurer, like all the Gumps; but he also had an extra-curricular responsibility.

"I can't go till after Saturday. I have to swim in the meet against Cal."

Saturday came and his breast-stroke victory helped to win the meet. Sunday he and his mother were en route to Seattle and thence across the Pacific to Japan. They lingered a while in Nippon and then went on to China. Without warning revolution broke out in that country. Fighting commenced in Nanking even as they were approaching the real goal of their journey, Peking. Headlines in the newspapers at home carried the startling news that the Gumps were lost in China in the midst of a battle. But U.S. Marines came to their rescue. They never reached Peking but returned to peaceful Japan.

Mabel in her picture hat and dramatic prints always attracted admiring glances as she went sightseeing with her attentive tall son. But one day she created a sensation beyond her own or Robert's comprehension when she appeared on the street in Tokyo wearing a light green haori coat with cherry blossoms woven into the dainty fabric. Barefoot children followed them, laughing and pointing at her; then they called their elders from the little shops. She was embarrassed by the pointing fingers and unintelligible remarks. Robert realized that the fingers were pointed at the symbols on the back of her coat, but no one would interpret them.

It was not until many years later when his own studies of Japanese customs gave him insight into traditions quite unknown to Westerners of those earlier days, that he was able to explain this incident. Then he discovered that his mother had probably been wearing a coat designed for some geisha girl, whose name not only appeared in the woven symbol, but also in the symbolism of the flowers. Moreover, custom in Japan dictates the color a woman may wear. Mabel, oblivious of these traditions, continued at that time to wear the clothes she liked, quite unaware that a married woman in garb and colors intended for youth was not only undignified, but also the object of derision. She returned to San Francisco with her light green coat and several more luxurious haori coats in her luggage, as well as others of a less expensive type known as ha-pi coats.

When she paraded the new possessions before her appreciative husband, he was especially taken with the texture and feel of the light-weight ha-pi coat. His merchandising instinct led him to order a hundred of them to experiment on the buying public. Thus started the fad of the twenties for these comfortable and attractive coats. Few of their owners realized that the little symbols on the back were merely advertisements.

Mabel and Robert had gone to the Orient expressly instructed not to do any buying for the store, but this chance personal purchase led to a profitable venture. As for other shopping, Robert concluded that his father must have notified their agents to show his family every courtesy except a jade tree. They were offered many things, from second-rate down, but the real treasures were evidently saved for the store.

During the summer of 1922, following the return of Robert and his mother, the younger son, Richard, met with an accident which changed the whole course of his life. He and a high school chum were spending a week end at the Gump summer home—"The Wilderness"—in the Saratoga foothills. The two boys took their shotguns and started off on a rabbit hunt. Richard came home on a stretcher, the accidental discharge of one of the guns having shattered his leg.

Medical skill saved the leg, but as the weeks of convalescence began it was apparent that he would be permanently lame. The shot had paralyzed a nerve. For a boy whose play hours had been spent on football fields and baseball diamonds, the future looked dreary. Dick had demonstrated prize-winning prowess as a swimmer and diver when the two boys had shared a daily hour at the Concordia Club with their father, who once held the Pacific Coast middle distance swimming championship.

A.L. had encouraged his boys to participate in every type of athletics. That their skills should be developed properly he had sent them both to a gymnasium run by Captain Wieniawski. This son of the Polish violinist and composer trained hundreds of San Francisco adolescents. The punch young Richard developed after five years of boxing lessons was gratifying to his athletic father; but now the accident seemed to nullify all that effort.

The prospect of a semi-invalid in the family posed a difficult problem. The Green Street home with its steep front steps, up which the children had bounded so heedlessly through the years, must now be abandoned. An apartment was found on Powell Street below the Fairmont Hotel. The British consul-general rented the Gump home which Edgar Matthews had planned so perfectly for their family needs, and the Gumps moved their paintings and tapestries to hang them on new walls. Opposite were great plate-glass windows through which the family could enjoy the moving panorama of the ship-filled inner bay.

Then A.L. bought a prefabricated penthouse for the roof of the apartment. There in sunshine and seclusion Dick began his adjustment to a different mode of life. All the energy restrained from physical outlet rushed to his overactive brain. With a private tutor he found that he could dispose of routine school work in far fewer hours than he had to fill.

Mabel had early recognized creative ability in this second son. Before this accident he had trudged up Nob Hill, sometimes accompanied by Robert, to the School of Fine Arts. Robert soon proved that it was useless to put crayons in his hands; but Dick lived up to his mother's expectations. In spite of his natural aptitude, the active boy had been too fond of the out-of-doors to be confined to piano bench or sketch book. Nevertheless, Mabel had insisted on enough basic education in both music and art so that he was now capable of diverting his surplus energy into productive avocations. She persuaded his father that he should have the best tools and instruction to make these enforced leisure hours profitable.

Just as he had found recreation in the differing skills of diving and football, he learned relaxation in changing from one artistic expression to another. With his T-square and blueprints he designed houses acceptable to his Uncle Milton. Then he began to draw designs for the reproduction of period furniture. His bed was littered with musical instruments. As original melodies began to flow into his brain, experimenting fingers would try them out on violin, piccolo, and saxophone. An old harmonium was drawn close, where he could reach the keyboard. His father's chauffeur spent hours pumping the foot pedals while Dick labored over potential symphonies.

For two years he thought and dreamed, discovering that harmony and counterpoint have their parallel in abstract use of line and color.

Then, partially restored to health, he was ready for his next adventure—a summer in Europe with his older brother. Robert had not returned to Stanford after the trip to the Orient. Instead, he had entered Harvard to study playwriting under Professor Baker in the "47 Workshop."

Both young men were prepared to appreciate the culture of Europe as they toured together in that summer of 1924. Richard visited cathedrals and chateaux with his Kodak, later studying and evaluating the pictures of the architectural wonders he beheld.

That fall A.L. saw both of his sons acquiring new experience. He felt that Robert was ready to participate in the business and he mapped out a schedule which would give the boy a basic understanding of the processes of receiving, storing, shipping, and selling merchandise. Robert was assigned to one of the younger executives, Martin Rosenblatt, for training. His day was divided into two hours of office work, two in the basement, and four as a salesman on the floor. This period of meeting customers was painful to the shy introspective young man, who completely lacked his father's enthusiastic approach to selling.

Dick registered at Stanford; but he found it an unhappy experience. He resented his physical inability to participate in athletics, where he would have been so well qualified. After two years of freedom from classroom routine he found it difficult to adjust to an institutional education. Life in the big sandstone freshman dormitory was too distracting. He left with "incompletes"—to the bitter disappointment of his father, who craved for his sons what had been denied to him.

That circumstance did not bother Dick. He felt that the family store offered better opportunity for self-expression, and he would be paid as he acquired his knowledge of its various angles. Like his father and brother, he served apprenticeship from the basement up, revealing in every phase an artistic creative personality.

It was a boon to A.L. to have his sons near him during this particular period of his life. His increasing blindness was taking a greater toll than he was ready to admit. Before his public in the store he put up a brave front, compensating for what he did not see with his acute hearing and his incredible memory. But he was exceedingly sensitive to an audience and deeply wounded if listeners penetrated his pretensions. In his home life this led to grief in small matters as well as in great.

Robert had learned this very early in life. Like all youngsters he had thought it Father's Sunday morning duty to read the funnies. One morning when he asked this favor A.L. said to the little boy,

"What will it be?"

"The Katzenjammers."

He climbed upon his father's knee with the paper. But he was bright beyond his years and knew more than his father gave him credit for. As he looked over the paper, he discovered that A.L. was supplying words that were not there.

Bursting with exasperation he exclaimed, "I don't want you to play games with me. I want you to read me the paper." Then, quite unexpectedly, tears welled up in the father's eyes.

Little Robert ran in distress to his mother. She gently explained to him that his father could not read, that he was gradually growing blind.

That had been a minor incident, but as the years increased his malady, A.L. grew more easily irritated over bigger things. Temper often flared in the Gump household. Mabel, whose sympathetic understanding had been the blessing of their early married days, wearied of the monotony and confinement of life with a husband who withdrew from the gay society she craved. As the children grew older she again found release in participation in amateur dramatics, sometimes bringing Robert into the cast. Then when her father's death gave her an independent fortune she began to spend more and more time abroad.

It was on one of those trips in 1925 that she wrote the letter which blacked out the flickering light of happiness for A.L. Robert was with his father on a trip to the Northwest. As was his habit, he was reading the mail aloud without a first look at it. He was suddenly too deep into its message to ease the blow for the listener. His mother wanted a divorce!

From that moment, whatever light had been visible to A.L.'s clouded eyes went out. As normal people are sometimes said to have "blind spots," so A.L. had certain "light spots." The condition of his eyes was such that with effort he could focus in some directions. But his vision cleared only when physical health was at a maximum. The blow to his pride and ego in that request from Mabel shattered whatever nerve stability helped to control the wavering lines of communication from eye to brain cell.

All fight went out of him as he dictated his consent to Mabel's request.

Now more than ever A.L.'s frustrated affections were bestowed on the store. Customers welcomed by the suave smiling gentleman were often unconscious that he really did not see them or the art he sold with such an air of authority. But he no longer went in search of treasure. Failing health had forced Alfred to give up his share of the buying several years earlier. When Richard was twenty-one A.L. decided to gamble on his son's ability as a buyer. He sent him to Europe again, this time with his mother who was returning to congenial Parisian circles after her divorce was final.

Mabel shared with her son the cultural inheritance he was so ready to absorb. He, too, enjoyed all that Paris had to offer; but A.L. knew that Richard must have training in the intricacies of buying as well as in the development of taste and appreciation. Accordingly he arranged that Stanley Corcoran, who had assumed the

European buying for the firm after the war, should take the young man under his tutelage.

While Richard was serving further apprenticeship abroad, Robert had qualified as a department manager, now in charge of the growing rug business. Even in his childhood he had been fascinated as he listened to his mother read about the ancient art of rugmaking and the caravans of traders who first brought examples from Persian looms to China. His own travels in the Orient and his training under Rosenblatt had widened this interest. Now he undertook careful study of his own and enlarged the scope of the department to include rare and costly imports from the Near East as well as from China.

Robert soon felt that he had done enough research to write a book on Chinese rugs—the first of its kind in English. One other was available in German; but there was real need for some publication that could be understood by Americans. The firm distributed Robert's book to libraries, museums, and schools all over the country. Very soon customers from the Middle West and East began to inquire about rugs he had described in these pages, and a different group of connoisseurs was added to Gump's enlarging clientele.

Naturally Robert felt himself an authority. Thus he resented his father's intrusion into his territory. But he learned one day that it takes more than knowledge to become an effective salesman. A caller wearing a gray derby came into the rug room with the air of one who is oblivious to convention.

Robert thought, "This man probably has so much money that he does not care about public opinion. He must be important." Following the rules of the establishment, he sent for his father.

A.L. recognized the stranger's voice as soon as he greeted him.

"How do you do, Mr. Leiter," he exclaimed. "It is a pleasure to welcome you back to San Francisco," and the two began to reminisce with complete disregard for the twelve-thousand-dollar Imperial rugs Robert had spread out in the Oriental Court. The younger Gump fidgeted impatiently until his father bid the visitor adieu. Then he turned to his parent, his voice full of rage.

"Dad, you'd better stay in your Jade Room and let me sell rugs. You paid no attention to what I was trying to sell Mr. Leiter, and now he has gone."

"No, Robert, you are mistaken," replied his father calmly. "Mr. Leiter is an old friend. You must learn to let me handle such people in my own way."

Robert was not so easily put off, and flung out of the room angrily. "From now on, you stay out of my rug room. I'll know better than to let you distract good customers."

A few days later A.L. called Robert into his office. His smile was whimsical as he handed his son a letter.

"Here is the order from Joe Leiter," he said. "He wants two of those rugs sent to his Washington home, and two to Chicago."

Shortly after this experience A.L. had another letter to share with Robert—a letter which started them off together on a new adventure. This message came from Honolulu—signed by Mrs. Alice Spalding Bowen, who was representing their firm in connection with her own interior decorating and landscaping studio. "My dear Chief:" she wrote, "Our business out here is expanding to such a degree that I wish you would come over to look into the proposition of buying a larger place . . ."

This suggestion was a tonic to A.L.'s depressed spirit. He had liked Mrs. Bowen from their first meeting, and their subsequent business relationship radiated mutual enthusiasm. It had been a red letter day when, a few years before, she had obeyed what she later told him was a whim of the moment and walked into the store, asking to "see Mr. Gump."

Her impulsive suggestion that he might like to join in the venture she was planning to undertake in her home city of Hono-lulu, following a course of study in interior decorating and land-

scape architecture in California, met with such immediate response
that she was almost terrified at her own audacity.

A.L.'s courtly reply to Mrs. Bowen's proposal that he call Mr.
John D. McKee of the Mercantile Trust Company for personal reference had cemented their friendship.

"Madam," he had said, "I am a student of psychology. I do not
need to inquire for your reference."

He remembered how confidently she had sailed for home in
1923 with an album of furniture photographs, a small case filled
with fabric samples, and a few plates and goblets to display in her
home studio.

The letter which Robert was now reading told A.L. that Mrs.
Bowen's neighbors, Mr. and Mrs. Gerrit Wilder, had recently met
his daughter in the South Seas. Marcella had suggested that the
Gumps purchase the Wilder home for an enlarged Honolulu headquarters.

Robert readily accepted his father's invitation to accompany him
on a quick trip to the islands. They planned only a two-day visit,
which would permit them to double back on the same Matson liner;
but they soon discovered that the proposition was not so simple as
it had first appeared. A recent zoning ordinance made a business
establishment taboo in the district where the Wilder home was
located.

It was no hardship for father and son to linger awhile at the
Royal Hawaiian, its gardens fragrant with ginger flowers and bright
with hibiscus. Except for a lone garage and the Milnor shops in the
two large hotels—the Moana and the Royal Hawaiian—this land of
play was uninvaded by commerce. The idea of breaking this spell
had been suggested on shipboard. Nate Milnor had been a fellow
passenger, and the two merchants had played a game of bluff with
every meal, proposing to merge their luxury lines. In spite of the
poker technique he had used, A.L. began to toy with the idea that
Waikiki might indeed be the place for a Gump's of Honolulu.

A "For Sale" sign on a grassy plot across the street from the Royal Hawaiian indicated that the owner could be contacted at their hotel.

"Why not?" Robert urged his father. But A.L. hesitated. He was anxious to retain the noncommercial flavor Mrs. Bowen had given to their experiment; but it might be too radical to build a shop in this purely recreational area. He finally decided it would be the part of wisdom to be somewhat nearer to the business district, and made a substantial deposit on a site about four blocks farther away from the hotel. This decided, they sailed for home on the *Manoa,* one of the smaller Matson vessels.

But scarcely had they begun to make preliminary plans for building when a man representing the owner of the lot opposite the Royal Hawaiian called at Post Street. The proposition he offered had many advantages. A.L. dispatched Martin Rosenblatt to Honolulu to reconsider. Further study convinced him and Mrs. Bowen that the Gumps should pioneer in the heart of Waikiki.

A.L. was compensated for the forfeit of part of his deposit when he learned that their Chinese competitor, the Fong Inn Company, had purchased land adjoining the site he had first selected. His new store would now be several blocks away from his rival.

When Richard came home in October of 1928, after eighteen months in Europe, he found his father and brother absorbed in plans for their venture in the Pacific. Mrs. Bowen's letters told them how kamainas (old residents of the Islands) were astonished at the malahini (newcomers) who were audaciously expecting a business to succeed in Waikiki. The mood of that vacation land was purely fun. Beaches swept clean each morning, breakers bearing bronzed beach boys with their outrigger canoes and exhilarated surfboard riders, hula dancers swaying in the moonlight, honeymoon couples dining and dancing on the lanai of the Royal Hawaiian—that was Waikiki, a place where carefree vacationers forgot all business and gave themselves up to pleasure. Those who knew it best warned against commercial investment here. But Mrs. Bowen sided with her Chief and was carried along in his enthusiastic plans.

Richard shared zest for the gamble, especially when he looked over the plans drawn by Hart Wood, architect of many of the island homes most appropriately suited to that environment. They all shared the determination to make this a unique building, more like a residence than a place of business. The imagination of the architect chosen by Mrs. Bowen was equal to A.L.'s vision. Gump knew now that through all the years since he had decided to remain in San Francisco instead of accepting Huntington's offer to build in that other tourist paradise, Southern California, he had been subconsciously planning this dream store.

Varied complications were encountered as soon as they tried to carry out their plans. It was not easy to build on this flat coral land. The basement kept filling with water as excavations were attempted but finally the Gumps had word that a nine-foot cement basement was anchored deep in the coral-filled ground. As the building neared completion, Mrs. Bowen wanted to roof it with Chinese tile in Imperial yellow; but A.L. had a favorite color—blue. Although he had sent to the Orient for workmen to give authenticity to his Post Street showrooms, he was sure that the perfect Chinese blue which his fellow San Franciscans, Gladding McBean, achieved in their California tile works would add distinction to the Hawaiian building.

Mrs. Bowen landscaped the gardens with Chinese, Japanese, and native plants. In February, 1929, the island public was invited to a gala opening. Despite their great interest, there were no Gumps present. A.L. and Robert were too busy with the overwhelming business which the San Francisco store was enjoying in that year of peak prosperity. Richard was starting to Europe again, now entrusted with all the Old World buying for the firm.

When the books for 1928 were balanced the Gumps found that the firm had made more money than in any previous year. Only the fair era of 1915 had anywhere near approached its revenue. A.L. felt he could well afford to indulge his most extravagant fancies in building up the inventory of both stores. He followed Mrs. Bowen's accounts of the response to the carefully selected jades and porcelains assembled for that miniature treasure house, and he gave Richard carte blanche to purchase the very best that Europe could provide.

Mail time was an hour of supreme satisfaction as Robert read to his father the exciting reports from Honolulu and the less exuberant but interesting accounts of the progress the younger son was making in his initial experience as a buyer on his own.

Richard's search for unique adornment for the homes of newly rich Americans taught him many lessons as he went from country to country; but unlike Ed Newell on his first trip to old China, he did not find kindly consideration for his inexperience.

Wherever he went he discovered that word had preceded him, preparing the dealers to unload their "junk" on the young man who was presuming to judge art and antiques. Weeks passed before he was offered anything he considered worthy of investment. But the great grandson of the Heidelberg linen merchant was equal to the test. He learned early to trust to his inborn sense of the genuine rather than to listen to insistent "advice" or rely on the signature—which could be forged—in judging a painting. In addition to his own "inner voice" he also had plenty of advice from San Francisco, for A.L. followed his son's travels with wise letters.

Richard Gump was practical as well as artistic. His youthful interest in furniture design had been supplemented by careful instruction during his apprenticeship in the store. In those lavish spending days of the twenties Gump decorators were furnishing homes all over the West, especially in Hollywood. During this time Liljestrom's staff of Oriental designers was supplemented by talented young artists directed by the new head of the Interior Decorating Department, Henry Judson Allen.

When Newell was advanced to the position of General Manager

this expert designer and artist, another former member of the Chicago Art Institute staff, had supervised the installation of the period rooms planned before the exposition. Richard had learned the secret of furniture making as the Gump factory carried out Allen's specifications for reproductions of antique Italian, French, and Spanish cabinets, desks, chairs, and tables.

Guided by sure knowledge acquired from such instructors, Richard visited every shop he could find—whether in the cities of France, Spain, or Austria, or in obscure villages of the Pyrenees or the Italian Alps. He soon found that he could not depend upon intuition alone. It was too easy to be fooled by the many copies of antique furniture offered in the dealers' shops where the European commissaires— counterpart of the compradors in China—took him. Having designed and built reproductions himself, he knew enough to look for details often overlooked by buyers.

When he visited these shops he did so as a fellow craftsman, not as the buyer for a San Francisco dealer. Thus he had an inside look at the method used by a French manufacturer who was copying the marquetry of the middle eighteenth century with expert finesse. That manufacturer even used hand-made nails and hired small boys to rub the new surface until it resembled pieces worn by age. Everything was cut by handsaw, no machinery was used in any step of the process; he was known to have thrown pieces off the parapets of the old castle where he worked just so he could repair and give them the authentic appearance of antiques.

This familiarity with backstage operations prepared Richard for his test in Florence. Like his father in Shanghai he was called upon to show his hand in the presence of pomp and ceremony. He was invited by a dealer to view a collection of rare Ventian furniture. He looked over each piece with appraising eye. Then he turned to the man and said,

"You might add this up and tell me how much you want for the lot."

With typical Latin exuberance, the man listed the pieces, elaborating on the good fortune of his young customer in arriving at the moment when he had such valuable objects to offer. Richard took the sheet of paper, cast his eye down the list, and wrote under the total the name of the town he had last visited, where he had just placed an order for exact duplicates—at a third of the price. He had decided in that town to take home a few of the best reproductions he had yet found, as examples of what modern craftsmen could do with old designs.

He handed the paper back to the dealer, saying,

"That's how interested I am in your offer."

For a moment the dealer feigned surprise and pain at the attitude of his presumptuous young customer. Then his face wrinkled slowly into a knowing smile as he shook Richard's hand and congratulated him on his shrewdness.

"Now I will show you the real thing," he said, as he led the way to a back room. There he brought out of hiding some of the best specimens of Venetian chests and drawers that Gump's has ever handled.

Both orders were shipped across the world—the first as excellent reproductions, the second for the elite who could afford to possess genuine antiques verified by experts. Richard had won his spurs as a buyer!

In June a cable came from home. "Proceed to Constantinople. Lay in a stock of Oriental rugs." This was a new field, one in which Richard lacked experience. But luck, better than he could have wished, was with him. Buying through the same dealer was Mr. Hinsky, head of the rug department of Marshall Field's, and recognized as one of the wisest men in the trade. Hinsky and his associate took a fancy to the young San Franciscan.

"You would do better to buy one of these, rather than two of that kind," they told him, as the Armenian dealers rolled out their bewildering array of Bokharas, Shiraz, Hamma-dans, and Tabriz. "We know that people expect to find the unusual at Gump's."

Richard expressed his appreciation for such practical help through invitations to lunch in the gay tiled restaurant over the near-by Spice Bazaar. There they enjoyed swordfish kabob and rich Turkish pastries as they looked out at boats scurrying hither and yon across the Golden Horn. And over dinner at exotic Taxims, Richard listened to fascinating reminiscences by these two experienced buyers. He absorbed from their conversation much of the lore of rugmaking in the Moslem lands which for centuries had provided the world with its most prized floor coverings.

Robert was astonished when the rugs Dick bought reached San Francisco. They were not at all what he had told his brother to buy; even when Richard had followed instructions, he had chosen the wrong colors. Nevertheless, they all sold.

What was more, Richard had made good use of his opportunity to browse through the canopied bazaars in which traders from Europe and Asia had mingled for hundreds of years. With his quick-appraising eye, Richard had selected enough worth-while articles to more than pay for his trip. He had sent home hammered brass and copper coffee trays with folding stands carved from strange woods, and various-sized boxes of minute inlaid mosaic. The jewelry department immediately claimed squares of Persian miniatures painted on mother-of-pearl. Ancient towels and wedding bands embroidered with metallic thread on Egyptian cotton were useful to decorators; while the many fine icons and paintings purchased from refugee White Russians were valuable enough to repay the whole venture.

Richard came home to find that money was being spent easily in San Francisco during that summer of 1929. Gump's was receiving its full share of nation-wide prosperity. The Honolulu store was booming. Gump decorators there as well as at home received fabulous orders for refurnishing old homes and designing custombuilt furniture for new dwellings.

During these halcyon days their broker approached A.L. with a plan for expansion. He told the president of the firm that he could easily sell five million dollars worth of stock and convert the organization into one of the most important distributors of exclusive art goods in the world. The plan seemed sound enough, in that A.L. and his brothers would still retain control. Other firms were succeeding in like ventures; but that inner voice which so often spoke insistently warned A.L. to beware. In discussion with Alfred they agreed to seek counsel from a disinterested friend and customer.

Arthur Curtis James was in San Francisco. This eastern railroad magnate was often in Gump's selecting fine bronzes and jades for his collection. A.L. waited for his next visit. Then he asked Mr. James if he could spare the time for a chat in the office. Gump laid the proposition before him and asked his advice.

"Do you need the five million?" inquired the experienced financier. "If you do, call on me in New York. I can easily arrange such a loan for you among a group of my associates; but I would not like to see your firm entangled in any such promotion deal. Moreover, it would de-romanticize your business. Your best customers would naturally be your stockholders. The mystery and glamour of your Oriental art would be lost if your collectors were simultaneously regarding your firm through the cold figures of a balance sheet.

"No," he laughed. "Keep your trade secrets to yourselves and let us enjoy the atmosphere you have created. I, for one, am willing to carry my part of the overhead."

A.L. appreciated his adviser's viewpoint and his confidence. Alfred readily agreed with his brother's decision to turn down the stock-selling deal. A few weeks later, however, he suggested that on the basis of the recent experience the firm needed a comptroller to guide its financial affairs.

A.L. concurred in this idea; but disagreed violently with the candidate Alfred proposed, a man who knew nothing of the Gump business. A.L. reminded his brother that everyone of the family and most of the executives had learned the details from the basement up. They had developed their staff with care, training each one under exacting supervision. Each employee in authority had reached his position through rigorous study of the details which made for perfection. They had consistently refused to hire a man at top levels before he knew the problems of the shops and shipping rooms. If Alfred wanted his protégé to begin as the rest of them had done, A.L. would consider employing him, but he would not appoint the stranger as comptroller.

The word battle became heated. Neither one would compromise. Suddenly Alfred blurted,

"Buy out or sell out!"

Quick as a trigger, A.L. acted in character. Of course he would buy! When he asked Alfred to name terms, his brother snapped back,

"Book value."

A.L. needed no comptroller to tell him this was a good buy—knowing as he did the large factor of appreciation over original book costs that applied to a considerable portion of the firm's holdings. The deal was promptly closed on this basis. Forty per cent of the agreed price in cash passed between the brothers; the balance to be paid in annual installments of $100,000.

When his anger cooled, Alfred regretted his decision; but A.L. was adamant. The bargain was struck and he fulfilled his financial commitments although he weakened on the personal side after a few months. Alfred, fed up with leisure and longing for his old habitat, became a "dollar-a-year" man with an office and no responsibility.

With the power he now possessed, A.L. ruled his empire as a beneficent despot. Willie, still part of the firm, took orders from the top as he had done heretofore. Need for a strong hand on the helm came soon. With the stock market crash in September their best clients were hard hit. Then the Gumps were grateful that they had followed Arthur Curtis James' advice. Suppose they had been obligated to pay dividends on a large stock issue!

A.L. took Robert into his confidence and shared with him the wisdom inherited from the older generation who had weathered financial storms before. Solomon's experiences in the seventies and nineties, as well as that of 1907 when Alfred and Abe had carried the burden of maintaining solvency in the face of panic, had taught them all how to carry on a luxury trade regardless of general business conditions. They had learned the importance of setting aside profits from prosperous years so that they would have cash available in lean ones—recognizing that an art dealer must plan from peak to peak, or depth to depth, of financial cycles.

Approximately one third of their assets were invested in securities. A second third was in real estate, part of which in the period just passed had been used to purchase the Post Street property which housed the original half of the store. So when the Depression struck they had been relieved of the overhead of rent.

The remaining third—actually a little larger proportion because of Alfred's overenthusiasm in stocking his departments—was in inventory. The gradual liquidation of this surplus, often at prices that yielded a net loss, nevertheless provided the badly needed cash which ceased to come in from the luxury side almost as soon as the Depression started. With this cash they were able to take advantage of opportunities to purchase objects of fine art from people who were forced to part with them to make up for other losses, and if necessary Gump's could hold these treasures for long periods until returning prosperity should re-establish a market.

With this program to carry out, the appointment of a comptroller became necessary. The older Gump son, Robert, was the logical appointee, although his only preparation had been a few reports

worked out with Rosenblatt's guidance. They engaged an internationally known firm of auditors to install a new accounting system
and Robert spent long hours in close cooperation with them as well
as studious evenings devoted to books on store management.

While Robert was mastering the economics of the business Richard was assigned the directorship of the galleries. The sense of risk
and leadership in matters of taste which had seemed to make each
successive generation of Gumps sensitive to current demand—and
often prophets of coming trends—was inherent in Richard's character. Yet, as well as he knew art, he was not as acutely aware of the
state of the public mind as his predecessors had been. His sense of
mission made him more of a prophet than a mouthpiece of his contemporaries.

Richard's sanguine expectation of raising the standard of art appreciation in San Francisco to the levels he found in Europe diverted
his thoughts from practical recognition of the relation of the stock
market to the satisfaction of good taste.

During his years abroad he had been swept into the prevailing
controversy over trends in the art world. Some galleries had been
crammed with distorted interpretations by disciples of the contemporary school—Vlaminck, Segonzac, Puzetta. At the same time he
was impressed by a popular swing back to the Old Masters. In
Vienna where he had gone to combine buying with the satisfaction
of hearing good music, he had found the art-minded populace re-
newing its appreciation of middle-European masters—Tischbein,
Verhaecht, Pynacker, von Honthorst, and others.

In his enthusiasm to share these discoveries with his fellow San
Franciscans Richard had invested heavily in canvases by these men.
In France and Italy he had purchased other paintings, more gener-
ally known to Americans. This latter collection included Hogarth's
"Midnight Conversation," a pair of portraits by Franz Pourbus,
"The Children of Israel Before Mount Sinai" by von Haarbim, "Por-
trait of a Young Man" by Robusti (better known as Il Tintoretto),

one of Van Dyck's earlier works showing a strong Rubens influence, and "A Holy Family" by Pontormo.

This last was hailed by the art critic of the San Francisco *Chronicle* as "probably the finest painting of its type ever to come to this city." This "Old Masters Show" was Richard's initial presentation in his new position. In the fashion of earlier Gump openings he had elaborate illustrated catalogues, prefaced with a line from Shakespeare. "Our court shall be a little academy, still and contemplative in living arts."

Intrigued by favorable comment in the art columns, San Franciscans flocked to the store. The stairway to the galleries was so choked with visitors that a new elevator service was required. But the public came to look—not to buy.

As the weeks went by it became evident that the net result of this extravagant buying expedition had been to freeze an undue portion of Gump funds in an investment that showed no prospect of moving. With the stock market sliding steadily down toward the depth of the Depression, few of the regular customers had spare cash for investing in old masters. The products of the mid-European school which had attracted Dick's interest in Vienna definitely did not appeal to the average American purchaser.

Even a collection of Rodin drawings, arriving somewhat later than the main group of paintings, failed to interest buyers. Dick had counted on those. He knew how San Franciscans enjoyed "The Thinker" as they crunched across the pebbly outer court of the Palace of the Legion of Honor, and admired Rodin's "Three Shades" marking the Pacific terminus of the Lincoln Highway. News that Rodin's original sketches for some of his most famous masterpieces were to be seen at Gump's brought new crowds—but again few purchasers. Only one drawing was sold, and that to a lady from Southern California!

Recalling European interest in the modern school, Richard concluded that he had "missed the boat" in confining his acquisitions to old masters, and the Rodin sketches. He dashed to New York to acquire canvases of modern artists whose work had most appealed to him in the salons of Paris—Picasso, Matisse, Derain, Dufy. But when these were displayed in the Gump galleries he was disappointed to find that these paintings were *too* advanced for his customers. They knew little and apparently cared less about modern art.

Richard had an ally in Guthrie Courvoisier, son of one of his father's early competitors. Guthrie was also trying to devise ways to introduce new art trends into San Francisco. The two cooperated in presenting the unusual; but neither store succeeded in eliciting any appreciable public response. Dick and Guthrie had another practical impulse. They would persuade the City Fathers to make quarters in the abandoned Palace of Fine Arts available to struggling young artists caught in the Depression with no means of support and no outlet for their experimental canvases.

The Art Section of the Commonwealth Club invited Richard to speak. He plead for public encouragement for creative artists.

"Why not underwrite these people?" he asked, "and occasionally buy a work of art for the public to enjoy? We spend municipal funds on parades and banquets for movie stars . . . why not do something for artists?"

Moved by his eagerness, the members of the section voted to form a group resembling "La Peau d'Ours" of Paris. They would buy the paintings of young artists, hold them several years, and then sell them for much or little, depending upon their later reputation.

Richard himself enrolled in evening classes in the splendid new School of Fine Arts which had opened in 1927 on the bayward slope of Russian Hill. Spencer Macky, dean of the school, praised his creative efforts; but in spite of this incentive toward further personal achievement, he became discouraged with art life in San Francisco.

Favorable comments of the critics who visited the Gump exhibitions and sporadic purchases by such specialized groups as that

THE PACIFIC OUTPOST

Set among its tropical gardens, Gump's of Honolulu with its blue-tiled roof embodies A.L.'s lifetime dream of a beautiful treasure house.

formed in the Commonwealth Club, had not been enough to justify Richard's extravagant buying. Even A.L. had to agree with William that Gump's was not in the business of educating public taste. Their investments were heavy. They had to see some returns from their ventures.

After two years as head of the galleries, Richard resigned from the Gump staff. The sight of a Union Oil tanker steaming out of the Golden Gate one morning lured his roving spirit. Why should he putter around among unsympathetic people when the Pacific was still to be explored?

His sister, Marcella, was living in the South Seas—on the island of Moorea—her husband being the son of an English gentleman and a Tahitian princess. Richard decided to pay them a visit. In those exotic surroundings new melodies might weave into his brain, or strange sights set patterns for his drafting.

Following the wake of earlier Gump voyagers, Richard sailed out of the Golden Gate, Tahiti-bound. A few months later he came back to California; but not to San Francisco. Using ideas wafted in on the winds of tropic seas, he began writing songs and designing sets in the movie colony, earning for himself the dubious title of "the greatest unpublished song writer in Hollywood."

CHAPTER TEN ∽ *Seeing Fingers*

and Sporting Blood

THE NEXT CRITICAL Depression years tried A.L.'s optimistic nature. He had heavy obligations. Although the Honolulu store made a fair profit in its first year, that ledger now showed red figures. The very people who would normally have flocked to the playland of Waikiki were the hardest hit by the break in the stock market. Yet the intense interest shown by the public in that first year convinced Gump that this gamble would be worth the long view. Accordingly, he continued to pour effort and fortune into the perfection of every detail, backing Alice Bowen in her constructive planning.

At home he took the same approach. He had long ago mastered the rules of a game he called "plunging in art"—a form of speculation that did not fluctuate with the stock market. A.L. had acquired the Oriental habit of regarding fine paintings, jade, and other permanent artistic expressions as a stable form of wealth. While others were meeting disaster via the stock market, he felt that he could chalk up permanent gains on the Board of his Treasure Exchange.

This contention was verified by the experience of an acquaintance, George Seeney of New York. A.L. understood Seeney's reasoning when he told how his hobby of art collecting had made a new start in business possible after all his Wall Street investments had been wiped out. The returns from his first art auction had netted him over a million dollars.

Seeney told Gump that he had only one regret about his plunge in art, which was that he had not put ten times as much into collecting when he had the means. He felt that he would have been just as well off when the Depression hit, and he could have lived with that much more beauty all the intervening years.

Men like Gump and Seeney knew that no matter how deep the Depression there were still some people who had both taste and money. The important thing was to contact these purchasers. Even in normal times A.L. always kept his ear to the ground. If the bookkeeper told him that the year-end figures indicated a likelihood of a loss, Gump always seemed to know just the person who wanted a necklace of matched jade, a Coromandel screen, or a period porcelain. Letters that were practically irresistible crossed the continent or ocean, calling attention to some item in his stock that he was sure should belong to that individual. The plan usually worked and Ralph Simmons would be surprised when the final statement for the year showed a net gain instead of the loss he had expected.

A.L. had an uncanny sense of timing—or maybe it was just plain Gump luck. There was always a Charles Crocker, a Mrs. Carolan, or a Mrs. Havens. In the thirties there was Barbara Hutton.

The first time the young heiress to the Woolworth fortune saw the Gump store she met the pleasant man with a red carnation in his buttonhole. She was standing by the grandfather clock on the mezzanine landing when he came there to wind it. Attracted by the little girl, A.L. stopped to explain the Chinese fairy tales which were painted on its white surface. She had been fascinated to know how one of the girls in his design room had brought him a picture of a clock painted that way and asked if she could try to copy it. The little girl had listened with serious interest as he told her how Bertha Reid had painted big grandfather clocks and little grandfather clocks, some white, some red, but all of them with Chinese fairy-story characters on them.

Barbara had told Mr. Gump her name and explained that someone in Paris had described the beautiful things in his Jade Room and she wanted to see those green birds and flowers carved out of stone. He took her up there himself and told her all about the great Emperor Ch'ien Lung and the artists the Emperor kept working in the Palace compound. They had talked together a long time that day and they remained friends on through the years.

Now Barbara Hutton came back, in 1933, to buy the most valuable pieces of Ch'ien Lung jade that had ever come out of China— the two huge beakers that were part of the ceremonial set Joe Wheeler had struggled so long to secure. She bought many other wonderful treasures which A.L. assured her had been waiting for her collection. Her visit helped to keep the balance sheet the right color.

There were other good customers who took advantage of the presence of such dependable art investments. Mr. and Mrs. Paul Fagan were as excited as A.L. over the pair of Imperial wine pots that had also been part of the Ch'ien Lung set. The graceful handles were superb; but the feature that amazed everyone was the long curving spouts. These were pierced so that wine could flow through them, although they curved upward and out. These wine pots were fashioned from a single block of nephrite, and years of labor must have gone into the tedious process of shaping the vessels and hollowing out these slender spouts.

Art values had stabilized since the days when Ed Wheeler had warned A.L. to set a high enough price on his Oriental importations. Now that public information about this art provided a basis for judgment, A.L. paid more in China for the quality that brought well-informed customers, and both his buyers and his clientele knew the genuine from the false. Transactions running into high figures demanded the guarantee of authenticated history with each piece, and Gump's was prepared to assure such purchasers that they were making a safe investment.

Another device for balancing the books was A.L.'s letters to men who had let their unpaid balances run into high figures. These usually produced the desired result. If the need for immediate cash arose he would dictate a reminder of an overdue account with suave assurance of the customer's desire to cooperate. That did not always work, of course, and Robert once found himself commissioned to collect in person from an internationally famous client, whose large balance had only one element of usefulness in those stringent times. It had helped to make "accounts receivable" impressive to their bankers for some time until A.L. decided that his patience had run out. The task given to Robert proved a little more difficult than the bill collecting Abe had undertaken in his youthful days when his uncle had sent him to Morton Alley.

On his first attempt the young Gump comptroller had the door shut in his face by a well-dressed New York butler; yet their lawyer's investigations revealed that this particular client owed everybody from the local butcher to Gump's of San Francisco. After a "forced sale" of that man's art collection the account was finally settled; but for a fraction of what the valuable pieces involved had originally cost Gump's.

The lavish buyers of the late twenties were not all good risks. One of them not only failed to pay Gump's for the elaborate decoration of his Beverly Hills mansion, but ended in jail himself in one of the spectacular oil scandals of the period.

A.L. learned to take these business losses with equanimity. Robert came to him with a question from one of his own close friends, the heir to a fortune that had grown with America, but one of the unfortunates whose own portion had been in the wrong place to survive the depression.

"Dad," said Robert, "G. . . wants to know what you think is

going to happen. He regards you as a wise person and he'd like some advice."

"Well," answered A.L., "I've been through three crashes. There will always be crashes; there will always be recoveries. Whether you recover or not depends upon whether you have courage."

Courage he had in full measure, this man who had overcome physical darkness with the light of understanding—who could enjoy a Flower Show for its fragrance and post a notice that every employee must be sure to *see* the beautiful exhibits.

From his earliest childhood Abe Gump had relied on his inherent muscular strength. The teacher who had taken him in her arms and thanked him for ridding the school of its bully—when he had expected to be rattanned for fighting—had implanted a self confidence which grew with the years. Throughout his life he regarded any difficulty as a bully to be overcome and banished from his environment. He was always at his best when he tackled a tough problem.

While there had been zest in the thriving business of the twenties, that era had been too easy. All he had to do in those days was to sell and sell, order and reorder. Now depression became a foe challenging his nimble wits.

He persistently cultivated the illusion of unconcern. He even entered a new field—that of collecting old silver. A few years before, in the middle twenties, L. Stanley Grohs had joined the Gump staff to install a modern silver department; but A.L. had a secret yearning to become a dealer in antique silver. One of his early clients, Francis Garvin, had opened his mind to the possibilities in that field when he told Gump how much his hobby had netted in New York sales—profits that Garvin had added to the endowments of several universities. As Drewes had become A.L.'s pupil in the study of Chinese porcelains, so now Grohs began serious research into the history of old silver.

As individual collectors and dealers began to need cash to meet the emergencies of the early thirties, A.L. was in a position to buy wisely here as he had done earlier in the field of Oriental art. The Peruvian consul in San Francisco came in to sell A.L. some rare brocades. Finding that the firm was interested in silver, he brought them a fascinating collection originally from old Spain. In this group were some rare shaving bowls, fashioned in shell-like form, curved to fit under the chin. One of these, reputed to have been brought into Mexico by Cortez, was later sold to the Honolulu Museum.

The fame of this collection brought other fine pieces to Gump's. Grohs was on a buying trip in New York when an agent representing the daughter of Grand Duke Michael, who had been "regent for a day" in Russia, contacted him. The agent told Grohs that this Russian noblewoman had been able to get the family plate into France, but that she could not sell it in Europe. There were over a hundred pieces, all bearing the Russian double eagle and the family coat of arms. Although the set looked English it was stamped St. Petersburg, 1857. A.L. answered Groh's query with an affirmative telegram. He was most pleased when the shipment reached San Francisco. One samovar set of solid silver gilt in its beautifully lined case with leather cover and straps made a sensational display.

The front section of the first floor in the Gump annex was remodeled to give better emphasis to the growing silver department. Gump's engaged designers to follow the craft made famous by Cellini in ancient times and by Paul Revere in colonial America. They set up a window patterned after the Revere shop in old Boston and had Porter Blanchard demonstrate to the public how his beautiful hand-wrought serving pieces were made.

As the Depression gathered force and A.L. saw his fellow art dealers fall victim, he had to acknowledge his indebtedness to Alfred's insistence upon keeping a large stock of "bread and butter" merchandise. A.L. appreciated the cash that he was able to hack out of this backlog at a time when other owners of irreplaceable treasures had to sacrifice them to escape poverty.

Alfred himself did not live to face this issue, nor to enjoy the luxury he could have had from the sale of his share of the business. His death occurred in 1932, only three years after his break with A.L.

The next year Mabel came home from Paris to suffer through a long and fatal illness. Abe was at her side every day, the past and all it contained of misunderstanding and bitterness forgiven and forgotten. Her private fortune, too, had dwindled to a fraction of that to which she had been accustomed. Nurses, doctors, and hospital bills were mysteriously paid. A.L. never acknowledged to anyone that it was he who provided the money. Like every good deed on his part it was done in secret.

Although he had acquired the reputation of miser and tightwad because he was so unutterably opposed to organized charity, he was responsible for many kindnesses behind the scenes. Having grown up in a different era when the city was smaller, A.L. failed to realize how many there were now who were alone and friendless and in need of general charity. He was unsympathetic, too, toward people who made excuses of handicaps. He had overcome his; had, in fact, made capital of it. But when an individual's need came to his attention, he was very generous.

It often became the lot of his secretary to order groceries or send a nurse when another employee had illness in the family, but she was sworn to secrecy. No one else knew the tenderness that lay beneath the exacting attitude of the ruling head of Gump's. One small gesture revealed his kindlier side among his business associates. When in the depths of the Depression a letter came from a referee in bankruptcy saying that Vickery, Atkins, and Torrey were prepared to pay so much on the dollar of their indebtedness, A.L. wrote promptly to cancel the interfirm account. The amount was small;

but the spirit in which it was done was a flashback to the days of old San Francisco neighborliness.

As one after another of his contemporaries were forced out by the declining buying power of their clients, A.L. continued to put on a brave front. One day he wrote Dick in Hollywood asking him to design the best-looking delivery truck he could. "Everyone is having a hard time," he wrote. "We should have some new trucks." Richard designed stunning chromium-trimmed black bodies which began to symbolize Gump taste on the streets of San Francisco.

But after all it was in the realm of creative art that A.L. put his greatest trust. Marcella had introduced to her father and brother a young Russian sculptor whom she had met in Paris. In spite of the dwindling demand for mere decoration, the Gumps undertook to acquaint the Far West with the work of Boris Lovet-Lorski. Richard gave him a show in 1930 and A.L. sent him out to Honolulu, where Mrs. Bowen not only presented his work but also saw that he met socially the people who would be most interested in his unique statues.

Lorski used unusual media. That very fact made his contribution appropriate to the Gump atmosphere. Like the cosmopolitan collections in the rest of the store, his marbles had come from all over the world. There was the finest Carrara from Italy, black marble from Belgium, other types from Crete and Sweden, onyx from Mexico. In addition he used bronze, slate, and lava, pewter, copper and brass.

When he wrote to A.L. from Hollywood in 1933 asking if he could put on another show, it took a gambler like Gump to believe that there were enough people with financial resources to patronize the most expensive sculptor in America. Nevertheless, A.L. took the chance. He advanced money for freight on the valuable marbles, provided an expensive hotel suite, and entertained for the visiting artist in pre-Depression style. Over five thousand visitors came to admire the month-long exhibit. Mr. and Mrs. Lawrence Dorsey (she the granddaughter of James J. Hill) sat for portraits in marble. William Randolph Hearst chose a graceful silvery bronze statue seven and a half feet high for his collection at San Simeon.

That statue almost met the fate of the treasures lost in 1906, for while it was in storage in the Gump basement, fire broke out among the packing cartons. Hot flash flames from burning corrugated boxes blackened the silvery lady. Some overhauling was necessary to make her presentable for company.

That fire was just another of the trials Gump endured during these challenging years. Efficient work on the part of the fire department saved the store, but rampaging hoses made havoc of fine china and glass, marble crumbled to ashes in the heat, and once again A.L.'s boasted courage was put to the test.

Government regulation of business was another hardship to the Gumps. It had become an unwritten rule since the beginning of the establishment that every member of the group was part of the whole, ready to step into whatever place most needed him. "Do" had become the watchword of the establishment. In spite of his blindness A.L. could wrap a package with the sure touch acquired in his youthful apprenticeship. Even as president he was not above doing a menial job if need arose. But when the time came for the annual holiday exhibit of beautifully set dinner tables in 1933, N.R.A. rules almost prevented carrying on what had become a Gump tradition eagerly awaited by the public. These tables had to be prepared after regular working hours and no one not accustomed to the precious accouterments used in the displays could be trusted with their handling.

A.L. appealed to the local government administrator for permission to use his regular trained personnel—on overtime pay, of course. He told the official that he would willingly engage some of the unemployed for routine tasks, but that this specialized handling was too important to trust to inexperienced persons. The regulations proved inflexible, however. A.L. turned to his executives; each

of them had come up through the ranks and under his leadership
they willingly went back for the night to the jobs of their apprenticeship. With the head display man as boss, department managers
turned porters, Robert set up tables, and by the early morning hours
the perfectly appointed dinner services were in place.

A.L. was a hard taskmaster, who expected every one to tackle a
given job with his own tenacity. As he assumed the attitude of "the
master of the household" he trained his clerks to regard visitors as
guests rather than potential purchasers. He was exceedingly proud
of the widespread interest in his rooms, filled with treasures garnered from the entire world, and he succeeded in inculcating the
same proprietary attitude in his staff.

At one time he was twitted by Lord Duveen, the famous English dealer, for bothering with such a large clientele when he could
make more money through one or two major accounts. A.L.'s reply that he would rather have thousands of visitors who had learned
to appreciate the beautiful summarized Gump's whole philosophy of
business. He was gratified when the rooms he had planned so
carefully as proper settings for his possessions came to be regarded
as a museum in the business center of a great city. When he talked
with the men and women selected as caretakers, he impressed upon
them that they were to make all comers equally welcome, whether
they were just looking, supplementing the education of young people by examining the relics of the past, or were serious connoisseurs
and collectors. Although at times A.L. allowed his enthusiasm to
overpower his customer's resistance, that was against the principles
of salesmanship he taught his employees. They were to find a happy
medium between high pressure and the disinterested stand-off attitude of museum attendants.

As assistant hosts and hostesses of the House of Gump, his staff
came to take pride in introducing their paterfamilias, even if behind
his back they nursed some secret grudges over his proprietary claim
to the consummation of every large sale. To be sure they had their

monetary reward in commissions, but A.L. liked to take the credit.

Nevertheless, all shared in the results of the reputation which led Frank Lloyd Wright to inscribe prophetic words in the Jade Room guest book:

"To Mr. Gump, a Western pioneer, who will be built into the history of culture in our 'West.'"

The achievement of this renown had not been easy, involving as it did faculties beyond the normal requisites of an art dealer. His seeing fingers and his sporting blood made him unique among his contemporaries, and the mental images implanted in the years when his eyes could partially serve him added to his reputation as a dependable critic and a sagacious businessman. It might have been natural for others to try to take advantage of such a man. But it was hard to get the better of A.L. Gump. The unerring tactility of those fingers which had been such a revelation to Samson in Paris, still guarded him well in many deals.

An overenthusiastic salesman came into his office one day with a figurine reputedly from Italy. Gump's buyer was evidently convinced of the quality and brought the owner in to show A.L. what a fine piece he had to offer. Gump took the little statue in his hands, fondled it awhile, and then turned to the would-be seller.

"Why do you try to palm off such stuff on Gump's?" he queried. "This is not Italian workmanship. It was made in Mexico."

Crestfallen, the salesman admitted his deceit and carried off his statuette in search of a less discriminating buyer.

Although they had become accustomed to his understanding of porcelains, Robert and Richard never forgot the evening when their father had turned to them after dinner, saying,

"Come on down to the store. I want to show you two magnificent rugs which came in from China today."

The rugs were already hanging with the rest of the stock in the Treasure Room. A.L. went through the entire collection, feeling the nap and tracing the pattern. Sure enough, he picked out unerringly the valuable new ones.

Perhaps the most subtle tribute to the perceptivity of this art dealer's seeing fingers is found in the portrait by Alfred Jonniaux, which hangs on the first landing of the stairway leading to the art gallery on the second floor of the Post Street store. It depicts a smiling gentleman, wearing his traditional red carnation, his favorite jade ring on the fourth finger of his left hand, and fingers of both hands deftly "appraising" the beauty of a magnificent ox-blood vase. Beside him on the table stands a lovely jade Kwan Yin, its color blending delicately with that of the ring.

This portrait of A. Livingston Gump made a vivid impression on a visitor from a faraway state. As the man remembered the message of the portrait, he wrote to Gump,

"If you think so well of that jade figure to desire it as part of your portrait, you may consider it sold."

And the little green image was shipped to Oklahoma!

Family and staff cooperated loyally to help maintain the legend of his "seeing fingers." After A.L. ceased to participate personally in the world-wide quest for treasure he made it his business to know and evaluate each important piece as it came into the store.

His fingers and mind had to test and approve whatever the eyes of his associates discovered. Then these objects became his, not alone through study of their form, but also because he insisted upon accurate information about their origin and historical significance. Each example thus acquired was catalogued in his retentive mind. He had to be told exactly which room, what shelf, what space these individual pieces occupied. He knew the floor space of the store by heart for he had a mental map of the entire establishment—a map that became a chess board on which he played the game blindfolded, cleverly manipulating thousands of pieces. He could walk up to each sculptured horse, jade carving, or great screen with its realistic pictures colorfully outlined in semi-precious stones and ivories. Using the sure knowledge of a connoisseur, he would describe the value and significance to his surprised customer.

There were times, nevertheless, when embarrassment resulted. One day he picked up a famous still life to show a visiting English lord. He launched into an enthusiastic description of the merits of the painting, not realizing that he was holding it upside down!

Another group was even more perplexed one afternoon when A.L. invited them to look at some tapestries. He was especially proud of these woven scenes. Various members of the staff had contributed to his knowledge of them. Eleanor Finch of the decorating department had taught him the feel of the weave. Ed Newell had patiently traced the historical background, while Robert had read aloud the Bible story and Richard had named for him all the musical instruments depicted. The composite information grooved itself into his mind.

A.L. ushered his guests into the galleries and stopped before the wall where the tapestries had always hung. Words and phrases came forth as though mechanically unloosed. He knew his piece well and was launched on an enthusiastic recital while his audience stared puzzled at a blank wall. Quickly a passing clerk realized the situation. He slipped up quietly to whisper in the ear of one of the visitors,

"You know that Mr. Gump does not see. Those tapestries were just removed and he has not yet been informed."

The callers listened courteously and went their way, perhaps more impressed with the knowledge and dignity of the dealer than they would have been if the tapestries had still hung where he assumed they did.

There was, of course, a certain amount of bluff in all this front; but one would not be justified in terming as insincere this man who thus tried to compensate for the lack of formal education and defective eyesight. He always had a ready answer, even though his audience might have presumed too much on the extent of his learning. Suppose the tapestries had been where he thought they were, and his customers had asked his opinion of similar ones hanging on the wall of a museum he had never seen. A.L. would probably have bluffed there, too, yet his listeners would never have known that he was treading on unfamiliar ground.

"Of course," he probably would have said. "Those are very wonderful, but not equal in historic value to the ones you now see!"

Perhaps bravado helped to ease the loneliness of advancing age, but A.L. Gump met his friends of other years with courtly grace and insisted on acting as personal guide for any new patron of importance. Not only did he know his art treasures by heart, but he remembered their purchasers by voice. He kept a mental catalogue of Gump's patrons, their interests, and their geographical location. If a new lot of marine paintings, Japanese swords, or inlaid snuff boxes had just arrived, he would immediately recall a patron who was particularly interested in such things.

He would be able to remember the description of the man's collections, hear his voice, and place him in a distant city; but the name would be momentarily lost! He would appeal to Edythe Larsen, to Ralph Simmons, Robert, or Wheeler, telling them in exasperated tones that of course they *must* remember the man or woman. Finally they hit upon a system. Every sale of importance was recorded and the details card-indexed by cities, objects purchased, and individual names and addresses. Then when a new shipment arrived and A.L. remembered that a lady from Washington looked well in aquamarine jewelry, or a collector in Minnesota appreciated Japanese ivories, the name was easily available. The friendly letter that crossed the continent had the warmth of personal recollection.

His daily tours of the establishment were looked upon with mingled feelings by his employees for although blind he had an uncanny ability to sense damage to his stock. His fingers would rub along the edge of an antique desk and rest on a chip in the

finish; or if a catastrophe befell a vase or piece of fine glass he would
be sure to sidle up to the showcase before the frightened clerk could
gather up the pieces.

On the other hand he regarded all the members of his staff with
a benign concern, stopping to ask about the baby at home, or the
college career of a son. Fred Malley's repair shop had a special
fascination for him, and was incidentally the source of information
which enhanced his reputation as a clairvoyant.

"What are you doing today, Fred?" he would ask.

"Repairing a lamp base broken in the first floor Oriental."

Then A.L. would hasten to the department and ask immediately
for the missing vase.

He and Malley became fast friends, exchanging jokes on every
occasion; but A.L.'s sense of humor almost went too far one afternoon. He reached for a plate which the repair shop had just
mended with infinite patience. It was worth at least $350. Touching
the forefinger of his right hand to his lips to wet it, Gump balanced
the plate on his fingertip and turned to Malley, saying, "I'll bet
you can't do this." With that he sent the plate spinning above their
heads. With the expertness of the Chinese jugglers from whom he
had learned the art he brought the plate back to safety.

On leisurely afternoons A.L. would hunt out Joe Wheeler in
the Lotus Room and reminisce about the collectors who had distributed the spoils of his Oriental treasure hunts all over the world.

Many a time they laughed together over a tale of the past, and
wondered what had become of some rare piece. Most often, however, one or the other knew just where their trophies had gone.

They were proud that Gump's was represented in almost every
great Oriental collection in the country. They could recall the exquisite peach bloom which went from their Porcelain Room to the
Morgan collection, and the magnificent Chinese screen purchased
by Joseph Leiter. A.L. remembered with special pleasure his frequent visitor, John J. Raskob, whom he regarded as one of the

nation's most discriminating collectors of jade and other art works. Wheeler agreed with his chief that the beauty and quality of Raskob's collection would measure up to any in the country.

Joe Wheeler liked to twit A.L. about his super honesty in dealing with another of the world's richest men, Lord Furness, head of the Furness Steamship Line. His Lordship had sailed into San Francisco harbor on a palatial yacht, accompanied by a group of English friends. Lady Furness and a guest made some purchases.

When they were about to sail, Lord Furness came to Gump's and asked for his bill, saying, "Would you mind taking a draft on my London bank?"

The statement was made out, totaling some eleven thousand dollars. A.L. took it to him, along with a blank draft which he sat down to fill in. Returning with it to the office, Simmons whistled. "Pretty good sale, Mr. Gump—over fifty thousand dollars in one order."

Startled, A.L. learned that Lord Furness had made out the draft in pounds instead of dollars. He took it back and said, "My Lord, you seem to have made a slight error."

"Have I, really?"

"Yes, you have written pounds instead of dollars."

"Deucedly stupid of me, wasn't it?"

A.L. had not done so well with another titled visitor. When he was showing the Duc de Talleyrand (husband of Anna Gould) around the store the duke had stopped, entranced, before an immense lacquer chest with beautiful gold inlay.

"Just the thing for my collection," he exclaimed with delight.

"Sorry, Mr. Gump," said a clerk standing near by, "that has just been sold."

Usually he would have returned later to that department to learn the name of the purchaser, but the day was busy. He went home without asking. The splendid chest was standing in his own living room! That very morning Mabel had selected it for their new apartment on Powell Street. The news was not received with equanimity. In later years, however, the boys often noticed their father stopping by the chest, sometimes almost caressing it. They knew that he had real satisfaction in keeping this collector's item to beautify his own home. Actually, as much as A.L. enjoyed selling to others, he had the acquisitiveness of a collector, finding lasting satisfaction in his personal accumulation of treasure.

Although the times when he allowed himself to be out-traded were few and far between, he was sport enough to relate with relish any story that showed him up. One customer asked the price of a sixteenth-century altar frontal piece with Hebrew characters embroidered in gold on the red velvet. A.L. named a figure of $190.

"All right," the man replied, "charge it to my account."

Once sure of possession, he asked to use the telephone, and called a dealer to whom he sold it for its historical value—$1400!

While Gump could tell that story with good humor, tales involving shoplifting drew bitter comment on the changing times. He liked to recall that in the days of the old Mechanics Pavilion shoplifting was unknown. The only protection provided for the beautiful objects of art, the opera glasses, Viennese fans of lace and ostrich feathers, and other accessories popular in that day, was a heavy canvas curtain lowered in front of the booth when the bell tolled. Yet not a single thing was ever stolen.

In sharp contrast, the success of clever shoplifters in evading the most thorough precautions exercised in the modern Post Street store, roused his anger. Two especially brazen and costly examples were cited when A.L. had occasion to reminisce on this unpleasant subject. One concerned a smartly groomed woman, who came in wearing a jade ring of great beauty, and asked to see a necklace to complete her ensemble. Handed a valuable string, she stepped to the mirror to observe its effect. Before the clerk could sense her intention, the woman slipped into a knot of customers and dashed through the doors onto Post Street. The clerk ran, too, but it was hopeless. The woman with the jade had cleverly lost herself in the mass of people.

Then there was the story of the Englishman who came in one day to ask if Gump's had any *fleur de pêche* vases. He was interested in an amphora, priced at a thousand dollars.

"I like this pretty well," he said, "but I really prefer something finer. I am going to China. If I do not find one I like better, I'll pick it up on my way back to England."

A.L. offered to put it aside pending his return, but he said no. In about four months he came in again and asked to see the peach-bloom. The clerk brought over the box in which it was kept, slipped open the lid, removed the satin covering and there was—nothing. Detectives put on the case could never turn up a clue as to what had become of the lovely vase.

AND SO the annals of treasure trade ran, always punctuated with the unexpected, sometimes a loss, usually gain. A.L. was like a miner—with the recurrent fever of prospecting constantly raising his temperature.

On the eve of a holiday in 1931 Gump again struck pay dirt, only it was stone—sculptured stone from a civilization even less known than that of old China. A.L. and his associates thought they were jade hunting again when George Washington Dinkelspiel brought word of the availability of the Hansen collection of ancient art in Bangkok. Dinkelspiel, a well-known San Francisco attorney, represented the kingdom of Siam as its consular agent, a procedure sometimes followed by a small country instead of sending one of its nationals to a foreign port.

He reported that the widow of Dr. C. C. Hansen, long-time American consular agent in Bangkok, wanted to dispose of her late husband's collection of Oriental art. Mrs. Hansen hoped that Mr. Gump or his authorized agent would make the voyage to Siam and examine the accumulation of a lifetime spent in the Orient. Since such a trip was impossible right then, A.L. wrote, asking for photographs and descriptions.

Before the letter reached Siam the impatient widow had everything crated and shipped to San Francisco. The hold of the vessel was so filled that there was no room for any other cargo by the time the five hundred and twenty-five cases were loaded, and the vessel started on what is reputed to be the first and only direct voyage from Bangkok to San Francisco.

Since Mrs. Hansen had exhausted her funds, there was nothing left with which to pay duty. Gump's helped out by renting the second floor of the largest bonded warehouse in the city, while they considered her offer of the entire shipment, for which she asked $100,000. A.L. sent Robert and Martin Rosenblatt to make a reconnaissance survey. With a crew of warehousemen they looked in consternation at the heterogeneous pile—two to three cases deep.

Mrs. Hansen had headlined her list with two iron vaults filled with jade. These she considered the basis for her high evaluation of the entire lot. But one look at these "eighth-rate pieces" was discouraging to Rosenblatt who was accustomed to dealing in the finest Ch'ien Lung and other selections from the discriminating Mr. Liu in Peking. They opened a few cases at random. The pages of shipping inventory gave no help. Here was a case marked "masks." That might be valuable, but no, it contained only a few papier-mâché items, worth about thirty cents each. They probed a few more, finding a few pieces of porcelain, some tables and chairs not worth the packing.

Then they ripped off the lid of a box marked "head." Out rolled a stone image, a magnificent piece, different from anything they had ever seen. Their knowledge of Oriental line and surface told them they had found a treasure. Quickly they segregated all the boxes marked "head" and "hands." Then they reported to A.L.

"This is worth a gamble," they told their chief. He bought on instinct again. He offered Mrs. Hansen several times the appraised value put on the "Siamese art" by American consular agents in Bangkok. It was hard for Mrs. Hansen to understand their enthusiasm over these broken fragments and stone heads and their decisive rejection of the jade and other items on which she had pinned her hopes for high returns. But she was pressed for funds. She

accepted the Gump offer and took her other "prizes" to the auctioneer.

When the boxes of Cambodian heads were delivered to Gump's
it was like Christmas for about five days. Excitement ran through
the store as one shapely piece after another was unwrapped and laid
on the receiving counter. Members of the staff took turns in coming
by to see what was going on, asking "how much for this one? . . .
how much for that?"

Finally Rosenblatt said, "Anything so high (measuring about
two inches with his fingers) is a dollar." And every Gump-trained
clerk and staff member carried off a trophy, unconscious of the real
value of such a "gift."

Now A.L. had a new field for study. He called in his sons and
his staff to do research. There were very few sources of information.
Dr. Hansen had built a reputation as a student of the ancient
Khmers and Thais, but the scholarly list he had kept of all his
possessions had disappeared. Mrs. Hansen could not locate the
valuable document which could have been a veritable Rosetta stone
to the struggling Gump researchers.

Robert Gump and Martin Rosenblatt delved into whatever books
they could find dealing with the history of Siam and Cambodia.
They discovered that the artists who had sculptured these amazing
heads had belonged to a race combining indigenous Melanesian
characteristics with Indian and Chinese cultures. Their capital at
Angkor-Thom was said to have been greater than Rome at the time
of Augustus. They learned, too, that the civilization represented by
these archaelogical fragments had apparently completely disappeared for over five hundred years.

Then in 1861—when Solomon Gump was running the blockade
out of the seceding South and David Hausmann was establishing
his little mirror shop in gold-crazed San Francisco—a French
naturalist, Henri Mouhat, had parted the thickets of the Cambodian
jungles and accidentally caught sight of the towers of Angkor-Vat, a

great temple equaling if not exceeding the then greatest monument of labor known in the world of their time, the pyramids of Egypt. There stood the towers in majestic silence, defying students who would pierce the mystery. Moats around them bloomed with lotus flowers, but no sign of human habitation in many centuries was revealed.

As the Gump staff sought further information, they turned to the French who had opened up the jungle, rediscovered the lost city of Angkor-Thom, and unearthed the fabulous treasury of ancient art created by priests from the ninth to the fourteenth centuries. So carefully had the French tried to preserve the setting that it had long been forbidden to bring out specimens except for such institutions as the British Museum. Dr. Hansen's private collection must have come to him as gifts and tributes. Gump's did not try to unravel that secret. It was sufficient for them to realize that they were the first Occidental commercial establishment to display examples of these sacred sculptures.

When the two San Francisco inquirers felt that they had sufficient information, they prepared a booklet on Cambodian art and called in the art director of their printing firm to photograph their best Khmer heads and hands. Robert held the lights and Truman Bailey clicked his camera. Students of archaeology and museum collectors were quick to respond. The images portrayed and described in those pages have since been scattered all over the world in museums and private collections of people who appreciate the contribution of these ancient artists, men who seemed to have worked in periods of peace and faith.

"Few artists have been able to translate into stone and bronze that vitality and spirituality expressed in the enduring sculpture of the Khmers and Thais," asserted A.L. "We sold the most superb piece in the whole collection, a splendid Ayuthian head, to the playwright Sidney Howard shortly before he met his tragic death in that tractor accident on his ranch. Perhaps, if his brilliant writing career had not thus been cut off, he might have penned some lines that would have done justice to a people who combined so remarkably the traditions woven into their Melanesian culture by migrations from India and the Chinese who seeped down from Yunnan."

Several months after the Hansen collection of Siamese and Cambodian art was offered to the public, H. G. Quaritch Wales, nephew of a renowned London book dealer, came through San Francisco. Wales, a British subject, late of the Lord Chamberlain's Department of the Court of Siam, had heard of Gump's acquisition and came in to show them photographs of the six Cambodian heads he had with him on shipboard, which he planned to offer to the British Museum.

In spite of their research, the Gump staff was not yet thoroughly grounded in Cambodian art. They welcomed this opportunity to learn from a world authority. A.L., Newell, Rosenblatt, and Robert went with Wales to the round-the-world ship tied up at the dock for the day. It was about noon when they decided to have a look at the six pieces and the ship was scheduled to sail at two. They moved fast. The hold had to be opened. Then the men borrowed a crate opener from a couple of longshoremen—opened the crates, saw the heads, and made an offer. The price agreed upon was exceedingly high, with no possibility of making a profit; but by this time A.L. realized that Hansen had never acquired a top piece in his life. The heads offered by Wales presented unparalleled opportunity to secure some of the best, ownership of which would give higher quality to their collection.

A.L. agreed to take five of the six heads Wales had to offer. But the traveler was not satisfied with a Gump check; he insisted upon a draft on the Bank of England. Time was slipping by. Taking Wales with him, Robert rushed to the Wells Fargo bank to have the firm's check converted to a bank draft on London. They returned to the ship, had the heads removed to the dock, and the Gump group waved the visitor off promptly at two.

Meanwhile the heads had not gone through customs and Gump's had no permission to own them. They left the Khmers sitting on the dock, gambling that no casual passer-by would think of picking up such oddities. Robert rushed to the customs office asking for the Far-Eastern arts man. He was not in; but associates said he was on his way over. Robert took the official to the dock and asked him to make out whatever papers were necessary. All the man asked was,

"Has Newell seen these?"

"Yes," answered Robert.

"And what does he say?" rejoined the official.

"We bought them," replied young Gump.

"Then they're all right with me."

This Cambodian art brought new collectors and museum buyers to hunt out Joe Wheeler in the Oriental Court, and A.L. soon realized that his gamble was proving more profitable than he had ever guessed that it could be.

The reputation of Gump's as a center for museum builders was soon further enhanced. In a shipment sent by Liu from Peking there were bronzes such as they had never seen before, marvelous examples of the skill of masters whose sense of rhythm and proportion excelled that of the Greeks. A.L. called upon the best authority in the bay area for identification—Dr. Alfred Salmony of the University of California. That scholar pronounced these bronzes as coming from the Shang dynasty (1765-1122 B.C.)—among the oldest relics yet divulged by the disturbed earth of China. The tombs from which they came had been opened quite adventitiously by the changing course of the flood-swollen Yellow River near Anyang, the ancient capital.

Along with the bronzes came strange pieces of bone and tortoise shell covered with inscriptions in Chinese characters. Research into their use and origin showed that these were "oracle bones," used by soothsayers to tell fortunes. They were engraved and then held over fire until they cracked and broke, the fragments were juggled, and the future was predicted from the results.

The bones had first been unearthed by a farmer near An-yang. Believing them to be dragon bones, highly valued for medicinal purposes in China, the farmer had collected as many as he could find and sold them to apothecaries. Because some of the bones had markings that could not possibly be ascribed to a dragon's structure, the old physicians would scrape off the markings before they prescribed pounded bones in a curious medicine for nervous diseases. Then in 1899 some of the bones came into the hands of scholars versed in the most ancient forms of Chinese writing. For thirty-five years these antiquaries labored over the deciphering of the inscriptions on the oracle bones until in 1934 they announced that by means of their markings it was possible to trace six centuries of Chinese history, hitherto considered legendary.

WHILE A.L. had thought his travel days were over, red figures on the Honolulu books became a serious enough problem in the spring of 1933 to make a trip out there imperative. He took Martin Rosenblatt and his wife with him this time, secretly glad of an opportunity to see for himself the fulfillment of his dream under those blue-tiled roofs which had brought him so many appreciative comments from other travelers.

On the first night out he accepted an invitation to sit at the captain's table and at once found a Jade Room patron as a dinner partner—Chris Holmes, grandson of the founder of the Fleischmann Yeast fortune. Holmes had recently presented a large group of animals formerly sequestered on his Santa Barbara estate to the new Fleishhacker Zoo in San Francisco. The two men exchanged anecdotes about collecting.

Holmes was as interested in antiques as in wild beasts, for he had often accompanied his mother on her jade hunts—a hobby begun under Gump guidance in the San Francisco treasure house. Mrs. Holmes had been another of the collectors whose buying power had not diminished with the Depression. When the Shang bronzes became available she was among the first to answer A.L.'s prompt letter. Her investments in these ancient pieces was rapidly making her the owner of the finest collection of such items in the world. A.L. was glad to hear more about her recent acquisitions from her son.

Chris Holmes had built one of the show places of Honolulu and he was enthusiastic over its decoration, for which Mrs. Bowen and her staff were responsible. A.L. completed his journey serene and confident, anticipating his own first view of what had been achieved in his Honolulu store since he had okayed blueprints.

As he returned to the Royal Hawaiian he was more than pleased that he had chosen to build across the street on the lot first suggested by Robert. Mrs. Bowen's gardens had grown rapidly in the fertile soil. A.L. entered the building through a doorway shaded by bamboo and the fragrant *mulan* of China. He found the rooms within like those of a private home. Long tables fashioned out of rare woods of the Pacific were laid with place mats of finely woven *lauhala* and set with translucent glass plates and goblets which captured the evanescence of island flowers in their sculptured designs.

He lingered in the Jewel Hall and felt the ingenious carvings and patterns lavishly wrought with semiprecious stones in bracelets, rings, necklaces, and pendants, the satiny touch of cool white jade, the warmth of honeyed amber, and the exquisite petals of coral roses. Glints of color penetrated through the haze that veiled him from distant objects and he held the finer jewels closer to his eyes that he might enjoy his favorite shade of blue in lapis lazuli and glowing Oriental sapphires. His fingers signaled to his brain the worth of the pearls he fondled—precious stones that warmed to human touch.

Then he went on to the Jade Room, rival in miniature to the inner sanctuary of his San Francisco treasure chest. Because space was limited and the clientele so selective, Mrs. Bowen had chosen the rare pieces temptingly displayed in those cabinets with incisive discrimination. A.L. found his fingertips tingling with ecstatic pleasure over mauve figurines and stallions carved from jade as black and smooth as summer midnight. The scepters, wine cups, bowls and images expressed to him and all who saw them the serene subtlety of ancient Oriental culture.

He delighted that he had clung to his determination to perfect this jewel box in every detail despite the threat to its existence which depression had brought. What he found convinced him that retrenchment was out of the question here. He stuck resolutely to his conviction that the treasures now gathered into these new storerooms had permanent value. He could afford to wait for returns on this investment.

He walked through the Moon Gate into the Willow Court and sat in its fragrant shade. As his feet slipped over the velvety moss of courtyards, which seemed to transport him back into Oriental palaces, he was loath to leave. But he was carrying away an indelible picture of tranquil beauty and a conviction that this venture should have his uninterrupted backing. He said Aloha to Mrs. Bowen and threw his leis over the bow as they sailed past Diamond Head. Although the return that legend promised might not be realized, there would never be any doubt that part of A.L.'s spirit would seek his Pacific outpost more and more frequently as the years pressed on.

He thought with proprietary pride of the contribution to the island community life made by Mrs. Bowen and her staff. Gump's of Honolulu had become not only a treasure house of beauty unearthed from the mysterious Oriental past, but also a center in which modern creativeness thrived. The blossoms sculptured imperishably on frosty glass were wrought from designs sent by Mrs. Bowen to a California artist who had never visited the islands to see for herself the ponciana or the night-blooming cereus. Nor did the Polynesians design the charming flacons which they carved to contain perfumes capturing the lingering fragrance of pikaki and plumieria. With wise foresight Mrs. Bowen had brought a Swiss wood carver from the Old World to teach native craftsmen how to work in the media of island hard woods. Both ideas inspired new industries for Hawaii.

Honolulu was more than a playground for the escapist: it was also a magnet for artists and writers, the melting pot of races, and

the legatee of two extremely different cultures. From the dreamy
Polynesian with his adventurous spirit and his closeness to nature
came the exotic; from missionary pioneers came the New England
tradition of austerity and education.

Alice Bowen understood both, adding to her sympathetic interpretation of the islands, which had always been home to her, the
broadening experience of travel and study in far places. As a hostess
she welcomed those artists of every calling who gathered in a land
which was so *simpatico*.

When Mrs. Bowen was invited to sit on the Board of Trustees
of the Honolulu Academy of Art, A.L. regarded that honor as testimony to the approbation of fellow citizens for the successful dream.
Visiting travelers often told him about her discriminating selection
of both Oriental and Occidental objects. From those who had been
guests in her home on Diamond Head he knew that the same care
and precision exercised in commercial displays had made its furnishings a distinguished example of art applied to homemaking.
That Mrs. Bowen's fellow Honoluluans made wide use of her
ability in helping to plan and arrange the art gathered in their
homes and public buildings fully justified his gamble in the Pacific.

But A.L. heard of one island visitor who had *not* consulted Mrs.
Bowen about the fine pieces she accumulated for her home. One
day in San Francisco a member of his staff, Gladys Donellan, came
into A.L.'s office with a letter from a woman who wished "to discuss a very secret matter." Mrs. Donellan answered the letter, inviting the writer to come to her office. When she came, the woman
confessed that she had in her possession a quantity of silver taken
from Gump's of Honolulu. She wanted to return it without
detection.

"But why did you take it?" the astonished Mrs. Donellan asked.

"My husband forced me to steal it. How can I get it back to the
store without anyone else knowing?"

"Ship it by express."

In about a week a large orange crate was delivered to Mrs. Donellan's office, addressed to her personally. She had it carried into A.L.'s office. Together they unwrapped from the bundles of newspapers two silver teapots, sugar and creamer, several compotes, a modern teapot, a jade box—in all about a thousand dollars' worth of merchandise.

Next came a letter explaining that there had been one more tea set, but that she had given it to her sister. She described it in detail and asked what it was worth. A.L. directed Mrs. Donellan to reply giving the exact cost to the store. A few weeks went by. Then a letter came enclosing the full amount, with the explanation that it had been necessary to sell part of her furniture to raise the amount. Of course, the address and name were fictitious, but as A.L. recalled the experience, he said,

"This was the most remarkable case of conscience and honest heart that I have ever known. How she ever got away with so much is a mystery. Mrs. Bowen knew that things were disappearing and even had a glass insert put into her office door so that she could watch what went on in the silver display room. Yet the thief was never caught."

A.L. had enjoyed the spring voyage to Honolulu so greatly that it did not require much urging the following year to yield to an importunate invitation from Marcella to visit her on the island of Moorea in the Society Islands. This voyage took him far from the harsh realities of the depression problems in the early summer of 1934. A.L. had the happy faculty of detaching himself from worry when he could do nothing about a situation. As he sailed out to the South Seas on a small vessel commanded by the same Captain Johansen who had been his host on the *Manoa* in 1928 he left behind all the perplexities that were complicating the business world.

Back in San Francisco Robert was coping with the difficulties of the water-front strike. While he was "wondering what Dad

would do" under the trying circumstances, a letter dictated by A.L.
was delivered after a month-long interval. It brought an enthusiastic
account of pleasant social gatherings in Marcella's tropic paradise.
A.L. told of interesting new friends he was making among the
writers and artists of this expatriate colony under the Southern
Cross, including James Norman Hall and Charles Nordhoff. He
described his pleasure in watching lithe native boys sliding up the
palm trees to knock down coconuts and the symmetry of dancers
expressing religious fervor in the flowing movement of ceremonial
festivities. He said that even his eyes were better in this relaxing
environment and that he enjoyed evening walks along the beach
with Clara Walker, a member of the store force whom he had taken
with him as secretary-companion.

Marcella's friends had related native folk tales of the tau-pau-pau
—ghosts—which were supposed to appear among the coconut palms
right after sunset. He seemed far more concerned over his failure
to verify the ghost story than over the vague rumors of industrial
strife at home which had filtered out to the South Seas! These he
dismissed with a casual postscript—"I hear you are having a little
trouble on the water front"—scant comfort to his harassed son.

Nevertheless, he cut his visit short and returned to San Francisco,
bringing with him pictures of himself surrounded by lei-covered
native girls, and one of a laughing sprite playing on the rocks—
Marcella's little stepdaughter, Hina Phillips, who had completely
captivated her adopted Grandad. He brought with him also some
exotic South Sea perfume which he sent on out to Mrs. Bowen, suggesting that they make this Polynesian fragrance part of their island
stock.

Once back in the routine A.L. had to know in detail how Robert
had met the general strike, being gratified to learn that theirs had
been the only large retail store in the city to keep on the pay roll
every employee who wanted work. Robert had really been prepared
to handle this challenge so paralyzing to San Francisco employers.

THE GUMP TOUCH IN JEWELRY

P'u Hsien, the All Gracious, and his elephant in coral against a circle of brilliant green jade. Turquoise with opal halo and gold lotus throne.

Peony of green jade, with leaves of pink tourmaline and gold.

Oak leaves and acorns in gold with tips of brilliant green jade.

Spirit of the leaf: coral deity rising in a golden cloud from a white jade leaf.

(Photograph by Frank van Eckhardt)

For six months before the strike occurred he had been reading *The Daily Worker* and spending as much time as he could along the waterfront, thoroughly familiarizing himself with the not-too-secret plans of the agitators. When the appointed hour came he was ready. He had drawn several thousand dollars in silver from the bank with which he paid the staff, telling them to keep it for emergencies. He stocked a commissary in the store so that all would be independent in case of siege. An emergency cafeteria was set up and all employees ate together at noon, picnic style, bringing cooked food from home for pot luck. Secretaries washed dishes and department managers presided over waffle irons.

A.L. was a benevolent human, even though he was a despot in his own realm. He was completely willing to match overhead against spirit and thus keep the loyalty of those who were responsible for the orderly handling of his business. So now he congratulated his son on his management of that situation and turned to the next assignment.

In spite of the uncertainties of business life in the depressing thirties, Gump determined to continue his jade hunting. Martin Rosenblatt was chosen as his scout. He had watched the developing knowledge of this younger man, a nephew of Mrs. Alfred Gump, giving him opportunity to visit museums, to work among Oriental collections, and to study under Newell and Joe Wheeler. He had also imparted to him many of the lessons he himself had learned through years of dealing with Oriental minds.

On this 1936 trip, just thirty years after the first pottery horses were unearthed in the awakening China, Rosenblatt was shown a fine specimen from the T'ang dynasty. This horse, resplendent with gold-leaf trappings, had become the object of intrigue and bargaining among dealers from two continents. The Peking dealer had placed a phenomenal price on it, actually triple what Gump's had ever asked for an antique horse. Rosenblatt hesitated, made what he considered a high offer, and was turned down. That evening he and his wife were invited to an elaborate dinner given by a local antiquarian of renown. It was a delightful social evening—no hint of business. But just as they were leaving, the hostess said in an undertone,

"I understand that you made a rather substantial offer on Mr. Hsia's pottery horse today."

"Yes," replied her guest, "but I imagine I do not have much chance of getting it."

Her smile betrayed ill-concealed satisfaction. "I know you are a newcomer. May I suggest that as a matter of face, you should not raise your offer."

The bamboo wireless that intertwines all deals in China had worked quickly! Gump's representative, sensing his competitor's desire to acquire the horse was at the dealer's shop early the next morning. His raised offer netted him the horse—a deal which later, through Gump's, made it possible for visitors to the Seattle museum to view one of the finest equine statues of ancient China.

Another piece of good fortune attended that buying trip. Rosenblatt was in the Peking compound when a Chinese apprentice walked in, carrying under his arm one of the finest of the missing objects from the Ch'ien Lung garniture, a piece sought by Gump agents for sixteen years. One look at the vase convinced the San Francisco buyer that it was authentic. The color, graining, and subtle perfection of its carving clearly identified it. The young Chinese would not divulge the secret of his possession, but there was no doubt as to its historical importance.

A.L. had told Rosenblatt early in his career he had discovered that chivalrous personal regard is an essential component of dealer-comprador relationship in Oriental buying. On one of these later trips Rosenblatt found the sound foundation laid by his predecessors most helpful in dealing with a man who considered himself a friend.

He was bargaining in Shanghai with a dealer who was a

stranger. Some Sung paintings were offered, but at a fantastic price. Rosenblatt asked the Shanghai comprador to see if he could bargain for one-fourth the asking price.

"Impossible," he replied.

Returning to Peking, Rosenblatt brought the old-time friend, Mr. Liu, back with him. Immediately he got the paintings for one-fifth the asking price. Liu had made the Shanghai dealers sell at a price fair to Gump's in spite of the higher local markings.

"They had an obligation," he said, "for they must not break the continuity of friendship."

On another occasion Rosenblatt forgot one of A.L.'s important admonitions, a phrase full of age-old wisdom—"Speech is silver; silence is golden"—especially when buying in China. He had purchased a dragon head weighing over a hundred and fifty pounds from a man who had carried it by camel-back hundreds of miles to the compound in Peking. The trader boasted that it was authentically "third century."

After Rosenblatt had purchased the dragon head the comprador proudly related the story of its origin, saying it had come from the "Pavilion of the Bronze Sparrow"—so named because it was built by an emperor of the "Three Kingdoms" (A.D. 221-280) on the spot where he had found an antique bronze replica of the little brown bird, omen of long life, health, and success. Since the ancient ruler's fortune had changed for the better with the discovery of the sparrow, he had erected the pavilion as one of his first imperial acts. The dragon head was stylistically of the period, artistically perfect, and its price substantiated the story.

Without thinking of possible consequences, Rosenblatt wrote out the complete story on his order copy, knowing how gratified A.L. would be to hear it. But the comprador was aghast when he saw the official paper. His fears almost severed their relations, for he told Rosenblatt that should this story become public property both he and the vendor might be accused of selling a public treasure!

From that time on the comprador was very cautious in what he told foreign buyers. In fact, he was so fearful of American "research" that when on a later trip Rosenblatt purchased a magnificent pair of horses from the early nineteenth century, the comprador insisted they were new. He was going to take no chances that he, like that other dealer caught at grave digging, would be accused of robbing an ancient tomb.

He even brought in a stone cutter and insisted that "this is the man who made them." When the horses arrived in San Francisco, Jacques Schnier, a local sculptor, confirmed Rosenblatt's conviction that they were genuinely old. Schnier had just returned from China himself, where he had been studying the work of the unknown artists of the past. From his own knowledge he was able to identify the period of these trophies. He said the patina and surface left no room for doubt. The comprador's dissembling could be explained only by the assumption that the pieces had actually been stolen treasure.

As interest in these antique pieces from far Pacific countries increased, the Gumps decided to explore farther. Robert convinced his father that Truman Bailey, who had worked with them on the brochure announcing the Cambodian art and other company publicity, should go through the Orient as a research man for Gump's. Places where the Gump scouts had never been he was to visit, as a man who could draw, photograph, pick out interesting materials—not necessarily knowing their value but simply their eye appeal—and bring back all the new ideas he could find. He was not a purchasing agent; merely a reconnaissance man.

Bailey started out in 1938, stopping in Honolulu to meet Mrs. Bowen and get the feeling of the Pacific outpost. Then he went to Japan, toured China and Cambodia, Siam, the Philippines, Australia, cabled for permission to go to New Guinea—thought again and decided not, and came home through Samoa and Fiji.

For Bailey, it was the beginning of a career that later took him all over the Western Hemisphere and the Far East as a photographer, designer, and creator. A.L. followed Bailey's career, gratified that he had a part in launching one who has contributed increasingly valuable knowledge of the Pacific area.

In the Philippines he ran into a collection of wood carvings owned by a widow, who, like Mrs. Hansen, kept saying, "If Gump's could only see them." Her price was not high. He figured that it would come within his expense allowance. In a minor way, it was as successful as the Cambodian experiment and it opened eyes at home to a phase of Philippine art with which they were then unfamiliar.

He became friendly with missionaries who were teaching handcraft to native Christians in the South Seas. They were making bowls in a traditional style, but had no original ideas. Bailey evolved some excellent designs to be executed under the supervision of the missionaries. The natives could not make enough to supply the San Francisco store, but Gump's of Honolulu provided a ready market. Many of their most beautiful wooden bowls and unusual woven mats came from these scattered islands of the Pacific, then little known.

In the meantime Robert had resigned, sold his Marina Boulevard home to his father, and left to use his Harvard training as a writer. Richard had on the other hand suddenly decided to give up his Hollywood experimenting and join the Gump staff in Honolulu. A.L. had many reasons for pride in his Pacific outpost, but the fact that its design shop was the means of bringing his creative younger son back into the fold gave it new significance. Richard's experience in modern design could be of use in the increasing business of decorating new homes in the islands in 1939, and certainly the atmosphere where he would work under Alice Bowen was more conducive to sustained production than disconcerting Hollywood.

Richard's Oriental designs began to earn recognition in nationally read periodicals such as *Vogue* and *House and Garden*. He also spent hours at his piano working out themes that eventually became his Polynesian Symphony. When time allowed, he visited the different islands, carrying with him paints and easel. And A.L. proudly hung water colors by Richard Gump on the walls of the home he had bought from Robert.

Celebrates Again

G UMP'S GALLERIES began to share an uptrend of San Francisco art appreciation. The hiatus of depression had forcefully removed American emphasis from getting and spending, as unsought leisure filled library reading rooms and art galleries with those who had previously been too preoccupied to pay attention to culture. WPA-sponsored projects furnished outlet for talents which otherwise might have gone unused. Where art had flourished in the past as the plaything of royalty, it now became important in the everyday life of a democracy.

Loan exhibits from the S. & G. Gump Company helped to acquaint strangers with Cambodian art in the de Young Museum and to decorate the walls of the new San Francisco Museum of Art with fine prints when that institution opened formally in 1935. The *55th Annual* of the Art Association coincided with the opening of this new center for creative art. A.L. felt that as his father had helped with the original exhibits, another generation of Gumps should participate in the inauguration of this outgrowth of the original aim of the pioneer group.

Here in the Veterans' Building at the Civic Center world-famed authorities in all realms of art gave public lectures, and school children attended free classes. A.L. followed this development with twofold interest, as knowledge of what constituted permanent values became ingrained in the populace. Leading sponsors were from families who had been patrons of the Gump galleries in his youth—the Crockers, Spreckels, and many others. He expressed the belief that this contribution to the cultivation of artistic taste in the community justified the philosophy he had explained to Lord Duveen. As he took note of changing patterns in American life he recognized that there would be fewer very rich men in the future, and he told his associates that he had been right in his desire to help thousands appreciate the beautiful rather than to follow the easy course of making a fortune out of a few accounts.

Very soon A.L. saw evidence of this truth in his own sales. Charles James, who had assumed directorship of the galleries after Richard left for Hollywood, reported that the Old Masters brought from Europe on Richard's ill-timed tour were gradually beginning to sell. The early favorites—Welch, Hudson, Gray, and Sparks—continued to attract purchasers, although new names were appearing in the catalogues. Monterey coast scenes by Arthur Hill Gilbert, which had previously been sold exclusively in the Del Monte Galleries, brought new comers to Gump's. Kenneth Slaughter, temporarily in the East, secured paintings by Frank Vining Smith. The marines and full-rigged clippers painted by this Massachusetts artist pleased A.L., who had heard so many tales of these ships from his father.

Juanita Vitousek brought over a floral study show from her studio in Honolulu and the art critics praised her pictures for their "spirit of life and growth" as opposed to the traditional flatness of most still lifes. Max Pollak, a Viennese, displayed his impressions of the Holy Land and Italy. Engraved invitations bade connoisseurs enjoy dramatic canvases painted in the South Seas by Viscount Hastings.

A.L. welcomed these and many more artists from far places; but he was also sponsoring local talent in competitive exhibitions started during the thirties. These had commenced in 1932, when the first prize went to Lucien Labaudt, a virtuoso in color harmony who contributed much to San Francisco's later art history. A local art critic praised the Gumps for offering this opportunity to California artists, saying that nowhere in America was there a greater wealth of good painters than in San Francisco, but that the public was unaware of their work.

A year later, in 1933, the winner of the water color competition was a young Chinese named Wing. This son of a former Cantonese jurist, now pastor of the San Francisco Chinese Presbyterian Church, told A.L. that he had never had a painting lesson in his life. The judges of the exhibit felt that his "Death of Cleopatra" revealed a great talent, praising the shimmering azure of the silken curtain behind the alabaster white of the queenly body. A.L. could not, of course, see the delicate lines of Wing's strongly colored scenes of Chinatown; but he knew that the heritage of ancient artists was expressed in the young man's understanding of his wise and humorous compatriots. Gump was proud to introduce the work of the Chinese-American artist in the galleries of his store—full of treasure from the land of Wing's ancestors.

Another young man who was winning fame in a different field was among A.L.'s Chinatown acquaintances. Ching Wah Lee, known to movie goers as Ching in *The Good Earth,* was a frequent visitor at Gump's. His father had owned one of the famous old shops of the eighties—The House of Ming—and he and his brothers had been brought up to know and appreciate the finest in Chinese art. Gump sympathized with this loyal young citizen's ambition to convince the world that San Francisco's Chinatown was not filled with "dens of iniquity."

Lee recounted to A.L. how in his childhood he had stood with clenched fists as he heard his home area so described to tourists by sensational guides; now he was carrying out the vow which he had made then that some day he would show the world the real story.

A.L. often sent visitors to see Chinatown under the auspices of Ching Wah Lee's modern guide service.

When Lee decided to open a Chinese Museum of Art next door to The House of Ming on Old Chinatown Alley, A.L. sold him some of the finer pieces from the Gump Oriental rooms. These he placed among ancient examples collected by his brothers in China or which he had secured from such New York dealers as C. T. Loo and Tang Yin. Skillfully grouped by the dynasties to which each belonged, this collection helped to visualize the history of Chinese art for museum visitors.

Lee often visited Gump's to discuss with A.L., Wheeler, and Rosenblatt the latest additions to his or their collections. As they talked about ruby-backed plates and third-century tomb pieces they knew that the public was acquiring more than aesthetic satisfaction in a deepening understanding of Oriental culture.

They spoke of the evidence—California universities were including more courses on Far Eastern history, language, and art; exchange students crossed the Pacific to share experiences with their own age groups. The Institute of Pacific Relations was making progress in coordinating basic ethnological, economic, and social information. Steamship lines with round-the-world itineraries had headquarters in San Francisco. Trans-Pacific commerce was building up trade relations with all the Orient.

San Francisco, which had so long remained indifferent and individual on her hilly peninsula, was caught in the surge of westward-bound travelers. No longer could the bay, with its friendly leisurely ferries, isolate this city of the pioneers from mainland neighbors. That body of water, so picturesque to those who viewed it from high windows, so sheltering to the ships that anchored in its stream, was becoming a barrier to progress.

Gump had often been among impatient motorists demanding easier access to and from the mainland. Like many others he had finished vacations in long lines of cars waiting for auto ferries at the Sausalito docks, or on the pier jutting out from Berkeley. Many a time he shared the frustration of men with business appointments in San Francisco who had honked through traffic only to see the gates close for twenty minutes at the Oakland terminal. There was only one answer. "Bridge the Bay" became a public slogan.

As the long steel structure grew across the bay, A.L. shared the pride of all San Franciscans in the wonders wrought by engineering genius. He reminisced with old cronies who had sailed with him on the windy bay in days when no one could have dreamed of tunneling through Yerba Buena Island or of driving from city to city across the largest bridge of its kind in history. Then when the longest single suspension span in the world was flung across the Golden Gate he agreed with fellow citizens that the city should pause for another celebration.

Brought up as he had been on the neighborly Mechanics Fairs, the camaraderie of Market Street on New Year's Eve, and the confetti-throwing waves of Portola Festival celebrants, A.L. entered into the hospitable ambitions of a city still sentimental over the Tower of Jewels and the Fine Arts Palace.

Since he now lived in one of the more beautiful homes of the crowded Marina District where the Panama Pacific International Exposition had been held, A.L. fully understood the dilemma of a city where there was no ground left on which to receive the guests! Once San Franciscans made up their minds to hold a fete, however, nature could not defeat them.

A man-made "Treasure Island" rose in the middle of the bay above Yerba Buena shoals, noted on marine charts for over one hundred and fifty years as a "menace to navigation"—since Don Juan Manuel de Ayala, first white man to pass through the Golden Gate, discovered them in 1775.

A.L. listened to descriptions of the process of making these shoals into an island, and spoke often of the lasting effect that the 1915 exposition had had on the life of the city. Expectation of new artistic attraction to this celebration came with word that Herbert Fleisch-hacker, president of the Park and Art Commission of the city, had sent Dr. Walter Heil, director of the de Young Museum, to Europe for several months in 1937-1938. Reports came back that the Vienna Museum had promised to send "The Princess Marguerite Theresa" by Velasquez, along with some canvases by Van Dyck and Titian; that the French National Museum would lend "Dame en Bleu" by Corot and that thirteenth-, fifteenth-, and eighteenth-century sculptures would come from the Louvre. But the most exciting word was from Italy. Raphael's "Madonna of the Chair" was among the twenty-nine masterpieces coming from that country. These also included Botticelli's "Birth of Venus" and many famous paintings and statues by Titian, Tintoretto, Donatello, and Michelangelo.

When the commissioners invited a former member of the Gump staff—Kenneth Slaughter, who had recently returned from the East —to direct the Fine Arts Building, A.L. had a personal interest in the splendid assortment of paintings and sculpture secured by Dr. Heil. Many of the canvases loaned by the great museums and galleries of Europe were clearly focused in A.L.'s mental gallery. Thus he could enjoy his discussions with Slaughter and with visitors who enthused over the fact that the finest collection of Old Masters ever to leave Europe was housed in the great fireproof building, one of the few structures to be built with permanent materials.

As opening day drew near, Slaughter told him of the arrival of the Italian collection, in charge of its own curator and with packers who were to remain throughout the exposition. He often relayed to A.L. some of Dr. Heil's experiences in the seventeen countries which he had visited with varying degrees of success. In most places the commissioners of the fair had paved the way so that when Heil presented credentials, officials were prepared. Sometimes, however, there was a cold reception.

In Belgium it was only because of a chance acquaintanceship with a young British diplomat, son of an English museum director, that Heil had been able after much difficulty to reach the premier. Then he was promised every canvas he sought. His own personal contacts had won him all he asked in France; but even though he dealt with Herr Goebbels in Germany and had his selections all promised, those, like the ones expected from the Soviet Union, were later canceled.

A.L. was especially interested to hear of Dr. Heil's success in persuading the board of directors of a charitable institution in Holland to loan one of Frans Hals's group portraits, for nothing like it had ever come to America.

Slaughter also brought him news of the achievement of Roland J. McKinney in assembling what he was sure would be regarded as one of the finest showings of American painting ever assembled. He said that McKinney, then director of the Los Angeles Museum of Art, had visited hundreds of artists all over the United States and selected personally the representative canvases that were now arriving daily to be hung in the great new building. Unlike the arcaded galleries of Maybeck's 1915 Palace of Fine Arts, this 1939 repository for priceless canvases was starkly utilitarian—in keeping with its projected future as an operating unit of the airport which was visioned as the permanent function of the man-made island.

The Division of Pacific Cultures, where A.L.'s greatest interest lay, brought the director of the Fogg Museum, Dr. Langdon Warner, from Boston to assemble specimens from China, South Asia, Japan, and the islands of the Pacific. A.L. knew that these examples of Oriental art in media of all kinds—wood, stone, bronze, gold, silver, ivory, and textiles—would greatly enhance understanding in the field where he and other dealers such as Vickery, Marsh, Bentz, and Shiota had long endeavored to develop popular taste.

Latin America had also been combed for its artistic contributions. Slaughter told A.L. of the unusual displays arranged by Dr. Grace McCann Morley, director of the new San Francisco Museum of Art, and Thomas Carr Howe, Jr., director of the Palace of the Legion of Honor. Both had flown from country to country in the southern half of the Western Hemisphere, encouraging participation by these near, but relatively little known, neighbors.

It was February 18, 1939, when great searchlights brought the Golden Gate International Exposition into focus against the backdrop of the night sky. There were many phases of the Pageant of the Pacific which had a direct appeal to A.L. He was intrigued with accounts of mysterious black light playing over walls sprayed with flourescent paint in hues representing Western Polynesian and Asiatic cultures. Listening to descriptions of walled-in courts for which architects had drawn inspiration from the towers of Angkor-Thom and the fabulous cities of the Mayas and Incas, this near-blind student of ancient cultures familiarized himself in imagination with all that drew new crowds of travelers to his city. He knew most of the men and women who carried out in stone and plaster the theme of the exposition—"Peace"—and joined in the wish which Franklin Delano Roosevelt had expressed in his dedicatory speech seven months before the formal opening: "that 1939 should go down in history not only as a year of two great fairs in America, but also as a year of world-wide rejoicing if definite steps could thereby be taken toward permanent peace."

Even the magic carpet of portulaca which spread before the elephant towers guarding the entrance seemed real to A.L. as he imagined the flowers blending like woven strands in Oriental rugs. He liked to feel the prows of great galleons with their figureheads carved by Tognelli as he walked through the Court of the Seven Seas. He listened to the tremendous metallic prayer curtain, behind Ralph Stackpole's hundred-foot statue "Pacific," as it fluttered in the breezes that constantly swept over the island. The fact that he could not see the Phoenix atop the Tower of the Sun did not diminish his appreciation of the Bach fugues played by blind Alec Templeton on the carillon.

Clara Huntington's heroic "St. Francis" standing in a garden bed of giant shasta daisies, Haig Patigian's "Creation," Millard Sheets' paneled history of California—he knew these and all the other symbolic objects as though he had actually seen them.

Two San Francisco artists of Latin American origin had visualized the essential unity of Pacific basin countries in their decoration of a gay pavilion known as Pacific House. Antonio Sotomayor who designed the large terra-cotta relief map in the center of this building had been a frequent Gump exhibitor. Miguel Covarrubias contributed animated maps educating visitors in the geographic, ethnological, and economic characteristics of this part of the world, maps which had also been displayed at Gump's.

While the peace theme was contradicted by headlines from Europe in the summer of 1939, Westerners still hoped that the friendliness of the Oriental countries who were participating so generously in this exposition might preserve the peace of the rest of the world.

As in 1915 San Francisco was gaily celebrating while Europe was embroiled in self-destructive war. The conflict still seemed far removed and the city acceded to public demand to reopen in the summer of 1940. This time European participation was impossible. Richard L. Tobin, another banker and art patron, who had succeeded Fleishhacker as the chairman of the Fine Arts Division, introduced Dr. Heil to some of the greatest collectors in the United States. From them and other American sources there came a new exhibit of Old Masters—El Greco, Van Dyck, Rembrandt, Murillo, and many of the newer French school—Fragonard, Delacroix, Courbet, Corot, Manet, Renoir, Matisse. The American section was enlarged for the second year, mainly because Dr. Heil had the cooperation of Herman More, curator of the Whitney Museum of New York, in assembling a notable display.

A new section called "Art in Action," the proposal of Timothy Pflueger, Vice-Chairman and Director of Fine Arts, added to the educative value of the second-year program. This exhibit took the public backstage to see the techniques of transforming common substances into beauty. Day after day Diego Rivera painted, high on a scaffold, bringing to life the fresco to be donated by the city school department to the new San Francisco Junior College. Dorothy Wright Liebes, who had assembled the remarkable exhibit of hand-loomed textiles from all of the world for the 1939 fair, demonstrated her flying shuttles. Other skilled hands molded clay into ceramic beauty, chiseled life-size figures out of huge wooden blocks, hammered metals into functional decorations, and fashioned daring and original jewelry.

Across the island from the Fine Arts, in the State Building, California played host to the world. One of its rooms was hung with canvases by Keith—now nearly forgotten by a public absorbed in pursuit of the more modern. On a day set aside to honor the Old Master of California, A. Livingston Gump was the speaker, sharing with this audience, as he had done for individual guests in 1915, his personal recollections of the artist he had never ceased to revere.

CHAPTER FOURTEEN ∽ *Elephants, Inro,*
and Ship Models

ENJOYMENT of the 1939-1940 exposition was largely a vicarious experience for A.L. Just as his selling of the bronzes of the earlier fair had helped to prolong its sentiment for many customers, so this time he took over the selling of the jades that had been on display. Not everyone had found this display of matchless gems and decorative carvings, hidden away within the replica of an ancient walled city of China; but those who had penetrated beyond the vermilion and yellow pagoda entrance had beheld objects they would never forget. There was a seventy-five-pound jade pagoda, fashioned out of a single block, the largest piece of fine jade ever found. It weighed nine tons before the jade cutters fashioned it into galleries and towers. The owner of the display, Mr. Chang Wen-ti of Shanghai, told his American listeners that it had required ten years' work on the part of 150 master craftsmen to complete his dream—a total of over two millions man hours. His comparison of the skill of the carvers to that of a brain surgeon working on a tiny nerve helped to visualize the precision attained by these artisans.

When the exposition was over the jade pagoda was taken on a tour of museums, part of the proceeds from its exhibition going to the March of Dimes. The remainder of the jade went to Post Street. Before the closing date its owners, friends of A.L., had said to him,

227

"These are for Gump's, if you want them." He bought about half the necklaces, ring jades, earrings, vases, and figurines. The rest, with the exception of the pagoda, which was not for sale, was left with him on consignment.

The Gump store was ready to show these pieces to advantage, for just previous to the fair the Red and Gold Room had been converted into an Outer Jade Room. A series of articles written by Frank J. Taylor for *The Saturday Evening Post* had introduced "Mr. Gump of GUMP's" to a wide circle who clamored to see the results of his "Jade Hunts" and his "Plunging in Art," as the stories were captioned. Clerks were spending too much time unlocking the original Jade Room and explaining to throngs of visitors the legends and history it represented. Thus glass show cabinets were substituted for sliding panels in the remodeled Gold Room and examples of jade in all its varying hues and forms were displayed where the public could more readily enjoy them.

Now with the Chinese exposition jades added to his collections and the former director of the Fine Arts Building back on his staff, A.L. was preserving some of the atmosphere of Treasure Island. Kenneth Slaughter, enriched by his experience as the host to art and artists of the world, had returned to Gump's as director of the Galleries. Their catalogues and shows began to list names quite new to San Francisco. The city understood—or tried to understand—the art of a new era.

A.L., however, had little patience with innovation, and no concept of what these strange pictures designated "modern art" could mean. He lost interest in the changing galleries and devoted even more time and thought to things Oriental.

During the exposition years his guest books had become a running commentary on the significance of the Gump establishment as a corollary to the international show on Treasure Island. Much that was represented in the polyglot city guarded by fanciful elephant towers spoke of civilizations to which Gump treasures had already

introduced his best customers. Now they came back to tell him how
they had found release from nerve strain and business pressure in
the absorbing pleasure of collecting along the various lines on which
he had started them. Diplomats, brokers, actresses, and writers
formed the procession who sought out "Mr. Gump" as soon as they
reached San Francisco. He always had some new item to complete
or add to the collection he had nurtured through adroit correspondence.

Personally, one of his favorite items was elephants, although he
was surprised to discover how many rabbits he had when the display designer started to collect a brood for an Easter ad. There were
tiny white jade bunnies, fantastic little wooden ones, clear glass and
even black onyx. His fondness for elephants, however, was more
deep-seated—a whim reminiscent of circus-devoted boyhood and
Oriental-inspired superstition. When he found a man like Matt
Brush of New York with a similar passion for these creatures in
any size, color, or material, he ordered his buyers to be constantly
on the lookout for unique examples.

"Brush," he said, "had over three thousand elephants of all sizes
and materials, many of them from our store. He was reputed never
to have purchased any of them himself; they were all gifts from
various friends who were intrigued by his hobby. He was a charming gentleman whose memory is very dear to me. The last commission I had for him was from his wife. When she ordered a
custom-made kimono for him she stipulated that the border must be of
elephants, all with their trunks turned upward to gather in good
luck."

David Belasco was another elephant collector. Although he and
A.L. never met face to face they corresponded voluminously about
this hobby and Gump's shipped elephants of ivory, crystal, jade, and
various kinds of quartz to fill cabinets in the playwright's New York
apartment.

A.L. also liked to tell how Sydney Myer came from Australia

"to make a raid on various works of art." Two years later when Myer visited again he told A.L. he had divided his living room into two sections. One set of cabinets he had designated "The Gump"; the other was named for a London firm.

With all his pride in these private collections, A.L. was most rewarded when the purchaser shared his possessions with the public. He pointed to Mr. and Mrs. William K. Vanderbilt as patrons generous with their private museum.

"I understand that at one of his suburban homes Mr. Vanderbilt opened his collections to the public several days each week," said A.L. as he described the Vanderbilt visit and their purchase from him of one of the finest Shang bronzes that had ever left China, a piece dated about 1200 B.C.

Other magnificent Shang bronzes selected by Gump buyers were given to the Fogg Museum in Cambridge by Winthrop Aldrich. The Cranbrook Foundation near Detroit received treasures purchased by George B. Booth at Gump's; while Miss Spooner of Boston gave many paintings from Gump's galleries to the de Young Museum in San Francisco and other collections throughout the country.

George H. Lorimer always brought his writer friends to listen to A.L.'s yarns, and consistently added to his art collections on every visit to the Post Street store. He told A.L. that a group of his Philadelphia associates had decided to spend their wealth for enduring objects of art, enjoy them during their lifetime, and will them to a gallery for the benefit of the public.

Other collectors were captivated by Japanese inro—tiny lacquer boxes to contain medicines, perfumes, and the like, sometimes inlaid with gold or semiprecious stones. When A.L. met an inro connoisseur he usually sent for Phyllis Marriott to spread out their assortment of these useful yet exquisite ornaments. Usually, she would explain, the inro, netsuke (emblem by which they were attached to the belt), and the ojime (bead on the cord) were designed as a unit. Some people specialized in the individual parts while others acquired large numbers of inro, complete with attachments. Mrs. Marriott learned about inro when she joined the Gump staff in the Oriental workshop above Podesta's Grant Avenue Flower Shop in 1915. Newell had brought some fine specimens with his early shipments of Japanese kimonos. These, along with a sword guard, were the only articles of personal adornment carried by gentlemen of the old school with their severe black haori coats.

Newell told her that the earliest netsuke were made of wood but later ones were fashioned from ivory, bone, and metal. No two were exactly alike and some had layers of tiny drawers marked with characters indicating the various pills carried by these noblemen, who seemed to need as many aids to health as modern man.

Gump's also stocked sundry swords, in their marvelous lacquered guards. These, too, were collectors' items because the Japanese had a secret process of making sword blades which has never been equaled. Some authorities believe these swords were even finer than Toledo or Damascus blades. The Gump Japanese collections must have been well known in the homeland, for twice Nipponese buyers bought up the entire stock of certain items. This happened first after the disastrous earthquake in 1925 when the Gump supply of wood block prints was cleaned out. Now in 1940 interested travelers from Japan purchased the complete selection of old swords. Price did not seem to matter, even though one blade was valued at $10,000.

Hobbies did not always lead collectors to the Oriental Rooms. They might stop on the mezzanine to buy new pieces for cabinets filled with Steuben glass or Doulton figurines. If they were accumulating paper weights or odd pieces of old china, glass, or other Americana, they would find an understanding guide in Clara Walker. She might even produce a bull's-eye lantern such as Paul Revere flourished on his race through New England.

A.L. was as insistent about the authenticity of his small items as he was about his old masters or his Chinese tomb pieces. Nothing pleased him more than to invite the public to see an historically correct display.

Such an exhibition brought connoisseurs to admire a "masters of tableware decoration" show. Tables were set showing the work of master handcraftsmen in pottery, glass, and silver. On one occasion the mezzanine floor was filled with examples of some of the greatest achievements in history, including china used by the Vatican, by Queen Marie of Rumania, Queen Victoria, the Prince of Wales, King Fouad of Egypt, and many other notables. Another time they held an "Old Masters sterling" exhibit, showing formal settings with matching flower bowl, candelabra, compotes, salts and peppers, in eighteenth century English, French Renaissance, Chippendale, Spanish Renaissance, and Modern.

A.L. took keen interest in each new phase of the collecting game, but one of his own inclinations was toward things nautical. Ship models were among his favorites. Some of the best of these were made by Harry Voss, a seasoned old sailor who had been one of A.L.'s cronies since those early days when he frequented the water front. Voss was a genius in his line. Some of his fine-scaled models were made with old ivory piano keys and wood from the planks of derelict ships. The two sea dogs enjoyed more than a business relationship; Gump looked forward to a yarn exchange with Voss whenever he came back from a new voyage. When A.L. returned from Moorea with several bits of loot for his friend to work over, he was saddened by the discovery that Voss had died in his absence. The death of the old sailor added new value to the models he had made. A.L. was careful to see that those who most appreciated the fine work should have the models. Whenever a collector showed an interest in miniature ships, A.L. felt it just as imperative to supervise the selection as he did that of his finest jades.

A search for model clippers, as well as Shang bronzes, brought Mr. Vanderbilt to Gump's store. That interest was easily understood, but A.L. was surprised to find a collector of ship models living high in the Rockies. C. K. Boettcher and his sister, Mrs. A. E. Humphries, from Denver purchased unique models—ships of all sizes in bottles—and ordered lamp shades to be decorated with a touch of the marine for the Ship Bar in Boettcher's Brown Palace Hotel. Then A.L.'s assistant, Nancy Reed, told him that Mr. Boettcher was interested in one of the rarest pieces of carved jade in the Gump collection—a Chinese junk beautifully fashioned out of green jade. As they conversed over the purchase, the hotel owner told A.L. that the ship would have a place of honor in a niche over the mantel in his own apartment.

It was in Hyde Park, however, that these ship models found their most famous setting. A.L.'s long correspondence with Franklin Delano Roosevelt began when a friend of the Roosevelts visited the Post Street store and told A.L. that the former Assistant Secretary of the Navy was making a collection of ship models and other items relating to the U.S. Navy. The next day a long letter went from Gump to Roosevelt. In 1931 when Roosevelt had become governor of New York, A.L. sent photographs of two models that he thought belonged in that collection. The first of these, wrote A.L., was of the clipper *Staghound,* evidently made from the original plans of the ship builder, Donald McKay of East Boston. He included the history of the clipper, which was built in 1850 and burned off the coast of Brazil in 1863 while bound for San Francisco from Sunderland, England, with a load of coal.

The other was even more interesting, representing the "74-gun ship of the line, *Ohio,*" really the *Oregon* of the Mexican War. A.L. wrote that he had never seen, nor heard, of another model of this ship, unless there was one at Annapolis. The hull of the model was of ivory and the masts of bone, with three complete decks and perfect in every detail.

Although at the time Governor Roosevelt felt that the price of these models was prohibitive, he wrote a cordial letter, asking Gump to keep him informed whenever he had any other naval items of merit. In the meantime Gump sold the model of the *Ohio* and wrote Roosevelt on March 10, 1931, that it had gone "to one of my Washington, D.C., patrons and when you are President you will probably see it there. This from an old-time Republican!" In the same letter he told the Governor that the entire family of the late Theodore Roosevelt were patrons, and added:

"I have at this time a dozen very interesting service plates, done in the old Lowestoft style, showing different ships (many of them American Clippers) on each plate. . . . Among the ships on these plates are the *Gamecock, Grand Turk, Flying Cloud, Westward-Ho* and the *Revenge.* . . . If you gave a nautical dinner it would be delightful to have one of these ship service plates in front of each of your guests. There are no two plates alike. . . . May I be quite candid in stating that your letter inspired me to do my best to acquire things that will be of special interest to you?"

In the midst of busy days, Governor Roosevelt evidently pondered this offer, for by the time he decided to purchase the service plates, other nautical-minded customers had acquired the few sets that Gump stocked. But he was not disappointed. A.L. shipped him the set he had reserved for his own home, and was rewarded with an enthusiastic acknowledgment, dictated just before the Governor sailed to join his mother who was ill in Paris. Roosevelt wrote:

"I must tell you how much I appreciate your sending me your own Service Plates. They are really lovely. However, I very much doubt that my guests will ever have a chance to look at them on the table. They are much too precious to be used. Before long I will find a place to put them where they can be looked at and admired, but 'please do not touch.' . . . Do let me know when you are coming East and plan to stop over here in Albany with us for the night or day or whatever time you can spare us."

The first model that Gump sold to Roosevelt was the *Flying Cloud,* which greatly delighted the collector. Not a half hour after the letter ordering this model was received by Gump, the grandson of Citizen George Francis Train, first owner of the original *Flying Cloud,* came into A.L.'s office. He looked over the model which was going to Albany and pronounced it the most perfect reproduction of the famous ship that he had ever seen.

A.L. wrote Roosevelt of this circumstance and closed his letter with a bit of philosophy: "In hectic times like these it is splendid to have some healthy hobby. . . . It will be my great pleasure to co-operate with you at all times in trying to find the unusual connected with our old fleets and the navy . . . I am sending the *Flying Cloud* with a cargo of my best wishes."

As the Christmas holidays of 1931 approached, their relationship had progressed far enough to justify A.L.'s impulse to send a gift to the Governor's Mansion, an old Chinese iron—Ming, of the early sixteenth century. The accompanying note suggested that "while this is a far cry from things connected with the navy, it makes a splendid ash receiver and goes to show how conclusively things eastern are opposite from western ideas. The Chinese, in place of heating the iron from the outside heated it from within by filling it with hot coals. I trust you are a smoker."

By the next Christmas season, another Gump-collected model— the *Niagara*—was in the Governor's mansion, and a new gift bore good wishes across the continent. A dozen glasses to go with the ship plates and a nautical tray especially designed for the recipient carried greetings from A. Livingston Gump in San Francisco.

On December 30 of that year, 1932, Gump wrote two letters to Albany, one telling his patron of a splendid model of the *Wasp,* a sixteen-gun brig used in the War of 1812. "The hull is of mahogany," wrote Gump, "the bottom copper, and many of the details are of ebony and ivory. It will really be an excellent addition to your navy, and I hope that it will be your first launching for the New Year."

The other letter informed Roosevelt of the fact that Gump's had recently come into possession of the Charles Wilson Peale portrait of George Washington, painted at Mount Vernon about 1791. He included a short history of the ownership of the famous painting, saying that it had belonged originally to Judge Gabriel DuVal, an associate justice of the Supreme Court of the United States, appointed by Thomas Jefferson, and describing the friendship between the Judge, Washington, and Jefferson.

Again he failed to make a sale to Roosevelt. The impressive portrait was eventually sold to the Honolulu Academy of Art, where its dignified presence helps to emphasize farreaching American influence in the Pacific.

A.L. introduced his next offer to the new President of the United States with courteous words: "It is with great hesitancy that I intrude on your valuable time, but I must obey your orders." This was in March of 1933 and he was writing to call the President's attention to "a superb sailor-made model of the *Raleigh,* first twenty-six-gun frigate of the United States Navy." As before, he related the main historical facts concerning this frigate, which was built in Portsmouth, New Hampshire, in 1776 and captured by the British in 1779.

The first reaction from the White House was negative; but in April a telegram came ordering the model of the *Raleigh.* In June Gump launched a third ship model in the direction of the White House, this time a gift. Along with the rare and fine model of the *Wasp* went A.L.'s flattering words, "In view of the splendid way you are navigating our country, and in appreciation of your expansion of our present-day navy, I am most desirous of being helpful in the development of your own personal fleet. For this reason, I am sending you today, by express, with my compliments, a model of the U.S. Brig *Wasp.* I have just returned from my outpost in Honolulu and am more than ever in sympathy with your love of ships and the sea."

The President replied that this model was "the pleasantest surprise I have had for a long time. It is a beautiful thing and is going promptly under glass." Although Eleanor Roosevelt became a regular visitor in many Gump departments and left her signature in the Jade Room—"with warm thanks for a beautiful hour"—A.L. never met his famous correspondent personally. He took pride in the fact that the President spent leisure hours wearing a dinner jacket from Gump's made to order at Mrs. Roosevelt's request.

A.L. once had a formal dinner invitation from his friend in the White House (later framed and hung on his office wall). Due to his visual handicap he was deprived of the pleasure of acceptance.

It was sometime later on one of Mrs. Roosevelt's visits that she purchased a set of jade after-dinner cups and saucers which she sent as a wedding gift to the Duchess of Kent.

Starting about this time, Gump interjected comments on world affairs into his business letters. Based as they were on his studiously acquired knowledge of the Orient, these written words came to have prophetic meaning. The first expressed concern over American policy regarding the World Court and was dated March 30, 1933.

In this letter Gump told the President that his close contact with the Orient had led him to know that Oriental psychology was in many cases diametrically opposed to that of Americans. He warned that if the United States were to enter the World Court at this time, after the withdrawal of Japan, it would be misinterpreted by Japan and the Orient, for to them it would appear that our representatives did not wish to sit in the World Court with Japan. He predicted then that eventualities might arise that would cause trouble in the Pacific and on this coast, and hoped that the splendid work Roosevelt was accomplishing would not be interfered with by outside ramifications.

Following this, letters and telegrams were exchanged with the White House touching on many matters of vital concern, not only regarding relations with Oriental countries, but domestic problems affecting industry and national defense. Gump was concerned over the plight of skilled workers in industries connected with the decorative arts—especially glass and pottery—and had considerable correspondence with officials of the National Recovery Administration. He never hesitated to write or wire his opinions to the President or the proper cabinet officer when occasion demanded.

But it was on July 30, 1941, that the art dealer placed himself on record as a prophet in ways far removed from art and business when he wrote:

"MY DEAR MR. PRESIDENT:

"Having done business with the Orient for the last fifty years I am familiar with many of the idiosyncrasies, and any gesture of kindness or appeasement is misinterpreted by the Japanese as significant of fear.

"If at any time it comes to pass that a firing war should open between this country and Japan, may I suggest that we do not fail to take full advantage of the element of surprise.

"Turning back the pages of history, you no doubt will remember that Japan struck at Russia at Port Arthur and declared war after the first naval engagement. Russia, from a naval point of view, never fully recovered from this initial blow. Of these circumstances I am sure you are familiar.

"I have great feeling for you, my dear Mr. President, in these heartbreaking, stirring times, and I know of no one who would measure up to this superhuman endeavor in a more enlightened way than my President.

"Most earnestly,
"A. LIVINGSTON GUMP"

CHAPTER FIFTEEN ∽ *New Roles*

W HEN THE FATEFUL WORDS, "The Japs are attacking Pearl Harbor," broke into A.L.'s radio enjoyment of the New York Philharmonic Orchestra concert on Sunday, December 7, he realized that his prophecy had been too mild. To this man who had devoted so much of his life to understanding and presenting Oriental culture, the treacherous triumph of the militarists was a personal defeat.

Most Americans, refusing to think through the truth, had placed unlimited faith in the frontier defense of their Pacific outpost. Honolulu, with its forts and Pearl Harbor, plus the magnificent modern Hickham Field, had seemed invulnerable. A. L. was one of the minority who knew that trouble was inevitable unless the foreign policy of the United States was tempered with fact-facing realism. His own convictions had been bolstered by those of his son, when Richard had returned from the islands in the spring.

They had had many long and serious talks, not all concerned with Gump policies and the new position this son had come home to undertake, that of assistant to the president. As a matter of fact, Richard doubted whether he would be long in the peaceful pursuit of merchandising. His first act on returning was to enlist in the Coast Guard Reserve, his old injury making him ineligible for active military duty in any line. Robert had applied for enlistment on December 4.

War in the Pacific ended a phase of treasure-trading which had dominated A.L.'s life. He was grateful for the trove garnered so

safely in his own storehouse—or was it so safe? Like all Californians, he wondered. He was more conscious than most of the cunning and deceit that was as natural as breathing to the type of
Oriental who had wrested control from the men of learning and
art. He knew the threat to the Pacific Coast and to all of America
should those now in the ascendancy not be stopped. He wired the
President again.

"May I suggest that intensified precautions be taken immediately
to prevent the sabotaging of our bridges. I cannot stress too forcefully its importance."

Until America's entrance into the war it had been possible to
continue to import some merchandise from Europe. Family heirlooms had come out of their vaults to be turned into cash as the
burden of war taxes in England steadily increased; many a shipment
had arrived bearing evidence of Luftwaffe attacks on the British
Isles. A candlestick had a bit of shrapnel imbedded in its base, while
a card in one shipment of Victorian silver that was unpacked in the
Gump warehouse in the summer of 1941 bore testimony to the
valiant efforts of the British merchant marine. The card said, "Glass
for butter holder broken during enemy action."

Even the paintings hanging in the Gump galleries that first week
of December, 1941, reflected the foreboding that was shrouding the
outlook through the Golden Gate. Alfred Jonniaux had a room full
of portraits of San Francisco personalities painted during his year
on the Coast. The compassionate eyes of Bishop Edward Lambe
Parsons, a man who had devoted the best of his years to a dream of
world peace, looked across the gallery on stalwart sons of his fellow
citizens in uniform. These were the grandsons of the pioneers who
had answered the call for volunteers and were preparing to assert
their convictions wherever their country might call them to service.

In the year since Kenneth Slaughter had come back from Treasure Island to direct these galleries, their tone had been modulated.
They were reflecting on canvas the swift-moving changes in the

world of art, changes that in turn mirrored the reaction of a generation of disillusioned and dislocated minds. Men and women who had grown up between wars and had felt the insecurity of the Depression allowed their restless groping to stiffen their brushes and vivify their colors. The younger school strove not for softness but for steel-hearted realism. There were more city dwellers among them, and they painted what they saw—skyscrapers, factories, struggling masses. As in the literature of the period, romanticism was dead.

Slaughter's understanding of the need for perspective led him to offer a contrast to these harsher scenes with an exhibition from the more softly blended palettes of the Barbizons. In collaboration with the Dalzell Hatfield Galleries of Los Angeles, he brought to the Gump Galleries French masterpieces of the nineteenth century— atmospheric portrayals of nature breathing Corot's sympathetic interpretation and impressionistic portraits by Manet. Another Renoir, this time a world-famed painting, "Gabrielle and Coco," hung in the gallery. A.L. thought back to that canvas his father had brought from the Latin Quarter so many years ago. He remembered the soft rose tints of the sunshade which threw a coral glow over the graceful figure of the young girl. What satisfaction Solomon would have had to know that the then obscure artist whose work had captured his imagination had now become so famous!

As the war raging in the Pacific swept to a crescendo, Gump's galleries began to feature canvases stark with personal realism— paintings and drawings that filtered back from battle scenes. As officers and enlisted men passed through this great port, those who were able to record their experiences on canvas were offered opportunity for one-man exhibits.

Young naval Lieutenant Carter Morningstar made names of places familiar to readers of headlines strikingly real in his "Water Colors of the Pacific." Louis Maccouillard pictured in tempera and water color his trek from Key West to Attu. E. L. Bloomster presented a graphic record of American exploits on the oceans of the world in an exhibit called "America Rides the Seas—U.S. Ships in Peace and at War, 1779-1942."

Good as these exhibits were, no group pulled at the heartstrings like the poignant sketches by Donald Dang, made in the Santo Tomás prison camp in Manila. This talented young Chinese-American had worked on scraps of paper while Japanese guards were not watching. Other pictures were sketched while he was ostensibly making portraits of Japanese officers—a commission which gave him freedom to use his pad and pencils.

Art galleries had other roles to play in those dark days. Charlotte Vickery, wife of W. K. Vickery's eldest son Fred, who in 1944 had been appointed director of the Crocker Art Gallery in Sacramento, discovered this when she came upon a young serviceman from a near-by camp sitting quietly day after day before a large painting, "The Grand Canyon of the Sierra—Yosemite," by Thomas Hill.

"It makes me feel so safe!" said the boy in response to her friendly smile.

The Gump guest book reflected the same response. Officers and men of all ranks agreed with Sergeant Karl Herlinger, Jr., who wrote in the book: "What a great honor and privilege to pause for a few moments and reflect upon the priceless history the Jade Room represents."

Across the Oriental Court, in the Galleries, art-minded servicemen and civilians could study history of another sort. Slaughter borrowed canvases from many United States collectors and offered the public an opportunity to review the progress of art from the fifteenth to the twentieth centuries. Art that is timeless taught harried visitors the significance of truly great painting.

The Gump exhibition included Cranach's "Mount of Olives," Tobias Verhaecht's "Tower of Babel," Sir Henry Raeburn's dignified "Portrait of Dr. Benjamin Bell," as well as Corot landscapes

A SAN FRANCISCO ROOM DECORATED
BY GUMP DESIGNERS

(Photograph by Frank van Eckhardt)

that took thoughts into peaceful French countrysides and helped
to banish the horror that had engulfed the world.

Gump's of Honolulu, like the home store, had its doors open to
those who sought respite. Mrs. Bowen wrote her chief about two
servicemen who had worked in the drafting room while they were
on leave. She enclosed a letter from one of them which said that
"this association has given us a spark of confidence to face the
future. It has shown us the way out of a rank-conscious army into
a world of people and individuals." She also enclosed another from
a battle area, saying that a brochure from Gump's "helped a few of
us to escape from the reality that is war, to the unreality that beauty
and peace now seem to be."

The Pacific outpost was one of the first to project a postwar
program for the employment of injured veterans. They invited
any who had even a slight knowledge of packing, shipping, and
cabinet work to apply at their store. Gratitude poured in from
front-line hospitals, especially when word of this offer reached Japa-
nese-American soldiers from Hawaii serving in Italy. Mrs. Bowen
had the satisfaction of helping several young Nisei who had been
decorated for bravery to win the harder battle of adjustment to
civilian life as disabled veterans.

War had its personal meaning for A.L., as it did for most of his
friends. Robert left early for service in the army which took him
from Panama and the Galápagos Islands to the Philippines and
Japan, for which theater his Oriental associations had fitted him.
Marcella sailed in the other direction, as a Red Cross staff assistant
in North Africa and Italy. Richard took on the difficult task of
maintaining Gump's as a going concern in a period when all their
accustomed sources of supply were cut off and public attention was
diverted from the aesthetic to the insistently realistic.

True to family tradition he was not daunted by the seeming
futility of the moment. He had been chafing to do the unusual

since he returned from Honolulu to find the business sticking too close to conventional patterns. When Rudi Blesh, head of the Design Room, came to him in 1942 with the suggestion that Mexico was the only place left where they might find contemporary material suitable for modern homes, Richard replied with typical Gump decisiveness,

"We'll go!"

They called in Eleanor Forbes of the Decorating Department, and the three prepared designs for the articles and materials they hoped to secure.

Not one of these designs was used. As soon as Blesh and Dick crossed the border they began to see what they wanted, and it was always better than they had anticipated. Like the early San Franciscans who had known the Chinese only through Cantonese coolies, most Californians had failed to appreciate the artistry of their next-door neighbors. Mexico had sent a small exhibit to the 1915 exposition and it was stranger to most eyes than anything from Europe. In 1939 they had sent more in quantity but it was so obviously of the showy *tourista* quality that few realized the potentiality of their artisans. Only Diego Rivera, painting his mural in the Fine Arts Building, gave a hint of what his country really could contribute.

Since the middle thirties, tourists had begun to venture into Mexico, coming home with gay serapes, lacquered bowls, utilitarian pottery; but it took Dick Gump to recognize in their craftsmanship a basis for future styles in California homes. He did not like their traditional designs, nor did he agree with their color harmony—or lack of harmony. He and Blesh set up headquarters in Mexico City. Then they toured the villages, learning that each community had its individual specialty. In Toluca a blanket weaver brought in a bright serape. One stripe in it appealed to Dick.

"Can you weave me a whole pattern like this?" he asked, indicating a tweed-like portion in soft brick red. In two days the man

was back, proud to show his *patrón* that he could produce what
was requested.

There were rugs in Patzcuaro bordered with stylized birds—no
weird colors to jar the simplicity of modern American homes. They
bought some of these and ordered others.

In Guadalajara they watched glass blowers swirling their blue
plates on long prongs pushed into glowing furnaces; and they interrupted their search for the modern to admire the great Murillo
painting in the cathedral, recently brought from its hiding place in
the basement where it had remained concealed during the Revolution. Here were people instinctively artistic, creative, productive,
conditioned even by their conquerors to appreciate great artists from
another world.

The pottery works at Tlacaquepaque offered commercial displays
of colorful jars and dinnerware. Guided through a maze of narrow
cobbled streets they found Panduro, the Indian clay modeler. As
they watched the white-haired man teaching his grandson the
ancient art of making figurines, they looked into the eyes of an
artist. He had nothing to sell them, but they paused to admire the
skillful fingers fashioning a tiny Honduran general on horseback
and picked up a clay peddler not over four inches high but exact
in every detail, even to the spiky pineapples in his pack. Working
contentedly in his whitewashed patio, surrounded by grandchildren,
chickens, dogs, and flowers, he typified the beauty-loving peon,
passing on his skill to the next generations, unhurried, undisturbed.

Panduro was too old to grasp new ideas. He would have smiled
benignly if the two young *Americanos* had tried to explain their
designs, but he would have gone right on making traditional figurines for his Central American patrons. He had all the fame he
wanted. His physical needs were few and satisfied.

Gump and Blesh went on in search of younger artisans, men
who could and would cooperate in their projects. In Puebla they
saw Indian workmen tracing delicate designs on handmade tile,

and a room filled with picture squares which invited one to linger and piece together some legend or story. At the pyramids of Teotihuacán (place where the gods worshiped) natives offered black and white pottery made from charcoal dust mixed with lime and fashioned in antique design. They lunched in La Gruta, a restaurant in a cave where they were served by Indian girls with such Asiatic features that, except for the costumes, they might have been at home in Chinatown.

A museum guide told them that a Chinese scholar visiting the pyramids had determined that the hieroglyphics on certain stones dug up near by were exactly the same symbols as those used in ancient China to designate "adobe," "sandals," and other common objects.

Everywhere they went they found primitive conditions, workers producing contentedly in home shops, and gathering once a week in the native market to bargain and gossip—none of the competitive struggle for wealth that complicated life across the Rio Grande. No wonder that artists were beginning to gravitate to Tasco, that gem of a village preserved as the Spanish left it in the sixteenth century. In the plaza facing the tall-spired cathedral they found clean, well-dressed Indians displaying gay baskets and native foods. In tiny shops under the white adobe houses, built tier on tier up the steep hillside, they watched silversmiths fashion the metal from the great mines which gave the town its birth. They visited the Spratling shop started by a young American and saw Indians carding wool, spinning yarn, and weaving serapes. Upstairs native artisans were working in tin and silver.

The two San Franciscans found welcome wherever they went. They, too, were craftsmen. They spoke the same language artistically, but they had a new purpose for the wares they saw. They wanted the workmanship applied to designs of their own choosing. At first the Mexicans demurred. Their skills were traditional, the design and method passed on from father to son to grandson, as Panduro had been doing in Guadalajara.

Richard and Blesh returned to their Mexico City hotel and drew up their own designs and color charts. Then they contacted the workers and waited to see what could be produced. They were delighted at the response, and after two months returned to San Francisco to transform the mezzanine floor of the Post Street store into a hacienda decorated in original and tasteful style.

The experiment worked so well that Richard returned to Mexico City for a six-month stay in 1943. He found that he was no longer a pioneer. Many buyers had learned their secret and the southern city had been invaded from the North. Mexicans were not prepared to produce in volume. They would promise gayly, but *mañana* became steadily further away. They were happy; they wanted to see their customers happy. Tomorrow?—who knew what that would bring forth!

Then they became canny. They would produce only if paid in advance. The inevitable race among Yankee traders began. Someone would put up a higher ante, and the goods promised to one firm went to another. In the effort to make more, shoddiness resulted.

Like Newell in his early buying days in Japan, Dick found it difficult to purchase in quantity—but for a characteristically Mexican reason. In one market place he was attracted by a display of *battea* (wooden bowls) offered by a *señora* in a stand near that of the chair manufacturer who was producing the specially designed models he and Blesh had suggested on their first visit.

"Ask the woman how much she will take for the lot," he requested of the chairmaker.

The woman's face fell when the question was put to her. She shook her head sadly. The agent reported that she would sell her complete stock this time, but that she was very unhappy. She had worked all week to make those bowls, just for the joy of bargaining in the market. Now her pleasure was gone. There was nothing more to do all day!

"Tell her that we will buy all she makes every week," persisted Richard. The woman refused. Her prices went up, and in order to fulfill the demand, the chairmaker had to rebargain for every lot.

Despite the newly created market for their products, Mexicans were not ready to grasp the trade opportunities offered in the war years. They were not prepared for the complications of the mechanical age. Richard Gump sympathized with their reluctance. His two short stays among the happy beauty-loving people who grew bright geraniums in every tin can and sold their fruit and vegetables from geometrically designed displays in the sidewalk markets convinced him that industrialization would be disastrous to their spiritual well being.

When Richard returned from Mexico in 1944 a new responsibility awaited him. He became general manager, and the administration of the firm passed to a third generation.

For a time Mexican metalcraft workers continued to turn his blueprints to chairs and tables, desks and settees. Furnishings from Gump's were going into homes whose owners had never patronized the Oriental Rooms. The store clientele was expanding beyond connoisseurs of fine art. Studios and bungalows, penthouses and modern offices accepted the casual and unusual touch Richard's staff of designers visualized with these simple functional articles made in the modern mood.

A.L. had not responded so readily to the furniture, textiles, and ceramics from Mexico as he had in days past to the Oriental motif. While he took paternal pride in the artistic accomplishments of his son, he was primarily a merchant interested in the high quality of his stock. He resented the inferior texture that crept into Mexican imports.

He was saddened personally in those days by the mounting

casualties of war, taking sons of his friends and employees. Martin Rosenblatt's assistant, Norman Koussis, met death in the air forces. Then Clara Walker's son Bob succumbed to war injuries. This was as if he had lost one of his own. He had insisted that Bob go to Stanford, had helped to make it possible financially. He felt the cruel waste that was depriving the world of so many young men of promise. His nostalgia for the past and his sympathies for those who were suffering in the difficult present lessened his enthusiasm for Richard's experiments.

Richard, however, understood the trend of the times better than his father did now. The San Francisco in which he was working was in the midst of another upheaval more drastic than the gold-crazed days when his great-uncle had first seen it. The largest mass migration of workers in the history of the country had filled its streets with strangers. No longer did trim-suited old-timers leisurely window shop on Grant Avenue and Post Street. In their place, grim-faced men and women in all manner of uniforms jostled with dungareed shipyard workers.

The great landlocked harbor of San Francisco was coming into its own once again. Those docks which had received fabulous cargoes from all the world had lost much commerce in the years just passed—commerce diverted by labor troubles to the port of Los Angeles enclosed within the man-made San Pedro breakwater. Now the bay was once more filled with ships. The docks were alive with tramping feet. As long lines of convoys threaded their way through the channel protected by submarine nets, some of the world's largest craft found safe harbor within the Golden Gate.

The gay colors of Treasure Island were buried under the drab dark gray of Navy barracks, and the shores of the bay were lined with shipyards from whose ways Liberty ships headed toward the battle areas.

While train loads of steel were being riveted and welded into war craft, Kaiser and other shipyards celebrated week after week with launching parties. Looking about for appropriate gifts for the sponsors of these ships, a representative of Kaiser dropped into Gump's. Another firm to whom they had given orders for hundreds of silver trays had been unable to meet its commitment. Stanley Grohs was equal to the challenge. He was sure that among the friendly dealers of the East he could find one who would supply the needed metal. But his letters brought only negative replies. He took his problem to A.L.

"You'd better fly East yourself," replied the dealer, who reveled in the dauntless optimism of his associate. There were others in the firm, however, who took a defeatist attitude and persuaded A.L. that "no one can get such an order in these times."

A.L. called Grohs to his office and said regretfully, "You'd better skip it."

Grohs tossed on his bed that night . . . there must be some way to keep up the Gump tradition.

At two o'clock in the morning he rose and called the Western Union operator, amazing the girl with the length of a night letter to an eastern silver manufacturer with whom Gump's had dealt perfunctorily in the past. Although the orders had not been large, Grohs had always maintained a friendly relationship with this firm. His persuasiveness was effectual. The middle of the next morning he walked into A.L.'s office with a telegram announcing that this firm would take care of Gump's orders. From then until the end of the war their shipments, running into hundreds of trays, were unfailing.

Between the shipyards and troop trains and transports, the pulse of the city beat as rapidly as it had in gold rush and bonanza days. The fevered populace wept and played together in frenzied effort and reckless spending. Cocktail bars vied with U.S.O. and church- and civic-sponsored hospitality centers for the leisure hours of the service men and women. While the unscrupulous fattened their purses on the susceptibility of the homesick, groups of higher-minded citizens spared no effort to give the service folk hopeful reassurance on their way out, or a friendly hospitable welcome back.

Richard found a resurgence of artistic creativeness in his own community. One of the constructive avenues of service developed in the San Francisco war effort had been the Red Cross program of arts and skills. Dorothy Wright Liebes, who had discovered the widespread interest in craftsmanship in her world-wide search for materials to be exhibited at Treasure Island, recognized an opportunity for talented persons to share their ability with bedridden veterans. Her friends—not only weavers but workers in ceramics, lucite, metalcraft, and jewelry, as well as cartoonists, finger painters, and wood carvers—all contributed time and enthusiasm. Professionals and amateurs good enough to pass a rigorous jury test were soon working side by side with occupational therapists in helping fill long hospital hours.

Hobbies developed to meet this community need led workers to devote full time to their avocations. The Gumps discovered among their neighbors and patrons, artisans whose products were superior to importations. A new section was added to the business. They called this part of their first floor "The Discovery Shop," and began to display the work from homes and studios in the bay area.

The pioneer craftsman whose ceramic decoration filled a need was Merlin Hardy, a descendant of an old San Francisco family. At twenty-two he had achieved fame for his work with Lucien Labaudt on the murals of Coit Tower on Telegraph Hill. His one-man shows had been held in galleries and museums as far from San Francisco as the Corcoran in Washington, D.C. His canvases had been hung in the Fine Arts Building at Treasure Island.

Hardy had changed his métier to ceramic decoration because of a conviction that a fundamental duty of art is to provide practical articles of beauty within the reach of the average homemaker. In this thought he found a responsive listener in Dick Gump. They also had a common interest in Mexican design, since much of

Hardy's recent work showed the influence of the churrigueresque architecture of Mexico. The overglaze painting that Hardy was using in his ceramic work was readily correlated with Gump-designed furniture used in recent California homes.

The Discovery Shop idea fitted well into the pattern of San Francisco life. A new generation was pioneering in studio garrets and basements. The fact that Gump's offered an outlet for their creations brought more craftsmen and artists to settle in the community. Among them were those who had already achieved success in other countries.

Marguerite Wildenhain was an expatriate from Germany who had received her training in Weimar under Dr. Walter Gropius, who later became head of the Department of Architecture of Harvard University. After Hitler came to power Mme. Wildenhain had operated her workshop in Holland and had won honor throughout Europe. She came to the United States in 1940 and Richard Gump was quick to recognize the exceptional quality of her pottery. A.L., too, enjoyed the feel of her jars and dishes, understanding well when she explained her technique and her philosophy.

"Pottery is fired at a temperature similar to that of stones fired by nature in the hot mass of the earth," said Mme. Wildenhain as they discussed their common interest. "Clay is an earthly material, as are the minerals and materials used in the glazes. They should not lose that quality of having come from the earth."

Shortly after the shop was established, its direction was placed in the hands of Phyllis Winterburn, who had left her drafting board in the Navy to join in this exciting civilian venture. Her coming increased A.L.'s personal interest in the project, for when Richard had mentioned his new aide, his father's acute memory flashed a signal.

"Ask Miss Winterburn to come to the office," he said. When she appeared he met her with an expectant smile.

"Are you related to Charlie Winterburn?" he asked.

"My father," she replied, and A.L. extended a hand of welcome to the daughter of his old school friend, a man with whom he had often sailed on the windy bay in the later years of their youth. Their paths had drifted apart in adult life, but the fact that a member of the Winterburn family was lending her taste and training to the development of this new phase of the business added validity to his belief in it.

As an art teacher in the Katherine Branson School in Ross, and a craftsman herself, Phyllis Winterburn had been well prepared for her new role in Gump's. Her acquaintance with other talented persons in the bay area helped to increase the variety of contributions brought to the Discovery Shop. Her own rigid standards of taste were in harmony with Richard's exacting requirements. Together they succeeded in developing a stock which so far surpassed the Mexican imports that Gump's was completely independent of that source of supply by 1945.

Potters' wheels and firing ovens were not supplying all the utilitarian art of that period. Hand looms had increased in popularity since exposition visitors had watched the beautiful yardage rolling off the looms in the Art in Action section. Dorothy Liebes' own studios had brought increasing fame for textiles to her home city. Women who had participated in the Red Cross arts and skills program respected the achievements of those who were making the ancient art a modern accomplishment.

Two Peninsula women, Constance Purrington and Frances Moore, brought in beautiful mats from their suburban home studios. These place settings for fine china and chaste silver, woven of English, French, and Irish linen with pure gold or silver thread accentuating their simplicity, became collector's items for textile enthusiasts.

As the demand for hand-loomed articles increased, Gump's established their own weaving studios. During the war years they supplied the decorating department with fabrics they were no longer able to import.

It was little wonder that eastern visitors who were shown the modern as well as the ancient accumulation in this western art center described it in the guest book as "the most creative shop in the United States."

Their appreciation was soon to be re-echoed by the most important assemblage of visitors San Francisco had ever received. On February 12, 1945, when it seemed that the overworked citizens of this crowded city could do no more, they awoke to read in the morning headlines that San Francisco had a new challenge to meet.

A communique from Washington said that world leaders gathered at Yalta to discuss a means by which close and continuing collaboration by all peace-loving people could be attained, had agreed that " a conference of United Nations should be called to meet in San Francisco in the United States on April 25, 1945, along the lines proposed in the informal conversations at Dumbarton Oaks."

Unlike the old woman who lived in the shoe, "the city that knows how" prepared valiantly for the arrival of more children from all over the world. Overcrowded hours were stretched to make plans for a welcome such as no other city had ever prepared. The War Memorial Opera House and the Veterans' Hall at the Civic Center were made ready to stage the drama on which the fate of civilization seemed to hang. Never in history had so many leading men and women been cast for important roles.

A. Livingston Gump, thoroughly conscious of the high honor that had come to his city, offered of his best to help to dignify the setting. He had among his most priceless possessions a pair of Gobelin tapestries woven in Rome in 1732 and 1736 from cartoons of Pietro Ferloni's "Jerusalem Delivered." These had formerly been owned by the Archduke Ferdinand, whose death at Sarajevo had precipitated World War I. Companion tapestries hang in the Metropolitan Museum.

When Mussolini had learned that Gump had these two he had tried to buy them for the private collection of Italian art he was accumulating just before World War II. Learning through an emissary that they were valued at $50,000, he had made an offer of this amount; but A.L. had refused to sell. Then the stubborn leader of the Italian people, unaccustomed to being balked, countered with a still higher offer. The final answer was that Gump's would not sell them to *him* at any price.

Now A.L. had found a place and an occasion worthy of his great tapestries. He presented them to the City of San Francisco, to be hung on the south wall of the vestibule of the Opera House where the plenary sessions of the United Nations conference were to be held.

As the day for the opening of the conference drew nearer, A.L. joined his fellow citizens in anticipation of President Roosevelt's opening words. Perhaps he might be the lucky holder of a ticket for that significant session!

Then the tragic news of the President's death came over the radio on the afternoon of April 11—further darkening the shadows that were closing in on the blind art dealer. Gump wired Mrs. Roosevelt his sincere sympathy, expressing his fear that the loss to the country would be irreparable.

With the zeal of a people entrusted with a sacred duty by the leader so suddenly taken from them, San Franciscans and their international guests approached the tremendous responsibility of the hour. A.L. sensed that even as his city had been evolving toward this destiny, the foundation of his own business—once thought "useless" by a conscientious banker—was in itself a plank in the credo of the times. He expressed his belief in the underlying idea in words that have since appeared on the back of every Gump sales slip:

ART KNOWS

no boundaries nor differences in race or creed. In
Gump's 40-odd international settings,
you'll find the nations united in
paintings, prints, handicrafts, silver and interior furnishings.
Visits to our Continental Room, Cambodian
Court, Mandarin Room, Georgian Room, Discovery
Shop, art galleries and Jade Room will show how all
nations have contributed to a finer, fuller life."

As the delegates arrived by ship, train, and plane, San Francisco's
homes and hotels opened wide doors of welcome. The Top o' the
Mark became a veritable Tower of Babel; ejaculations of wonder
burst in every language from those who looked down on the panorama of hills, bay, and bridges. Crowded Post Street with its navy
buses transporting the guests between the Civic Center and the
Palace, St. Francis, and other downtown hotels, became a more
cosmopolitan thoroughfare than ever before.

Now Gump's, which had played many roles in its eighty years
"on stage" in San Francisco, assumed a fascinating part in this unprecedented new drama. A.L., who often in these years had laid a
fatherly hand on the shoulders of servicemen relaxing from the fears
of the present in the oasis of ancient beauty, now rose in dignity to
extend his hand to many a notable. These men and women who
were concentrating all their thinking on the problem of restoring
peace and unity to the world, came to ponder their weighty task
in the detached atmosphere of the Jade Room or the Oriental Court.

One day it was an old friend, Sol Bloom, member of the United
States delegation, who wrote in the guest book, "After seventy years
you have still upheld the reputation of the Gump's of my time."
Sol Bloom, representative in Congress from a New York district,
had begun his life as a newsboy on the streets of San Francisco!

Signatures and appreciation in nearly every language filled these pages. From Egypt and Greece, South Africa, China, and Bolivia, members of important delegations found time to thank Mr. Gump for their pleasure.

Quite the most dramatic of all the visitors in those days when the U.N. struggled into birth were the princes of Arabia. One day Gump's was in a flurry of anticipation and excitement as preparations were made to receive the royal entourage. Everyone stepped back in respectful dignity while the handsome, black-bearded Arabians in their flowing burnooses started their tour of inspection. At this moment a young University of California art school graduate who was, at the time, Gump's window trimmer, backed out through the sliding door from the window and, turning, was face to face with a younger member of the group.

"Stinky!" she exclaimed in surprised pleasure, and he greeted her with equal enthusiasm. The young Arabian had studied at the university across the bay, where they had become good friends in International House.

The ice was broken; pomp and ceremony evaporated in the "small world" atmosphere which Gump's continually symbolizes.

CHAPTER SIXTEEN ~ *Exploring*

A S A.L.'S CLIENTELE had increased to include so many men of affairs, men who looked to him for important additions to their capital investment in art, he, like the emperors in the history he studied, had begun to command production at home and abroad. Had he been Oriental rather than a deeply ingrained disciple of democracy he might have gone down in history himself as "the last of the Emperors." Just as Ch'ien Lung and the late Empress Dowager enriched the world's storehouse of treasure by their commissions, so this imaginative Western art dealer was responsible for much in the modern era of production in China.

Encouragement of productiveness in others was indeed one of A. Livingston Gump's most important contributions to his age. This was not a matter of altruism. It was a question of meeting demand, and often of anticipating and cultivating standards of appreciation. He was never satisfied to accept just the traditional but constantly asked his designers and workers to strive for the unusual. Because of this insistence upon improvements and adaptations of old ideas to new uses, he had helped to bring the marvelous creations of Oriental workshops into all types of American homes.

The simple suggestion of adding ornamental handles to commonplace Chinese irons made these everyday household implements of ancient China into decorative oversized ash trays. They were used everywhere—from small homes where owners had a flair for the unusual to the White House where his own gift of a Ming iron had gone to the Roosevelts.

It was A.L. Gump who had the inspiration and sent the first order to workers in China for lovely boxes and other items carved out of chaste white lacquer instead of traditional cinnabar red. This led to commissions to craftsmen who had served imperial households to fashion Coromandel screens of white, as well as of black and red, skillfully decorated with enameled pheasants and peacocks.

Silversmiths who had supplied the Dalai Lama were commissioned to make a dinner service of repoussé silver over wood. Jade carvers wrought a spectacular dessert service of deep forest green, cool to touch and lyric in design. Such pieces, along with intricate chess sets and magnificent rugs produced by hundreds of Chinese workers responding to Gump commissions often surpassed in beauty treasures unearthed from past ages.

As A.L. gradually handed the reins to his son, Richard applied his trained mind to the demands of a newer generation, and found himself trying to translate high artistic idealism to everyday usefulness. His theory of merchandising differed from that of his father. A.L. with his infectious personality transmuted his ardor to the customer, sometimes almost intrusively. Richard approached business as an artist. His criterion of design and beauty was placed ahead of the inevitable "Will it sell?" The younger Gump counted on the sincerity of the design appropriately displayed to sweep the customer into purchase even though the piece presented might be quite unorthodox.

Richard applied these principles in expanding the Discovery Shop. He heard of Don Kirtland and his copper work. A teacher of adult handcrafts, Kirtland had established a workshop above his garage and labored at night hammering useful articles out of sheets of copper. When Gump's began to purchase his trays and bowls, his hobby became a profession, for burnished copper has a tone that blends well with modern color schemes, accentuating with dramatic effectiveness the simplicity of design so essential to Richard.

He did not go in quest of new artisans, but wherever he turned some new candidate appeared. Even recreation brought surprises. Richard was as fond as his father had always been of crossing the bay to Sausalito—with its old ships and sagging docks. One night at a picnic supper aboard an abandoned, half-burned lumber schooner he made a discovery worthy of his shop. The hostess, Loyola Fourtané, invited him to her workshop on the bridge. Shallow drawers, formerly used for nautical charts and maps, were filled with semiprecious stones. On the broad work table where the captain had charted his course were Mrs. Fourtané's drafting board and designs. On hooks above the board were pieces of costume jewelry fashioned of contrasting metals—silver and copper, white and yellow gold, agate mounted like a seared brown leaf, fish-shaped stones reminding him of the Honolulu Aquarium.

"We can use all you make," offered Richard, surprising the designer with his spontaneous decision.

As other artisans realized the opportunities offered by this adventurous buyer, Gump's was shown decorative and useful articles in a variety of media. Ellen Atkins, William K. Vickery's grandniece and a pupil of Marguerite Wildenhain, brought them her exquisitely fashioned stoneware. Daniel Rhodes, a successful young artist and muralist, told the Gumps that he and his wife had been on their honeymoon in the Southwest when he had stumbled upon some potsherds used by Hopi Indians when their civilization was at high tide. The lure of clay modeling had turned him from canvas and walls to the hobby which had led him to bring his own creations to the Gump Discovery Shop.

Variety continued to be added to the gift selection spread on these tables as they discovered John Dirk's fantastic animals carved out of imported woods, mostly from South America, bowls and platters made by Bob Stocksdale from these same hard woods, and the intriguing "enamel on copper" fashioned into soft-hued vases by several different craftsmen.

The reputation which Dick Gump was building as he created this center of distribution for the work of free-lance artisans was rivaling the Oriental fame established in the days when A.L. did the planning.

Encouraged by public acceptance of his innovations, Richard penned a plea to his fellow dealers. Under the heading "It's Time for Taste" he wrote an article for *Retail Home Furnishings* in which he chided manufacturers of decorators' materials for lack of artistic effort. In 1946 home building was a critical national necessity. Richard Gump urged that more attention be paid to artistic integrity in designing furniture, fabrics, lamps, glass, and chinaware to be used in the smart, practical houses that were being blueprinted.

The burden of his plea was that just as America had taken the lead in artistically designed automobiles, household appliances, and ready-to-wear clothes, so must the manufacturers of home decorations use trained artists. The label "made in America" should mean more than speed and efficiency.

He practiced what he preached and looked to the art schools not only for creators of his wares but also for artists to present them to the public. Gump's windows on Post Street began to attract startled attention because of the unconventional use trimmers made of the goods displayed.

At the same time the discovery idea was permeating all departments. Shoppers began to discover that they could step down the few stairs that bridged the two halves of the store and match their mood in porcelain, pottery, and silver.

As the war ended, European merchandise began to trickle in. The first came from the Scandinavian countries. Grohs received silver, flat and hollowware, designed by Denmark's leading craftsmen with the simplicity of line that pleased young Americans. Then he discovered that the silversmiths of Holland, known before the war for traditionally ornate designs, had begun to execute beautifully plain patterns in the modern manner. Since government regulations made the Dutch export 80 per cent of the output of their reconverted factories, it was soon possible to buy in San Francisco pieces that were impossible to find in Holland.

Then some Royal Copenhagen arrived and was assigned to the gift tables in the Discovery Shop. Except for the gray-mottled enamel on copper vases similar to those fashioned by local artisans none of this was modern in mood, but it was appropriately placed —in the nature of a rediscovery. Phyllis Winterburn took the figurines and vases to A.L., that he might touch their familiar lines and sense again that the world he had known was settling back to ways of peace and commerce. Swedish glass became available. The public welcomed these simple heavy pieces from the Orrefors and Kosta factories. They met the requirements stipulated by Dick in his article, utilitarian and simultaneously beautiful.

In spite of his ambitions for a new era of American production, Dick knew that a store such as his must still rely on the Old World for much of its finest wares. He would go exploring and find out what other countries had been able to revive in the way of artistic production.

On September 11, 1946, Dick and his wife left by plane, bound for France and Italy.

During their stop over in New York they visited the Museum of Modern Art, which had already begun to display decorative material from the Discovery Shop in San Francisco. Contemporary exhibitions at the galleries of the Association of Modern Artists attracted the two explorers. Richard was interested to see the recent work of Arnold Blanche, with whom he had studied for a while in 1931, when Blanche was on the faculty of the California School of Fine Arts.

Two weeks in New York and other eastern cities sped by. Then on September 29 they were landing in Paris, saddened by the empty cafes, the dimly lighted streets, the pitifully few things offered for sale, the unkempt look of buildings remembered as so immaculate. They found some prewar goods—hidden away underground by Parisians who refused to sell to their German captors.

In the glass-domed House of Baccarat, scintillating with prisms of light from myriads of crystal chandeliers, they learned that Baccarat had stood firm in his refusal to complete a set of glassware his factory had been commissioned to make for Herr Goering during the occupation—despite the lieutenants sent to threaten overseers with Lugers. That was a story to retell to A.L., along with the description of dinner services made for rulers of Europe and Asia and one very special design for Franklin D. Roosevelt.

They purchased the last yards of velvet, lamé, faille, and taffeta from the representative of one of the finest silk factories in Lyon. Gibson Bayh, their skillful young designer who a few years before had daringly guided scissors into ancient priest robes and mandarin coats, would welcome these precious tissues to add to the choice of materials he could offer Lily Pons, Norma Shearer, or Greer Garson for an evening gown. It was the Gumps' good fortune to be on hand before the spools of this factory were wound with synthetics as the supply of raw silk was exhausted.

They left the French capital in October and crossed the Swiss Alps to find Italy better prepared to participate in American trade. Representatives of the Italian Handcraft Headquarters, whom they had met briefly in New York, and their *commissaire,* M. Borelli, had mapped out their time efficiently.

Everywhere in Italy they were impressed by the unfailing kindness and courtesy of even the humblest employee. Both the Gumps came away feeling that it had been a privilege to meet the artists— unaffected, humble folk with the serene air that attests happiness and satisfaction in simple ways of life and work. This was particularly evident when they called on a little deaf man in the outskirts of Florence who was making copies of ancient porcelains, many of them even finer than the originals.

Richard's memory guided them up the almost invisible road that led to that miniature hamlet in the suburbs of Florence where he had purchased copies of antique furniture eighteen years before and had thus won his spurs as a buyer. The old man remembered the San Francisco visitor and chatted with them about the war and its hardships. But he confided that despite lack of any available market they had been able to use their hoarded savings and continue production. Consequently they were now in the fortunate position of having goods to sell.

The Gumps found much to admire in Italy—from the pretty women of Turin, with their black hair, fair skins, and icy-blue eyes to the glass blowers of Venice fashioning fairy bubbles with gold and silver flecks floating in their transparent and opaque shapes. They discovered the fantastic and amusing dolls in the Lenci factory in Turin and considered them works of art worthy a showing in the Gump Galleries.

Florence, with its centuries-old art, its beauty, and its modern artisans busy making porcelains, ceramics, leather goods, furniture, and rugs would have held them more than the ten days allotted, but news of an airplane strike warned them to be on their way to Rome to make new arrangements, if necessary, for the return to America.

Before they left Florence, however, they drove to Sesto to visit the Ginori factory, manufacturers of some of the world's finest porcelain. During the war the Germans had mined the huge factory; but the manager, at the risk of his life, had hunted for the lines and cut the fuses so that the TNT could not go off. Thus he had saved their entire collection of museum pieces as well as most of their modern stock. Then, for the remainder of the occupation, they had buried all their treasures under ground in some thousand cases.

After a few days in Naples and Rome the continued air strike forced the Gumps to return to Paris for new reservations. By mid-November they were flying back to share their memories and their trophies with friends and relatives in San Francisco.

Richard and Agnes arrived to find Old World atmosphere in its modern mood in the Gump Galleries. Kennth Slaughter had arranged for an exhibition brought straight from Paris—the first major postwar exhibit from École de Paris to be shown in America. Its offerings were in the spirit of the store which was making the Discovery Shop the keynote of its present mood. A new generation of Parisian artists had integrated the characteristics of their immediate predecessors—the between-wars generation—into conventions faithful to nature and taste, as well as to certain rules of traditional beauty. The catalogue which explained the background of this exhibition pointed out that some of these very young artists were new to America. They waited discovery by discriminating collectors who, if they could afford to wait, would be rewarded with ownership of famous paintings. Again, modern Gump's was gambling in art and advising their clients to take a plunge!

Richard was pleased to see this presentation of artists already well known in the land from which he had just come. He also shared Slaughter's ideas of promoting the younger artists of their own country, especially some of the newer California painters. In the spirit of discovery Richard planned with the Gallery director for an Employees' Show to be sponsored early in the coming year. The amazing number of entries good enough to hang proved to him that his idea of using artists not only to design and display but also to sell art was fruitful. Clerks and shop men vied with decorators—and with Richard Gump himself—for honors in the exhibition. There were water colors and oils, etchings and abstractions. Peter Rook-Ley of the Interior Design Department and Fred Malley, A.L.'s crony from the repair shop, submitted landscapes. Malley's of Yosemite, was in oil: Rook-Ley's in water color. Don Smith used sketch paper to demonstrate the abstractions that motivated his unique window displays.

Interest in this project somewhat assuaged the discouraging news that A.L. had received in reports from the other scouts he had sent across the Pacific. Martin Rosenblatt and his wife had returned from the Orient only a few days before the young Gumps had flown back from Europe. Their nine and a half months in the Asia the Gump buyer had known so long brought them home greatly depressed.

No longer were the Canton jade auction rooms thronged with carvers bidding against shopkeepers for chunks of the precious stone. The Jade Guild, which formerly had numbered many thousands of workers, was shattered. Rosenblatt told A.L. that there were probably fewer than two hundred people fashioning beautiful objects of jade. The armies, of course, had conscripted most of the apprentices. Many of the sculptors had found more remunerative occupations. The cost of living had risen so high that jade cutters could not afford to keep apprentices even if they were available. And most of those who would have been learning to draw the wire through ruby and sapphire dust were in the army or following it in the long trail of camp retainers. Brothers and cousins below military age were trekking after their teen-age elders—carrying their equipment and cooking their meals. The artistic heritage of the country was being dissipated in the struggle to survive.

Rosenblatt reported that Communists were in control of the Ming tombs and that rumors were current that they were rifling the burial mounds. No one knew what might be the fate of these ancient treasures.

While in Peiping Rosenblatt had been invited to pay a secret visit to a retired Chinese general. The comprador, son of old Mr. Liu, had told him that the elderly Chinese owned fantastically valuable treasures. The general had always maintained, however, that he would prefer to keep them in his family vault to parting with them for any sum of money. But when Rosenblatt responded to his invitation to a conference, the Chinese asked if he could pay for the education of his son by sending these treasures secretly to America.

A.L. wanted to know what had happened in the case of another wealthy family in Tientsin whose charming daughter had visited him in San Francisco. The Rosenblatts had gone, with their comprador and shipping agent, to the splendid house in the European section where this distinguished old Chinese family lived. The outer door was bolted and locked. A servant furtively opened a panel in the door, and with some reluctance took the letter of introduction from the daughter, along with the personal cards of the shipper and comprador.

After a considerable delay, the head of the house came to the door, cautiously opened it and invited the visitors to enter. He explained that it was necessary to keep the house barricaded because they had recently been robbed. The burglars had been apprehended; but the victim was afraid to appear in court to identify them lest they or their accomplices should ultimately murder him.

The Chinese gentleman showed the visitors his collection of porcelains and bronze mirrors, which he was quite willing to sell. But when it came to his gem jades, that was another matter. The porcelains and bronzes were bulky; but these tiny jades were so valuable that a hundred thousand dollars worth could be held in a baby's hand. In case of emergency he could conceal that kind of wealth in the same way that Marco Polo had sewed his jewels into the lining of his clothes and thus had taken his treasures secretly to Italy. The gem jades were not for sale.

It had been possible to find a few ancient pieces in the Peiping market. Some fine decorative jades, porcelains, paintings, and furniture—a surprising amount considering conditions—were available. The organization nurtured so carefully through the years since Newell's first visit had served well even in these trying times. But in the main, A.L. realized that this report closed one chapter of his life. The lush, fabulous days were ended. There would be treasures, to be sure; but the China which had caught the inner recesses of his mind and which had poured forth its wealth with such abandon was no more.

Content that he still had a goodly store of the best that the Orient had produced, A.L. turned his imaginative mind to another phase of the business. The Department of Interior Design was a feature of the Gump establishment where he and Richard could share constructive planning. Ever since Ed Newell had awakened his thoughts to popular need for guidance in matters of home furnishings, A.L. had followed the accomplishments of his designers with increasing pride, holding up to them his favorite motto from the old Doulton mug which Keith had sent him so long ago—"The best is none too good."

Now he had his reward in the reputation his firm had won through adherence to this goal. Some of those who had worked for him in this field had gone on to win acclaim in other places— Henry Judson Allen to Barker Brothers in Los Angeles, Ben Davis to establish his own modern furniture factory in Chicago. His line, known as TAPP, embodied the functional comfort and simplicity stipulated by modern Americans. A.L. heard Dick describe enthusiastically the prestige it was bringing to this former member of their establishment. He was further interested in the Davis development when Eleanor Forbes was invited to spend a few months in Chicago cooperating with Davis in introducing a Chinese motif in this furniture. The recognition which she received for this effort meant that Miss Forbes, who now headed the Gump Department of Interior Design, was accepted as one of the world leaders in her line.

A.L. was therefore entirely in accord with a suggestion which Dick brought to him one afternoon early in 1947, following a long conference with Eleanor Forbes. It was her idea that the design work of all departments should be correlated in one studio. She was anxious to return to her drafting board where she felt that with a proper staff she could contribute more by helping to correlate all Gump's design work—from advertising layouts to home furnishings.

Peter Rook-Ley was ready and able to assume the departmental responsibility she was giving up, and A.L. fathered the new venture with his old zest for progress. He knew how capable Miss Forbes was, for he had watched her development from the shy young student from the California School of Fine Arts who had come directly to Gump's to work under Ed Newell in the early days of the department. He knew not only that she could use her pencil and brush with exacting finesse but that she was also skilled in cabinet work and understood metal craft. She had been a responsive pupil of Newell and Allen, and through the years her original ideas had been expressed in many media.

As they discussed the unfolding of this latest idea, she told A.L. that the thought behind this pooling of Gump resources had developed through a casual circumstance. A client, this time a large corporation, had come to her for advice in carrying out the vision of one of their own younger architects.

American Overseas Oil Company had an Oriental theme to pursue in its decorating scheme for a new reception room. What was more natural than to turn to Gump's for aid? At that time Eleanor Forbes was assigned the task of assembling the various items to create the atmosphere they wanted. She found that she did not have to go outside her own organization for anything, even to the ash trays, which were made to order by one of the artisans contributing to the Discovery Shop. Under her direction special dyes were blended so that these accessories could become an integral part of the color harmony.

Because even conservative executives were surprised to see how much a harmonious environment could mean to long hours of conference, the success of this experiment led to a revolution in office furnishing in San Francisco. Eleanor Forbes had a personal approach to each assignment, and she found cooperation from the architect in charge. Together they studied the existing atmosphere of the rooms they were asked to change. Taking the pictures on his walls as an indication of an executive's interests, they made their plans accordingly. Then they chose a motif in keeping with their findings. One man was evidently interested in the sea and in early California. They selected a fine old ship model and worked their scheme around that. Another was apparently fond of hunting and the out-of-doors. Soft green walls and hand-blocked drapes in leaf pattern made him seem less confined behind his desk as he worked among his pictures of ducks sweeping up from the marshes.

They thought of a map panel for the wall of the Arabian-America Oil Company reception room. The architect designed a map of Arabia in sand-toned wood and Miss Forbes carried out a curving flat-topped desk for the receptionist that almost made the desk part of the Arabian peninsula. At one end she placed a small cactus garden in a plant box which was fashioned as part of the desk, hoping that the spiky leaves would eventually hide the typewriter behind the garden, its sage-green color accentuating the sand effect of furniture and carpet.

A.L. had listened with increasing interest to the details of this new development, realizing that Miss Forbes was carrying his philosophy into the daily lives of some of the city's most important council rooms. Professional men, as well as great corporations such as the California-Hawaiian Sugar, Haas Distributors, and others had followed the oil companies in providing functional and attractive settings for their business hours.

As the new Design Studio began to harmonize the creative efforts of his whole force, A.L. looked forward to each step in the process. His own activities were now mostly limited to telephone contacts with the various parts of his organization. It was no longer possible for him even to feel his way to familiar haunts.

"My headlights have gone out," he said one afternoon, half-apologizing to Marvis Raymond in the Kimono Room because he had to have guidance on his visit to that favorite spot.

Employees were becoming accustomed to his voice over the phone with the regular afternoon question,

"What's new with you today?"

Eleanor Forbes never failed to answer with an account of some intriguing development or problem. She might tell him about a spray of yucca she had designed for the jewelry department in response to a request from a young man who wanted to present his fiancée with a reminder of happy days on the desert; or she might describe the colors that were to be woven into a rug for a Sea Cliff mansion where windows framed the gray-blue vista of the Golden Gate.

That spring and summer of 1947 found the man whose forceful personality had dominated this now world-famous store-museum pathetically aware that his physical strength was ebbing. It was hard to let go.

Robert came home from service with the occupation forces in Japan and for the second time in their adult lives the two sons were working together in the business of the Post Street store. Alice Bowen flew in from Honolulu, bringing encouraging news of post-war plans for the Pacific outpost. Marcella paid him a visit.

His thoughts turned back to Mabel and he frequently called attention to her stunning photograph at the head of the family pictures that hung on his office wall.

"That divorce was a great mistake," he would say. "It ought never to have been."

Richard interrupted his father's reverie with news from the outside world that took his mind away from self and family. He had in his hand proofs of some Gump publicity which would soon appear in their national institutional advertising. It was a message

personally signed "Richard Gump," congratulating Pierre Monteux
and the San Francisco Symphony on their projected national tour.
A.L. listened to the reading of the column, smiling approval as Richard came to the concluding paragraph:

"As art dealers closely linked in the world's eyes with the artistic
development of the Far West—Gump's feels that the Symphony's
Grand Tour is an eloquent tribute to the cultural maturity of the
Pacific Coast and we are happy that the whole country can share
with San Francisco the delight of a Monteux concert."

His pleasure in the fact that the San Francisco musical group
was reversing a century-old tradition by taking an artistic achievement from West to East was repeated with personal emphasis when
Eleanor Forbes came in a few weeks later with an invitation to participate in a "Moderama" to be presented in the amphitheater of the
large Abraham Strauss store in Brooklyn. The letter said that they
planned to use her "Chinese Modern," designed for TAPP, in two of
the seventeen rooms which were to demonstrate to the public the
finest in current home furnishing.

A.L.'s sagging spirit was buoyed by this tribute to a member of
his staff who had had all her training within his Post Street walls.
He congratulated her heartily, expressing warm satisfaction that the
Gump firm, which had started so humbly less than a hundred years
before with its mirrors for saloons, was now able, thanks to the Design Studio, to accomplish something that possibly no other organization in the world could match. Without going outside their own
staff they could provide every needed article, individually designed,
to express the personality of the most exacting client—for home, office, or self.

They talked together about the meaning of this, recalling rooms
with wall coverings designed in their San Francisco studio and
painted in China on silk stretched over strong paper. With such a
backdrop, jade and ivory rested on teakwood tables; Chinese rugs
copied from those formerly in imperial palaces and woven to Gump

specifications completed the ensemble. They could picture the hostess receiving in a gown cut by Gibson Bayh from tribute silk and designed to set off jade jewelry matching the silk in shade.

Then Miss Forbes reminded him of the wide variety of homes they now could serve because of Richard's introduction of modern American design. She told him of ranches in Wyoming and Arizona where Gump-designed furniture in light wood, leather-trimmed and nail studded, carried out a completely different theme. The table in those dining rooms could be set with matching dinnerware and glass, hand-painted in geometric Indian design; even the pictures framed in rawhide would match the sinewy bronze horses and desert mountains. Every feature of the harmonious scene stemmed from Gump's!

A.L. had always held back on these innovations; but as Richard —newly elected president of the firm—joined the discussion, the father had to admit that even as his ideas had differed from Solomon's, so his son was now meeting the demands of another changing era.

"That's right, Dad," agreed Dick, "You see, being modern is not new. It is merely carrying on our family tradition."

CHAPTER SEVENTEEN ∽ *"Beyond Price"*

IN HIS LAST MONTHS, when his only light was reflected from glowing embers of memory, A. Livingston Gump found surcease in reliving his crowded years. He had kept the tryst made that day forty years before when he pondered the usefulness of the business of an art dealer while the jerking cable car bore him through the ruins of a devastated city.

He had lived through the years of rebuilding and expansion; weathered war, depression, and war again. Pondering with all thinking men what would come of the atomic age, his mind kept pace with the swiftly moving twentieth century. He heard the whirr of giant Clippers, soaring in from the Pacific and off again around the world in fewer days than the transcontinental trains of the seventies had taken from coast to coast. He remembered how proudly his father, familiar with months-long journeys in full-rigged clippers had boasted of a six-day trip by rail from New York to San Francisco.

He welcomed men and women from every clime with the air of a potentate ruling a small kingdom of inanimate but symbolically alive representatives of wide-spaced artistic ages. As he grew in understanding, experience and public recognition had taught him that business such as his could never be "useless." He learned and emphasized to those who worked with him that its inherent values were beyond computation.

Satisfaction blessed his declining years as he spoke of the great Sung painting of the Ho bird surrounded by smaller feathered com-

274

AN EXOTIC TABLE SETTING

Typical of Gump's are the appointments to be found on this table. The glass, severely simple, especially made in Venice; silver hand wrought in Denmark; mats woven of gray and silver by Iona Cahan. Black service plates and small plates with hand-painted Chinese actors were especially designed by Merlin Hardy, well-known San Francisco artist.

(Photograph by Frank van Eckhardt)

panions hanging now on the walls of the Honolulu Academy; of the Poyntz tapestries of the Battle of Solebay sold by him to George Lorimer and bequeathed to the Philadelphia Museum of Art; of priceless Chinese porcelains selected by his Oriental buyers, now in the Chicago Art Institute where students of ceramics could study their simplicity of form and subtle coloring; of the matchless blue of Imperial rugs and the soft-hued landscapes he had chosen for homes of patrons all over the world.

He often said, too, that he was glad he had kept his roots in the city of his birth. San Francisco to him was always more than a market place or a heterogeneous hodgepodge of close-crowded homes and apartments, touching wall to wall as sand dunes and hills were covered with dwellings. It was a port welcoming to safe shelter daring men and women from every land, hiding in its heart traditions of generosity and hospitality passed down by pioneers who had struggled together for its existence. He took pride in the remembrance of fame won by deserving artists whose first shows and humble beginnings had been sponsored by two generations of Gumps, and shared with his sons the knowledge that they, too, were serving the same creative purpose in a new era.

His part, like that of all conscientious dealers in art, had been well played. He knew in his heart that the man who interprets and saves for posterity the finest expressions of creative art, performs a service, not just to his own community or era, but also to all the progressions of human beings who travel the road to ultimate peace and true civilization.

He followed with particular gratification every trend toward better understanding, every acceptance of men as individuals and not as members of race or class. He was pleased when he heard that the new Joseph Magnin store in Honolulu had Chinese-Americans on the board of directors and that Gimbel Brothers included Nisei on theirs. He listened to news from Lake Success with eager hope that the purpose of the United Nations might be achieved; but he grieved over what he termed unjustifiable uprising in Palestine, expressing foreboding of dire consequences.

Like all who understand the universal language of art and culture, he perceived in the far-reaching program of UNESCO a possible foundation for world friendship. That two San Franciscans, Dr. Morley and Helen Crocker Russell, could play important roles in that drama was to him tribute to the city whose citizens look beyond the horizon.

As all of life had been to him a great adventure, so his spirit yearned to know what might be the next experience. Like Columbus sailing out on an uncharted ocean he was confident of finding a port beyond the mysterious sea. Only a few weeks before he set out on that last journey he mused, "Like all persons seeing the end of their personal highway ahead, I reflect sometimes as to where it may be leading. Frequently these reflections come to an impasse and can *prove* nothing. Yet, so many things that seemed like psychic phenomena have happened in my life that I cannot ignore the persistent thought that there is something beyond the grave that time will enlighten. . . . These are just a few groping thoughts, but I have come to one conclusion. Beauty cannot die. There surely is an art world beyond the grave."

A.L. was in a mood of happy reminiscence on August 29, 1947. He was back in Paris in imagination, walking out of the Hotel Crillon, down the Place de la Concorde, remembering the Luxembourg Galleries with their choice hangings and "the Louvre, of course—there is only one gallery like that in all the world." And because he was so vividly alive in that moment, he added, "If you go to Versailles, be sure that it is when the fountains are playing."

While his heart was warmed by these memories, his mind was alert to the present. Robert came into the office to tell his father about the sale of a set of glass and chinaware to an oil executive going out to Saudi Arabia to help build an oil pipeline. The older man's face lighted with eager pleasure as he visioned these appurtenances of gracious living serving an American-built home on sandy wastes now being tapped to provide energy for the future.

He said "Good night" to his sons and to Edythe Larsen and sat quietly waiting for his chauffeur. It was about five-twenty when he called Marvis Raymond on the telephone.

"Did my friends get up there all right?" he asked. "Nice people, aren't they? . . . I hope you showed them something they liked. . . . Good night."

Five minutes later the driver opened the door. A.L. was sitting in his accustomed chair, the smile lingering on his face; but he did not speak. His pulse was still; the tired heart had stopped. A.L.'s spirit had gone on a new quest.

So live, that when thy summons come to join
The innumerable caravan that moves
To that mysterious realm, where each shall take
His chamber in the silent halls of death,
Thou go not, like the quarry-slave at night,
Scourged to his dungeon, but, sustained and soothed
By an unfaltering trust, approach thy grave
Like one who wraps the drapery of his couch
About him and lies down to pleasant dreams.

—*Thanatopsis,* by WILLIAM CULLEN BRYANT

From A.L.'s favorite poem, read by
Rabbi Irving Reichert
September 2, 1947

Index